STYLE ANALYSIS

Analytic Hypotheses

Surface rhythm: vocabulary and frequency of durations and patterns.
Continuum: meter (regular, irregular, additive, heterometric, synco-
pated, hemiolic); tempo; module or dimensions of activity (fraction,
pulse, motive, subphrase, phrase, sentence, larger grouping).
Interactions: textural rhythm, harmonic rhythm, contour rhythm.
Patterns of change: amount and location of stress, lull, and transition
(S L T).
Fabrics: homorhythmic, polyrhythmic, polymetric; variant r:
density.

Rhythm

Large-dimension considerations: balance and relationship between move-
ments in dimensions, tempos, tonalities, textures, meters, dynamics,
range of intensity.
Evolution of control: heterogeneity, homogeneity, differentiation, spe-
cialization.
Sources of Shape
Articulation by change in any element; anticipation, overlap, elision,
truncation, lamination.
Options for continuation: recurrence, development, response, con-
trast.
Sources of Movement
Conditions: stability, local activity, directional motion.
Types: structural, ornamental.
Module: the pervading or characteristic growth segment.

Growth

Choice of timbre; exploitation of word sound for mood and texture;
word evocation of chord and key change; clarification of contrapuntal lines by forceful keywords; influence of word and sentence
intonation on musical line; limitation by awkward vocables; influence of word rhythms on surface rhythms and poetic meter on
musical meter; degree of adherence to text form (line, stanza,
refrain, da capo, etc.) in articulations and options for continuation;
concinnity or conflict in mood change, fluctuations of intensity,
location of climax, degree of movement.

*Text
Influence*

GUIDELINES
FOR
STYLE
ANALYSIS

GUIDELINES

FOR

STYLE

ANALYSIS

Jan LaRue

W · W · NORTON & COMPANY · INC ·
NEW YORK

CONTENTS

PREFACE

At the moment of publication many books claim to be new. This book, however, is old and derivative, yet possibly in a new way (the polyphonic thinking here matches the ambiguities of music): it presents a framework for understanding music based directly on the notes themselves, and the whole substance within this framework might be regarded as a summary, translated into words, of a wide range of musical procedures. There are two important reasons for this verbalizing about music. First, the acquired skill of comprehensive observation needs words as reminders and records; second, we can communicate very little of our insights and opinions without the aid of words. While historical musicology obviously makes the most direct use of verbal aids in observation and writing, music theory and performance also have an ultimately important stake in communicating their understanding of music. The present framework, though arranged categorically for ease in use, originated not as a theoretical method, but rather as a distillation of experience, organized systematically to remind us of the potentials of any piece whatever. Rather than a set of pigeon-holes, it is a flexible mesh through which the music passes, leaving a network of tracings from which we perceive the essence of a style. The specialist will always want to add his own detailed refinements and personal emphases (or limitations) to the present suggestions; but as a point of departure, this style-analytical framework can serve musicologist, theorist, and performer alike.

If there is anything new in this framework—and those who have worked with it seem to find an effective freshness of approach —it is the attempt to achieve both comprehensiveness and simplicity. Toward these objectives, accordingly, the whole framework expands from a simple central premise that music is a growth process, combining two aspects: first, the largely momentary impressions that we feel as movement; and second, the cumulative effects of this movement that we retain as a sense of musical shape. As pathways for exploring sources of movement and shape, the four elements—sound, harmony, melody, rhythm—provide familiar ground. Finally, to avoid or control confusions in overlapping observations (for example, the accent that controls a bar may not be the controlling stress in a phrase) as well as the omissions that result from musical myopia or hyperopia, the style analyst should systematically observe in large, middle, and small dimensions, changing focus in turn from movement to part and finally to phrase. In this way his observations of movement and shape will accumulate naturally in collections of comparable importance.

As the title implies, the *Guidelines* offer suggestions rather than directives, reminders rather than imperatives. For this reason there should be no deep conflict with any other method of analysis. All insights available from other approaches can provide welcome extensions for style analysis, and the open-ended character of the present framework can accomodate highly detailed and sophisticated techniques in particular areas without strain, including them as additional sources of observation and understanding. In reciprocation, the style-analytical scheme, owing to its comprehensive nature, may often suggest fruitful lines of development for other types of analysis.

Some years ago I began work on a detailed theory of style analysis (under the working title *Elements of Style Analysis*). Although this project moved forward steadily, it became clear that many years would be required to finish it, partly owing to the lack of basic research in many areas. Rhythm, for example, needs a whole army of researchers just to prepare the basic terrain. Yet for teaching purposes I urgently needed at least a brief statement of the style-analytical point of view—my students were working from ancient outlines and skeletal summaries. To solve this problem I decided to delay the larger book and extract from it a compact exposition of style-analytical principles, making use of the most mature and fully-tested material from the *Elements* to produce the present set of *Guidelines*.

For the purpose of this book musical style is regarded as a matter of music rather than as a problem of philosophy. Until the study of musical style purely as notes has advanced much farther, it will be difficult to test and validate the theories of estheticians, however persuasive their arguments. Taking a solely musical view, therefore, the style of a piece consists of the predominant choices of elements and procedures a composer makes in developing movement and shape (or perhaps, more recently, in denying movement or shape). By extension, we can perceive a distinguishing style in a group of pieces from the recurrent use of similar choices; and a composer's style as a whole can be described in terms of consistent and changing preferences in his use of musical elements and procedures. Even more broadly, common characteristics may individualize a whole school or chronological period. As these shared choices become increasingly general, of course, their application to any particular composer decreases. The only remedy for this statistical dilution is an increasingly thorough and perceptive style analysis.

These *Guidelines* are intended to fit in naturally and flexibly as part of existing courses devoted to musical analysis. The style-analytical approach makes a useful background for courses in "form and analysis," for example, since it trains students in the perception of articulations and relationships. The book can also be used as a text for a semester or year course (as in New York University) in style analysis itself. For such use, of course, the material in the chapters on "Growth," "Symbols for Analysis and Stereotypes of Shape," and "Style Analysis in Action" can be supplemented with additional projects. Most of the terminology used here is conventional, and if there is any objection to the main novelty, "growth," no harm results from a return to the more familiar term, "form." (As one studies the simultaneity of movement and shape in music, however, the word "form" seems increasingly unsatisfactory to describe the immense variability and flexibility of musical processes.) Working in a field in which so little accepted terminology exists, we have tried over a period of years to find the simplest available words for the musical procedures involved. Inevitably, however, some terms with a ring of jargon creep in and gradually become indispensable. Can anyone suggest a fully effective substitute for "directionality"? We would welcome suggestions. Another smaller point of usage: the book uses "bars" instead of "measures," a personal preference resulting partly from years in orchestral rehearsals and also from instincts of typographic economy—the principle of minimum space for a minimal unit of communication. All other specialties of style-analytical terminology may be located easily by consulting the index.

Within about a year we expect to publish a workbook to accompany the *Guidelines*. Already nearly finished but undergoing further testing, the workbook will consist of questions and examples for discussion and tear-out sheets of small and large analytical problems. There will be sufficient assignment material on several levels of complexity so that the workbook can be used for elementary, advanced, and graduate courses of either a semester or full year in length. Since a teacher's manual will accompany the workbook, material not used for assignments can be adapted as further illustrations in either discussion or lecture situations.

✿   ✿   ✿

This book is dedicated to those generations of students and colleagues whose nagging questions have made some attempted response inevadable. As a consequence, if there is any merit hereinafter, the credit is theirs; and if there are any mistakes and omissions, I hope they will accept full responsibility.

To many colleagues who have given valuable comment and support I offer a general acknowledgment in hopes that each will recognize his part. Of friends more directly concerned, first thanks go to Professor Betty Churgin of Vassar College. Her thoughtful consideration of ideas, careful evaluation of teaching and research applications, and her large-, middle-, and small-dimension encouragement were of inestimable importance. Equally valued were the profound and far-ranging suggestions of my colleague Professor Martin Bernstein, razor-sharp yet tactful, unique in their combination of scholarship, musicianship, and practicality. To Professor Elaine Brody of our University College I owe thanks for an unusual contribution to the progress of the book, since she encouraged the use of early versions of the *Guidelines* in all the historical work of her department. This important source of field testing yielded valuable suggestions and confirmed the utility of SHMRG for both elementary and advanced work.

Farther back in the pre-history of the book, two teachers of mine, Professors Walter Piston and Roger Sessions, deeply influenced my thinking about harmony and line, respectively. Later, at Wellesley College, two colleagues, Professors Howard Hinners and Hubert Lamb, taught me more in occasional informal discussions than I had learned in many a formal course. Mr. Hinners' profound insights into harmony gave me an ideal of meticulous observation and a deep consciousness of the structural influence of tonality. Mr. Lamb's concern with movement helped to focus my continuing attempts to explain at least in part this central mystery of music.

At the very interior of the project, of course, have been the cycles of students in style analysis classes and most particularly my research assistants, who have reacted, advised, criticized, checked, typed, dittoed, mimeographed, tested and taught beside me: Eugene K. Wolf, Marian W. Cobin, Elvidio Surian, and Floyd K. Grave. It is a pleasure to remember and record my debt to all of them. Among my doctoral candidates several have used and extended the style-analytical approach in creative ways that open important new avenues for future work. For this new growth I am grateful to Shelley Davis, Steven Lubin, Judith Schwartz, and Evangeline Vassiliades. To the executive secretary of the Graduate Department of Music, Mrs. Rena Mueller, and to the secretary of the Music Department of Washington Square College, Miss Barbara Brancato, I owe unending thanks for typing and processing drafts and stencils for class use over a period of years. Mrs. Mueller's special gift for layout and typographic planning has transformed many a dog-eared draft into a format of unexpected elegance.

In some circles, acknowledgments to a writer's family are thought to be overly personal. Yet when one considers a family's immense contribution, much of it hidden (though more like a quiescent volcano than an iceberg, perhaps), the family should really head the list. Fortunately there is a distinguished precedent

for informality in writings about musical analysis: if Donald
Francis Tovey, in his dedication of the *Essays in Musical Analysis*
can refer to Robert Trevelyan's habits in the bath (Trevelyan did
not sing in the tub), I may surely express intrafamilial appreciation.
My wife, Helen, has worked on so many phases and processes of the
book that it would be impossible to reconstruct the full range of her
assistance and my recurrent gratitude. Throughout the years she
has matched moral support with practical support, particularly
in typing hundreds of pages of fresh drafts when revisions made
the current pages contrapuntally indecipherable. My daughters,
Chari and Christine, perhaps to their surprise, also helped with the
book: when they would interrupt my work by shouting for the
spelling of a word (though there are unabridged dictionaries conveniently open on music stands on both floors of the house . . .
never overestimate the utility of supplying your children with
reference books), I was able to counterattack and interrupt their
homework by asking them to read a paragraph to see if it was
clear. For their comments at these times, both tactful and helpful,
I am deeply grateful. The next book will miss them.

Though the present style-analytical approach began to develop
when I was teaching at Wellesley, the first real impetus toward
book form came from the strong interest expressed by the late
Nathan Broder, then Music Editor for W. W. Norton. His encouragement was reinforced by Mr. Robert Farlow, Vice-President; and
as the book neared completion and went into production, I have
had the pleasure of working with the present Music Editor, Mr.
David Hamilton, and his associate, Mrs. Claire Brook. To all of these
I record my warmest thanks.

JAN LaRue

May 1970

CHAPTER ONE

FUNDAMENTAL ANALYTICAL CONSIDERATIONS

Music is essentially movement; it is never wholly static. The vibrations of a single sustained note, the shock waves of a clipped staccato induce motion even in isolation. Any sounds that follow may then confirm, reduce, or intensify the embryonic sense of movement. At the same time that a piece moves forward, it creates a shape in our memories to which its later movement inevitably relates, just as the motion of a figure skater leaves a tracing of visible arabesques on the ice when the movement has passed far away. It is the first task of style analysis to explain as far as possible both the character of movement and the enduring shape of music.

Among the arts, music has a special power because its materials and symbols are not fixed in their connotations. A succession of tones can mean an infinity of different things to composer, performer, and listener. A musical phrase may lack the specific meaning, the immediacy of words or pictures, but it also escapes their limitations. The attractive flexibility of musical connotations entails some penalties, of course, in the form of ambiguities that impose difficult tasks for those who attempt to explain the movement and shape of music. To cope with ambivalent effects produced by changing relationships between musical elements, analysis must occasionally create artificial situations in which the moving art-form is "frozen" so that we can study each moment by itself. Some of the meaning is certainly lost in this immobilization—frozen fruits can never equal the flavor of freshly picked produce—and other analytical procedures may also seem to violate the basic principles of art by reducing subjective feelings to objective quantities. Yet, although analysis can never replace nor rival feeling, it can enhance our perception of a composer's richness of imagination, his complexity (or utter simplicity) of material, his skill in organization and presentation. The performer and listener must incorporate these insights into the full context of their personal response.

The Style-Analytical Approach

If analysis at best can accomplish only part of the task of understanding music, obviously we must attempt to compensate by constructing a plan of exceptional completeness to ensure our observation of every nook and cranny of a piece, studying each of its musical elements in turn at various magnifications to fit all dimensions. Next we must try to understand the functions and interrelationships of these elements, so that we can make meaningful interpretations, identifying the significant aspects of each piece in relation to its composer and the stylistic relationship of each composer to his milieu. From these significant determinations we may venture to evaluate the music and the accomplishment of the composer. To keep all of these matters within a consistent perspective, we should begin with a general outline, a compact overview of the whole process and concept of style analysis. In the scheme on p. 3 there are a few unfamiliar terms, notably the substitution of "Growth" and its subdivisions ("Movement" and "Shape") for the concepts usually gathered together under the topic heading of "Form." These unfamiliar points will become clear in the ensuing pages.

By keeping firmly in mind the three main stages of style analysis—background, observation, and evaluation—we can find our way through the complicated interweaving of thoughts and responses involved in the complete plan outlined above. Though the divisions of the process do not exactly parallel the flow of music, the framework reminds us of all relevant musical facets; a less comprehensive approach can easily degenerate into a mere catalogue of momentary personal impressions. The general classifications and subdivisions

I. BACKGROUND
The Frame of Reference
Significant Observation: Selection rather than multiplication of evidence

II. OBSERVATION
The Three Standard Dimensions of Analysis: LARGE, MIDDLE, SMALL
The Four Contributing Elements: SOUND, HARMONY, MELODY, RHYTHM
(SHMR)
The Fifth, Combining and Resultant Element: GROWTH
1. Sources of MOVEMENT: Varying Degrees and Frequency of Change
   a. General States of Change: Stability, Local Activity, Directional
   Motion
   b. Specific Types of Change: Structural, Ornamental (Secondary)
2. Sources of SHAPE
   a. Articulation
   b. The Four Options for Continuation
      —Recurrence: Repetition, Return after Change
      —Development (Interrelationship): Variation, Mutation
      —Response (Interdependence):
         S: forte vs. piano, tutti vs. solo, etc.
         H: tonic vs. dominant, major vs. minor, etc.
         M: rising vs. falling, stepwise vs. skips or leaps, etc.
         R: stability vs. activity or direction, balance between mod-
         ules (4 bars answered by 4), etc.
      —Contrast
   c. Degrees of Control: Connection, Correlation, Concinnity
   d. Conventional Forms
The Style-Analytical Routine: Typology—Movement—Shape

III. EVALUATION
Achievement of Growth (Movement, Shape, Control)
Balance of Unity and Variety
Originality and Richness of Imagination
External Considerations: novelty, popularity, timeliness, etc.

inevitably produce some overlapping. For example, one can hardly discuss sources of Movement without citing some musical element in a specific function. Interconnections such as these, however, do not in any way produce a wasteful repetition or duplication: quite the contrary, they accurately reflect the interrelations, interactions, and interdependencies of the music itself. By approaching an inter-connection from two contributing aspects, we gain new understanding of each element, just as a picture gives different impressions when regarded first from the right, then from the left. Furthermore, the process is actually self-correcting: any redundancy that crops up in the observational phases will automatically disappear in the course of selecting the most significant characteristics for final evaluation.

The first preparation for style analysis concerns the background: without some frame of historical reference, some idea of the conventional procedures of similar pieces, we cannot make consistently relevant observations, for on the one hand we may impute originality and importance to what may be a matter of common convention, or on the other hand, we may entirely overlook the skillful sophistication of an advanced technique, simply because we do not recognize its rarity in its own time. To take a single example, the progression V^7–I occurs so rarely in the fourteenth century that it should immediately draw our attention; yet to comment upon this cadence in a piece written about 1750 would be completely superfluous.

The second preparation for style analysis concerns our own state of mind: from the outset we must concentrate on *significant observation*. Once we have established by the frame of reference that an observation is relevant, we must apply further tests and exclusions to make sure that it is worth recording. Otherwise we will quickly accumulate such quantities of observations that we will drown in our own data, a danger particularly noticeable in computerized analysis. Successful style analysis combines dissection with selection, insight with overview. If we mindlessly proliferate observed details, we may never reach larger understanding. Recently a respected university offered a semester course devoted to a single composition. Such an intensive approach may occasionally be justified as a demonstration of method; as style-analytical procedure, however, it shows a dangerously myopic trend that can transform the intended virtue of completeness into a trackless jungle of incommunicable personalized subtlety: a hundred notes produce a hundred thousand words. Meanwhile centuries of great musical literature lie virtually unexplored. If we are to make any general progress in understanding music, we must learn to be both comprehensive and intensive, stressing landscape as much as inscape. We may bear in mind as a cautionary guide that truly significant observations keep a balance between what can be deduced only after hours of study and what can be readily noticed by a careful listener after several hearings.

It must be emphasized repeatedly that each piece is in some respects a law unto itself, requiring the analyst to adjust the general framework of examination to bring out characteristic features of a specific composer, at the same time eliminating points from any initial working outline (see p. 230) that may be irrelevant or unproductive of insight for a particular situation. The purpose of these *Guidelines* is to establish an effective general method. The specific application rests with each performer and listener. In the course of laying down general principles for many areas in which opinions vary widely, we will often find it useful to arrange observations in three-part hierarchies. This "Rule of Three" derives from Aristotle's method of establishing means and extremes. For almost any characteristic we can propose a range of intensity from most to least, but any gradations in between can arouse justifiable disagreement. The practical solution is to consider "in between" as a third category. Though this may seem imprecise, in practice it will usually enable us to discover the emphasis of a given composer in treating a particular element of style. For most style analysis this will give us sufficient individualization to deepen our insights without burdening us with an endless series of unstable, arguable decisions. The experience of opinion researchers that the categories of "yes" and "no" are far more meaningful if there is a category such as "maybe" in between confirms this practical approach. And we must bear in mind that a comprehensive style analysis involves dozens, sometimes hundreds, of observations and interpretations; the fallibility of any one (or several) of these determinations will not seriously weaken a genuinely comprehensive evaluation.

The first axiom for the analyst seeking completeness is to begin by looking at the piece as a whole, not as parts, not even as a collection of parts. We can come much closer to the sense of flow in a movement if we try first to grasp its entirety. Furthermore, once we comprehend the wholeness, the parts fall into a proper perspective. The opposite process yields less insight, for a study of the parts does not usually help us to sense the whole; in fact, it tends to fragment any broader view, obscuring it with a multiplicity of detail. Hence, it becomes essential to begin with large overviews. The number of dimensions in which we examine a piece depends directly on the character of the piece. On one hand, complexly layered compositions with independent activity on many levels might require the analyst to apply many sizes of "yardsticks" combined with appropriate magnifications of musical microscopy and telescopy. On the other hand, a relentlessly consistent, motivic piece might yield most of its insights when examined within a single dimension such as the individual bar. To apply sixteen-bar yardsticks to a motivic piece would be as inappropriate as to apply only motivic dimensions to Bruckner. While the dimensions of analysis thus vary according to particular pieces, most works can be adequately explored by treating them in three general dimensions: large, middle, and small. These dimensions can be related to musical syntax as follows:

Small Dimensions	Motive
	Subphrase
	Phrase
Middle Dimensions	Sentence
	Paragraph
	Section
	Part
Large Dimensions	Movement
	Work
	Groups of Works

Again we must remember that not every work makes use of all the various units in the hierarchy above; it represents a composite generality from which we extract relevant parts to elucidate the work at hand. Also, dimensions may occasionally overlap.

Large Dimensions

Large dimensions concern musical wholes: entire movements, or even complete successions of movements if a larger unity can be discerned. At the largest, a musical whole might consist of a giant cycle of complete multimovement works, such as a series of descriptive symphonies. Even more extensive, a full understanding of

Wagnerian *Leitmotiven* could properly be based only upon dimensions large enough to encompass the whole *Ring* cycle. Large-dimension observations thus include comprehensive considerations such as change of instrumentation between movements (Sound); contrast and frequency of tonalities among movements (Harmony); thematic connection and development between works (Melody); selection of meters and tempos (Rhythm); and variety in types of forms employed (Growth). The five categorical headings (the acronym is pronounced "SHMeRG") include the broadest associations for each term. Harmony, for example, refers to all vertical considerations, including counterpoint and atonal structures as well as familiar chords, progressions, and modulations.

Many single movements, though functioning as parts of groups such as suites or sonatas, individually constitute musical wholes that require large-dimension observation. Investigating style elements for a mainly independent movement we concentrate upon the relationships of its parts to each other and to the movement as a whole. Questions such as the following result: Where are the most impressive dynamic climaxes? (Sound) Apart from the tonic, which keys receive most attention? (Harmony) Is there a symmetrical balance of melodic peaks or an upward progression between sections? (Melody) Are the layers of rhythm more complex in certain parts than others? (Rhythm) Are the main articulations marked by areas of greater stability or greater activity? (Growth) In each investigation we view the evidence broadly, taking into account the entire span of the movement in comparing the internal phenomena.

Middle Dimensions

In middle dimensions we concentrate on the individual character of the parts of a piece—the part in itself rather than as a contribution to the movement. We therefore attempt to show how each part governs its individual hierarchy of paragraphs, sentences, and phrases. Typical questions that the analyst would consider in looking at middle dimensions would include some of the following: How does the orchestration underline the entrance of secondary

sections in sonata form? Are the modulations tensional or merely
coloristic? Do we find both vocal and instrumental types of melody?
Does surface rhythm contribute decisively to thematic contrast?
What devices, other than cadences, does the composer use to
punctuate paragraphs?

The exact extent of middle dimensions cannot be fixed as
neatly and easily as large and small dimensions, because the boundaries vary on both sides; they are "in between" at both extremes.
For large and small dimensions, in each case one limit is fixed:
large dimensions cannot expand larger than the full piece or group
of pieces; small dimensions cannot shrink smaller than the smallest
notes. Yet we can master the seemingly slippery "in-betweenish-
ness" of middle dimensions by thinking of them functionally: they
concern happenings fixed at the upper limit by the main articulations of the movement and at the lower limit by the size of the
first complete idea (the word "phrase" will not always fit the concept of "first complete idea" perfectly—again we must use a generalized term). Middle-dimension functions, then, control the formation of musical ideas into sentences, paragraphs, sections, and
parts of a piece.

As an illustration let us imagine the somewhat confusing situation found when the first complete idea of a piece consists of a
motive one bar long, moving along with no stronger articulations
until we reach a double bar with repeats at the middle of the
composition. (This situation frequently occurs in movements of
Baroque dance-suites.) Here, lacking the middle articulations that
elsewhere may produce phrases and paragraphs, the middle-dimension observations must extend from the one-bar motive right up to
the half-way articulation. The main relationships, therefore, connect
motive and part, and we will rightly find rather little to observe by
comparison with the frequent articulations of a Classical exposition.
To restate the basic principle: middle-dimension analysis should
illuminate the handling of ideas within the parts of a piece. The
moment that we find ourselves comparing the handling of themes
in an exposition with the recurrence in the recapitulation, we have
moved up to large dimensions, since the comparison of parts
requires us to look at the shape of the piece as a whole.

Small Dimensions

In the other direction, distinctions of higher magnification come into focus clearly if we think of small dimensions as those involved with the structure and character of the smallest self-sufficient unit, the smallest complete idea. Within this contracted sphere of relevance new questions such as these arise: Does the composer use dynamic contrasts to define and individualize the subphrase as well as the phrase? Is the thematic fabric chordal or contrapuntal? Which types of melodic movement predominate—steps, skips, or leaps? Does the rhythm generate flow by motivic treatment or larger contouring? Do the subphrases balance statically or create a sense of progression within the phrase?

For some pieces the basic building-block or musical module will be the phrase, within which we study the interactions of the subphrases or motives that make it up. For other styles the musical module may be still smaller, consisting merely of a motive, within which we may not always be able to discover any smaller fractional components such as submotives. At this ultimate magnification, then, we can only study the bare bones of rhythmic patterns, melodic figures, and specific chords involved.

Small-dimension analysis contains one great danger: over-preoccupation with detail. Since performance problems tend to concentrate on the phrase level, our whole experience of practicing and learning music reinforces a minutely fragmented approach. As a result of mere routine and habit it is altogether too easy to feel analytically virtuous by piling up mounds of tiny observations—particularly if some of them actually contain points of genuine interest or novelty. Yet the main goal of detailed analysis, as of all style analysis, is not so much to admire the character of any single detail as to discover its contribution to higher structures and functions. We may find a beautifully organized plant cell in either a microscopic diatom or in a giant sequoia; in the latter case, however, the tree—not the cell—should receive our major attention. Similarly, musical understanding controls refined discriminations by the perception of generalized relationships.

The Four Contributing Elements and
the Fifth Combining Element (SHMRG)

To illuminate any work of music by stylistic discussion we require not only the approach in three analytic dimensions mentioned above, but also some way of subdividing the phenomenon of music into manageable parts. Continuing on the level of generalization already established by the three conventionalized dimensions, for style elements we must now also oversimplify initially if we are to avoid a vast quagmire of quibbling: numerous elusive problems arise in the attempt to define a set of categories that are satisfactorily distinct, yet without undue branching and proliferation. For purposes of comprehensive style analysis a division into five categories—Sound, Harmony, Melody, Rhythm, and Growth—can be strongly recommended on the basis of extensive practical experience: these five categories have withstood the test of a number of years of research and teaching by the present writer, his students, and various colleagues. The value of initial clarification provided by the easily remembered five-part division of style greatly outweighs the possibility of more refined distinctions that could be made available in a more complex framework. Furthermore, generalities logically come first; refinements can be more appropriately developed at a later stage, as elaborations within the more general plan.

Since the analytical separation of musical elements in a piece of music is an artificial device (though a helpful and necessary one), it comes as no surprise again to find occasional overlapping among elements. The nature of texture, for example, if we think of it merely as timbre or spatial organization, mainly affects the category of Sound. Yet, where various strands weave together in controlled vertical relationships, the textural observations may fit better among conclusions about harmony and counterpoint. Hence, we may properly speak at one point about "woodwind textures" in connection with Sound, yet later, comment with equal relevance on "fugal textures" while discussing counterpoint as part of the category of Harmony. At times the very categories themselves interact to produce overlapping functions such as harmonic rhythm, textural rhythm, or contour rhythm. In the observational process it does not matter at what point we test these potentialities. For interpretation and evaluation, however, they should be associated with whatever category appears to control a particular situation. For example, if we are seeking to show the exact location of a rhythmic stress, the evidence of harmonic-rhythmic effects would be weighed during the discussion of rhythmic features. On the other hand, if a sudden total change in the rate of chord rhythm produced a powerful harmonic climax, this contribution of harmonic rhythm would be discussed along with other harmonic phenomena. Furthermore, the same effect could even be cited with validity as an aspect of Growth, since any sharp alteration in harmonic rhythm would act as a powerful articulation, with obvious influence on the development of musical Shape.

The five basic elements do not stand on a completely equal footing. Taken singly in isolation, Sound, Harmony, Melody, and Rhythm in most cases cannot individually maintain successful musical structures. (The nearly independent functioning of Melody in chant or folksong is an instructive exception.) As a result, they typically function as *contributing elements*. Growth, however, develops a dual existence as both the emerging product and the adjusting matrix of the other four elements: it is the *combining, controlling element*, absorbing all contributions into the simultaneous processes of Movement and Shape. Owing to this combining function, Growth stands somewhat apart from the other elements in character, yet at the same time it usually maintains a closer relationship to each of them than they to each other. For three reasons, furthermore, it seems undesirable to place Growth on a wholly different level of consideration. In the first place, Growth resembles other categories in having some contributory aspects. For example, the use of external conventions such as the *formes fixes* of medieval poetry is a contributing, not a combining point of style; the fixed poetic schemes are joined with other elements in further processes that produce a final Shape. Secondly, Growth does not stand entirely alone as a combining element: other categories also coordinate and interact from time to time, as we have just seen in the combined function of harmonic rhythm. Finally, any separation of categories that continues earlier analytical compartmentalizations will tend to interfere with the clean sweep of a unified approach. For example, all divisions into "style and form" violate a basic tenet of our present comprehensive style analysis, i.e. that form in its full meaning (Growth) is as characteristic a part of style as any other element.

The many music courses dealing with "form and analysis" that are still to be found in college catalogues reflect another confusion in the stylistic arena, for the analysis in these courses usually consists of harmonic analysis. Yet any implication of division between form and harmonic analysis can be seriously misleading since, as we shall repeatedly find from actual experience with comprehensive analysis of style, harmony contributes in an absolutely central fashion to the articulation of musical growth, notably by color contrasts and tensional balances between tonalities. Both of these academic dichotomies—style and form, form and analysis—probably derive in a somewhat tortuous fashion from a common ancestor, the esthetic distinction between form and content. While this division may suit the needs of general esthetic theory, any functional theory of musical style analysis must include form directly as a part of the total content that we sense as the growth process of a piece. We obviously are aware of the changing content in any arrangement of repetition, contrast, recurrence, or other formal process. At the same time, content, as it is articulated by changes in Sound, Harmony, Melody, and Rhythm, actually builds and determines form. Musical form and content thus constitute a relationship of flesh and blood—not flesh and bone—which no analytical Shylock should attempt to split. The present approach, symbolized by the term *Growth*, reaffirms at every opportunity the interactiveness of music; it makes use of categorical divisions only to illuminate the richness of the interaction.

Movement and Shape

The analytical division of Growth into Movement and Shape is not a definite separation but a reflection of elusive coexistence between layers of the same phenomenon, a continuity of Movement created by sounds that leaves an impression of Shape in our memories. This musical coexistence again calls to mind the image of a figure skater. In music, Movement is a complex extension of Rhythm that results from changes of all sorts. Obviously the strength of Movement depends on the frequency and degree of change; the more clear-cut and coordinated these changes are, the more powerful the resulting Movement. Though we can easily identify a strong rhythm in small dimensions—think of Baroque drive motives—in middle and large dimensions, probably owing to irregularity of articulations as well as to distractions from other elements, we are less likely to observe the sources of Movement consciously, though we may be profoundly moved by the ground swell of motion that they create. Since composers as well as their audiences have rarely maintained a consistent awareness of Movement in middle and large dimensions, it is no surprise that these dimly realized, larger aspects of Rhythm have been insufficiently studied. To fill this gap, research on the phenomena that create Movement deserves a high priority.

Frequency and degree of change in music vary so constantly that some generalized conditions must be defined to help us recognize the basis for our general impressions so that we can seek analytical explanations and confirmations through all the elements. Three general states of change can be distinguished:

1. *Stability.* In an absolute sense "stability" means "no change"; obviously, therefore, the musical connotation of the term is merely relative. As opposed to quick echoes, a sustained chord is relatively stable, though its components, viewed acoustically, are cycling madly. A thematic passage in a single key is stable by comparison to the modulations in a transition. In a context of sixteenth notes, a group of double whole notes is deadly stable, just as stepwise motion can seem blissfully restful after the instability of a passage constructed of jagged leaps. We can even sense stability in Shape itself, partly from fulfillment of expectation, partly from regularity of design, by use of approximately modular construction in all dimensions—which is just another way of fulfilling expectation, of course.

2. *Local Activity.* In moving toward or away from stability,

music must demonstrate a lowered or heightened frequency or degree of change. Often, however, these changes do not really provide a definite movement away from the point of stability, serving instead merely to maintain fresh interest by viewing the home territory, as it were, from new perspectives. All changes that are approximately regular (i.e. returning to a starting point or repeating a cycle of some sort) tend to produce this effect of local activity, which might also be called "motion in equilibrium." Sometimes in the development section of a concerto, for example, the exchanges between a soloist and orchestra become so regular that we hear them as repeated unities; instead of recurrent contrasts, O-S-O-S-O-S, we unconsciously shift to the next larger dimension and hear the exchanges as repetitions of a two-part idea, OS-OS-OS, which creates an underlying stability. In harmonic treatment there are many types of local activity, such as ornamented pedal points, tonic-dominant oscillation, sequencing within a key, ostinato effects, and ground basses of all sizes. Similarly, any consistent patterning of melody or rhythm gives us a mixture of activity and stability—activity from the changes and stability from the recurrence of the pattern. Local activity thus provides a useful middle category of movement.

3. *Directional Motion.* Steady, cumulative increases (or decreases) in frequency or degree of change produce a recognizable sense of direction, a feeling of activity that carries us definitely away from the area of initial statements instead of oscillating or cycling around it. Common illustrations of this directional motion can be found in crescendos, either written or intrinsic; modulatory sequences that break away from the tonic orbit; profiles of higher and higher melodic peaks; and constant diminutions of rhythmic values: the mounting activity and excitement of each of these effects gives tremendous drive toward new goals, the most basic source of fundamental Movement available to the composer.

In studying the processes of musical change we face a constant need to separate the essential from the trivial, the bones from the flesh, or in style-analytical terms, the *structural* from the *ornamental*. These distinctions can easily become confusing if we do not maintain a consistent dimensional level, since a small-dimension change is ornamental if we are observing middle dimensions, yet a middle-dimension change that in its own dimension is structural, becomes merely ornamental as soon as we consider it from the perspective of large dimensions. As a general rule, therefore, events smaller than the prevailing dimension will rightly be regarded as ornamental, transitional, secondary. The prevailing or controlling elements also act as guideposts for classifying structural as opposed to ornamental functions. If the Movement in a passage seems to result entirely from harmonic changes, melodic activities obviously recede into an ornamental role. A piece also reveals its structural features in a confirmation of one element by another—for example, we commonly recognize as structural the harmonies that appear in positions of rhythmic stress. The identification of structural phenomena, therefore, is the key to significant observation; and although as a matter of comprehensive routine we will naturally examine all dimensions and all elements, true musical understanding emerges from the attempt to discover in each piece the *characteristic dimension* and the *controlling elements*.

As we listen to a piece, its Movement leaves us with a host of short- and long-term memories that together constitute our sense of Shape in music, more or less defined and vivid, depending on the character of the musical material. At the first articulation in the musical flow ("articulation" is a better word than "punctuation," since it connotes both interruption and connection) the composer faces his first crisis: What should he do next? And although the choice seems infinite, it actually resolves into *four basic options for continuation*: recurrence, development, response, and contrast. Keeping these options in mind as a guiding hypothesis of Shape, we can more quickly recognize which procedure has been chosen; and in the course of the piece, we will gradually perceive a characteristic range or pattern of choices.

In attempting to understand Shape, any classification by conventional forms (rondo, sonata, etc.) can be more misleading than helpful. In the first place, these forms are abstractions—notice how difficult it is to find a "typical" rondo or sonata form. Hence, any stylistic groupings yielded by abstract categories will obviously be mainly useful as initial generalizations, limited by the oversimplification endemic to such generalizations. In the second place, style analysis attempts to discover more the individuality of a piece or composer than the conventionality, which is often all too easily perceived. The most instructive classifications of Shape, therefore, will emerge as a spectrum of evasions of the obvious, of imaginative escapes from the convention.

A successful musical style employs a consistent choice of materials and control of functions to achieve effective Movement and Shape. Historically this achievement seems to be marked by an increasing relationship between musical elements, which composers gradually learn to control and then actively exploit to confirm levels of activity or processes of articulation and continuation. A particularly attractive term to describe the highest degree of interconnection and correlation between elements is *concinnity*, "the skillful arrangement and mutual adjustment of parts" (Webster). The measure of concinnity in a piece, therefore, which may connote well-adjusted conflict as well as skillful confirmation, furnishes an important criterion of style. A useful progression in control of stylistic elements can be suggested by categories such as these: connection, correlation (or coordination), and concinnity.

The Style-Analytical Routine

To assure completeness during the observational process each style element should be examined with a general program in mind. Like all of the self-starters that we shall develop in style analysis to stimulate our perceptions and systematize our methods, the initial observational program should be infinitely flexible, constantly open to revision by expansion and elimination, frequently redesigned for sharper illumination of particular problems in understanding. The major divisions of observation, of course, concern the phenomena pertaining to each element as these phenomena occur in the three standard dimensions. Within each dimension, to be certain of thoroughness in observing all relevant stylistic events, we can apply a three-part investigation to each element:

1. *Typology*: the total spectrum of SHMR events, and within this spectrum the preferred or predominant types.

2. *Movement*: contributions to the flow of the piece.

3. *Shape*: contributions to the processes of articulation and continuation.

This plan contains one apparent redundancy: If Growth already consists of Movement and Shape, how can it contribute further to them? The answer has already been hinted at above in the discussion of the dual character of Growth: while it is mainly a combining element, any parts of it that are contributory rather than combining must be studied for their effects on Movement and Shape. In a motet or madrigal, for example, the first text-section may be set in short, active phrases, followed by a second section of longer, relatively stable phrases. The "Growth rhythm" here, motion followed by rest, obviously contributes the fundamental sense of movement of the piece.

While the three-part plan above will keep us on the track in a general way, the spectrum of procedures within each dimension may become exceedingly complex. In observing Sound, for example, we get at the heart of the matter not so much by discovering merely the total range of voices or instruments but rather, to put it in a mildly confusing way, by identifying the range of ranges, i.e. the whole assortment, spectrum, or vocabulary of ranges employed for various instruments or combinations of instruments in the course of a piece. Similar typologies of fabrics and dynamics may tell us a great deal about a composer. And of course we extend the procedure to other elements, compiling vocabularies of chords and inversions, selections of dissonances, and routes of modulation; assortments of note values, classifications of rhythmic patterns, varieties of meter and tempo; tables of intervals, compilations of curves, cumulations of peaks and lows; weightings of articulation, measures of contrast, clusters of confirming features. By these collections of a composer's working materials we prepare the way for steps two and three, the recognition and interpretation of functional contributions by all the various aspects of each element. Descriptive analysis—the identification of all of these aspects, the construction of a full taxonomy—no matter how subtle its distinctions and comprehensive its categories, represents merely a first step that only partly illuminates a style. Only by studying the materials in action can we begin to understand the essential goal of analysis, the explanation of musical function and interaction.

In the process of forming the collections mentioned above we can to some extent organize the "evidence" as we proceed, if we bear in mind the idea of a scale of values as a sorting device. Thorough style analysis produces such a bountiful harvest of observations that "data control" becomes essential to avoid an embarrassment (and indigestion) of riches. In addition to obvious musical polarities such as low/high and soft/loud, other defining conceptual extremes for purposes of initial sorting and organizing of observations are: simple/complex, thin/dense, stable/active, disorderly/ orderly, bland/intense, light/dark (rather subjective!), close/remote, diffuse/concentrated. One danger: grouping observations according to various criteria of progressive intensity may tend to involve us with inappropriately refined subjective decisions, which for initial analysis simply waste time, even if at a later stage and on a higher level of detailed evaluation they may be essential. Instead, for this first sorting we need simple classifications that can be applied as objectively as possible, without time-consuming, hair-splitting decisions. Again, experience fortunately shows that the Rule of Three will yield rough but distinctly meaningful subdivisions: merely insert the word "middling" between any of the extremes listed above, and a collection of observations can rather quickly be sorted out into manageable order. Early in the observational stage it is not a matter for concern exactly where we fix the boundaries of "middling," since the purpose of the whole analytical technique is basically comparative rather than definitive. In comparing two pieces, as long as we use the same yardstick on both, the comparative results will be meaningful. In measuring two rooms, a yardstick thirty-five inches long will not yield exact yardages, but it will definitely tell us which room is larger. Returning to music for another example, between simple and complex curves the concept of curves of "middling complication" seems rather elusive and indefinite on first thought. But *merely for initial analysis* we badly need the Rule of Three as a grouping device to control the evidence, to sort out the types of curves. Following the suggestion above, one plausible application of the Rule of Three would be to define simple curves as those containing one directional change, e.g. the up-down of a parabola; "middling" can then be thought of as "compound," i.e. more than one directional change; and "complex" curves connote many changes. Here the distinction between simple and compound is clear, but the line between compound and complex needs further clarification. We would waste a great deal of time, however, attempting to decide whether a contour gives a complex feeling already with three directional changes or perhaps not until five. This is not the time to make such decisions, which might be appropriate for a closely detailed study of a composer's melodic characteristics *after* general analysis has revealed that melody is the most significant part of his style. We lose nothing by using simpler categories at early stages of observation; the material is all still there, ready for closer study if required. And we may avoid a great deal of unnecessary work by postponing this more detailed consideration until a later stage. A concrete illustration will show how the seemingly rough groupings of the Rule of Three answer all early requirements and, surprisingly, may even be all that is ever necessary. Let us suppose that we are trying to determine whether the thematic material for points of imitation in Palestrina's madrigals is more active than the analogous material in his motets. Among the elements that we would investigate would be melodic activity, which in small to middle dimensions can often be neatly compared according to types of curves. To set up three initial categories—simple, compound, complex—we might make an arbitrary first decision that all curves with more than three changes of direction will be considered complex. This arbitrary decision may not be the best possible ultimate esthetic distinction between compoundness and complexness, but we are not trying to make ultimate distinctions: we are merely making initial observations bearing on the study of a finite, immediate problem—thematic activity in Palestrina's madrigals and motets. By sorting his imitative phrases according to three working categories, we will almost certainly be able to determine which repertory is melodically more active. Only for an examination of thematic melody in depth would we need to fix an ultimate distinction between compoundness and complexness.

There is a further important reason why any single initial category need not be overly refined; the mere crosscutting of observations emerging from five style elements supplies a powerful statistical characterization. For example, to answer the Palestrina problem above we must investigate not only three categories of curves, but also SHRG activity of various kinds (M is already involved by the thematic problem). The correlation of all these other observations will almost certainly furnish adequate distinctions, even if by a rather small statistical chance any single contributory determination, such as the decision to draw the line between compound and complex at three changes of direction, should not prove to be fully effective in deciding whether madrigals are more or less active than motets. Again, therefore, for the purpose of general style analysis we need not agonize over the precise lines of distinction between attributes. Such definitive refinements will be required only for more specialized determinations—to formulate ultimate principles of esthetic theory, at one extreme, or at the other pole, to organize microscopically detailed studies of a single stylistic element.

In the foregoing discussion the whole question of texts in vocal music has been temporarily bypassed, since many textual characteristics lie largely outside music. For the observational phase, texts can best be treated as a separate category, with additional subdivisions derived as by-products from interaction with the five basic elements. In this way we can study text influence by means of questions such as the following: Does the choice of instruments reflect the character of the poetry? What words call forth the most striking harmonies? Does the composer avoid vocally awkward syllables on melodic climaxes? Can we find analogies between word rhythm and musical rhythm? Are the details of poetic structure confirmed by musical articulation and thematic recurrence? Then, during the final evaluative phase, the influence of the text will usually be seen to affect some elements more than others. The natural progress of this final commentary would then bring in relevant textual observations and interpretations as a part of the discussion of the elements affected rather than in isolation as a separate topic.

Evaluation

The ongoing processes of observation seek to discover the characteristic dimensional activity and controlling elements that produce individual Movement and Shape in a piece. Inevitably some evaluation occurs during the process of observation itself, particularly in the selection of significant observations. Evaluation also enters subtly into our expectations: once we detect a trend of sophistication in a composer, we expect more of him, which in turn also makes us more alert in recognizing profundity of feeling and technical excellence. Finally, in attempting to identify characteristic and controlling features, we inevitably compare the force of various stylistic events. All of these evaluations, however, look inward, preparing mainly for decisions about the piece itself. It now remains to look outward, to assess the qualities of the piece with regard to comparative standards fixed by analogous works.

Obviously we must begin by comparing the achievement of Growth in one piece with others of similar nature, proceeding gradually to review a complete genre, or to set the oeuvre of a composer against those of his contemporaries. It is quite likely that the majority of works in any repertory will not make a particularly distinguished impression, so that we may find ourselves comparing not so much total achievements—too few are totally achieved—as individual stylistic facets of particular interest. Where a convincing Growth exists, we are justified in going deeper to evaluate the balance between unity and variety: many a striking piece lacks consistency; many a controlled piece lacks contrast. The quality of originality, too, important though it is—historically and intellectually—does not necessarily contribute directly to beauty. Yet it is one of the potential values to be considered. As a final comparative value, the imaginative depth of a work, including range of expression and richness of resources and techniques, decisively influences our permanent evaluative response.

The last source of evaluation goes beyond comparative musical considerations to matters of a distinctly external nature, such as novelty, popularity, and timeliness. Though we may not accept popularity as a valid artistic standard, we can learn much from the opinions of other periods about a piece we feel we know. It is a distinctly healthy shock to find that contemporary audiences may have had quite different preferences within a given repertory, choosing pieces that later periods have found less meritorious. These historical preferences teach us much, not only about earlier audiences, but also about ourselves—our prejudices and possible insensitivities or oversensitivities. Novelty and timeliness are more debatable as standards for evaluation, since they lie partly within the province of chance, and largely outside of inherently musical considerations. Nevertheless, the "firsts" of music often reflect unusual perceptiveness if not actual prescience on the part of the composers; and the timeliness of certain works helps us to isolate the elements of style that create a specific turning point in music history.

The cumulated evaluation of a piece of music according to intrinsic, comparative, and external standards provides a sophisticated background against which to express personal reactions. No one need suggest, much less impose, a set of priorities among these values for another person; the important objective for all musicians —performers, scholars, and listeners alike—is an ever fuller appreciation of the wealth of potential expression, making possible in turn a correspondingly broad range of valid individual response. This omnivalent appeal is the rarest and most precious attribute of music.

CHAPTER TWO

SOUND

The style-analytical category of Sound includes all aspects of sound considered in itself rather than as raw material for melody, rhythm, or harmony. Observations of Sound group naturally under three headings:

1. *Timbre*: the vocal, instrumental, and other colors chosen by the composer.

2. *Dynamics*: the intensity of the sound, both as indicated by markings and as implied by the disposition of forces employed for the piece.

3. *Texture and Fabric*: the arrangement of timbres both at particular moments and in the continuing unfolding of the piece.

The relationship of these three aspects may be expressed visually as follows:

By organizing typologies for each of these characteristics we become fully aware of a composer's expressive approach to the element of Sound.

Timbre

Timbre refers to acoustical tone-quality, the character of the sound wave produced by various frequencies in single or combined sources of sound. The aspects that should be chiefly considered in characterizing a composer's style include:

Choice of timbres: strings, woodwinds, brass, percussion, electronic sounds; exotic, *concrète*, or other nonmusical timbres, such as tapes of external sounds; female, male, child, castrato voices; combinations of all the foregoing. In some cases, particularly for early music, we may need to proceed partly on assumptions or even speculations regarding appropriate settings.

Range: total spectrum of frequencies employed; preferences for particular ranges (tessituras) and combinations; interest in exploiting or forcing extreme ranges, emphasizing split or partial rather than continuously balanced range.

Degree and frequency of contrast: the amount of timbral contrast used by a composer and the frequency of these contrasts. Both observations contribute significantly to a composer's style profile. He may shift from high to low instruments, either within or between families or sections, or he may subtilize the degree of contrast by gradual changes among mixed groupings of either voices or instruments. The timing of these changes, ranging from sudden confrontations to gradual transitions, can exercise a profound influence on the effect of a composition.

Idiom: recognition (or ignorance) of special capacities of instruments, such as ability to leap easily from one part of a compass to another between open strings; felicitous effects of idiomatic combinations of bowing and tonguing, or figures that fit registers or hand positions with ease; effects peculiar to one type or family of instruments, such as pizzicato, double stops, and harmonics for strings; double, triple, and flutter tonguing for winds; muting and stopping for brass; and the like. These groups idioms may also reveal a composer's more generalized capacity to write with notable effectiveness for families of instruments, such as the characteristic string lyricism in many Tchaikovsky melodies, the impact of massive brass chords in Gabrieli canzonas, or the delicate woodwind traceries in Ravel's *Daphnis and Chloë* suites. Even more important, the style analyst must recognize a composer's innovative extensions of instrumental technique, such as Liszt's writing for piano, Paganini's unusual demands on violin, or Wagner's new concepts for brass. At his subtlest, a composer may differentiate between various uses of the same instrument, for example, Beethoven's differing treatment of violin in the symphonies as compared with the string quartets. Analogous subtleties of vocal idioms include strategic use of climactic skips, unusual ranges, special techniques such as falsetto, *Sprechstimme*, and exotic voice-production (e.g. African glottal stops, Asian "narrow throat" singing). And for both voices and instruments composers may develop characteristic patterns of surface articulation—slurred and staccato notes. Related to these finer points we should consider the evidence of a composer's awareness of lip and lung fatigue. At times we can sharpen our perception of composers' skills by taking a negative approach: for example, by noting infelicities of orchestration such as rapid figures across register breaks or trills that require cross-fingering. Yet at the same time we must not lose sight of the possibility of a final, almost obscure subtlety, *reverse idiom*, i.e. the deliberate exploration of difficult, harsh, awkward, or otherwise unidiomatic procedures for special effect, such as Stravinsky's repeated staccato vocal chords (*Symphony of Psalms*: "Laudate Dominum") or the strained, high bassoon at the opening of *The Rite of Spring*.

Dynamics

From experiences with performance we all tend to think of dynamics in terms of written indications such as piano or crescendo. As a style-analytical category, however, *dynamics* must include all aspects of intensity in sound, whether indicated by dynamic markings or not. Particularly for the late nineteenth century, of course, dynamic markings offer a shorthand summary of the fluctuations of intensity, as well as giving a measure of the composer's care and his knowledge of the media. We must train ourselves, however, to observe actual as well as indicated dynamics, calculating the intensities produced by the disposition of forces within the fabric, not overlooking the subtle increase of intensity produced by higher ranges or the curiously unpredictable effects on intensity produced by some doublings. Clarinet doubled with trumpet, for example, seems to blur and partly muffle the trenchant brass tone, yielding less rather than more intensity; on the other hand, a string quartet, when compared dynamically with a string trio, gives the illusion of considerably more resonance than the one-third gain that might be expected from the single additional player. To make a reasonable evaluation of a composer's use of dynamics we must consider the following points:

Types of dynamics: in this vocabulary of dynamic effects we must include both indicated and implied dynamics, from loudest to softest, at the same time noting the most frequent and characteristic dynamic levels, as well as individual details such as addiction to *sforzando* or eccentricities such as *pf*.

Degree of contrast: differences of expression in different eras produce surprisingly varying degrees of dynamic contrast. While *piano* to *forte* suffices for most Baroque and Classic composers, Beethoven expanded the degree of contrast at least one level in each direction, and Mahler's dramatic sensibilities sometimes require close juxtapositions of *fff* and *ppp*. Less obvious but possibly even more revealing of a composer's style is the *frequency of contrast*: the interval of time-elapse between different dynamic levels, ranging from immediate succession of sharply contrasted dynamics, through more gradual changes such as crescendos, to longer gradations of increasing or decreasing intensity. Taken together, degree and frequency of contrast produce two main dynamic procedures:

1. *Terrace (or block) dynamics*, in which phrases and sentences of a piece establish contrasting dynamic levels, as in organ registration or, less sharply, in the alternation of tutti and concertino forces in a concerto grosso; and

2. *Tapered dynamics*, in which gradual changes in forces and instructions make a sloping transition to lower or higher plateaus that continue for a substantial amount of time and therefore contrast with each other only in a rather general way. The principles of terracing and tapering may occur in all dimensions, of course, determined simply by variations in the composer's timing of dynamic contrast. Concerti grossi of Corelli, for example, apply terrace dynamics on a tiny scale, sometimes echoing back and forth between tutti and concertino in half-bar responses. The entrance of the

tutti at the end of a solo episode in a Bach or Vivaldi concerto, however, represents a major sectional change of considerably greater weight and larger dimension.

Texture and Fabric

Since texture changes from moment to moment in music, the main problem of the analyst lies in discovering some useful generalizations under which to group these manifold textural observations. Vertical details may be described directly by terms such as thick or thin, simple or doubled, continuous or gapped, alternating or overlapping, balanced or top- (bottom-)heavy, pure or mixed between voices and instruments. The predominant pitch area in which a composer sets a section, part, or movement may conveniently be indicated by the word *tessitura*, which, though merely the Italian equivalent of "texture," through much usage in discussions of singers' ranges has tended to acquire a more restricted and specialized connotation. (This specifically musical connotation of tessitura to mean "most-used pitch area" will also be used in the discussions of Melody below.) These textural terms do not entirely suffice, however, for we often need to differentiate single textural events precisely from the total continuum of the music. Hence, it is a good plan to restrict the meaning of *texture* to refer to particular, momentary combinations of sounds; then, pursuing the analogy with textiles, we can use *fabric* to refer to the whole continuous web of combined textures and dynamic levels. In the course of music history various types of musical fabrics have emerged and survived as successful conventions of textural extension:

Homophonic, homorhythmic, chordal: referring to styles in which the textural events take place more or less simultaneously.

Polyphonic, contrapuntal, fugal: referring to styles of higher textural vitality resulting from greater rhythmic and melodic independence of the various strands or layers of the fabric.

Melody/bass polarity: the characteristic texture of the Baroque, elaborated in the *trio-sonata fabric* (typically two violins plus thoroughbass).

Melody plus accompaniment: the chord-oriented, thematic fabric familiar in much of Classic and Romantic music.

Sectionally specialized textures: more sophisticated arrangements developed by composers to give smoother orchestral effects by assigning sustaining functions to brass and doubling or antiphonal functions to woodwinds as support or alternative to the fundamental melody, accompaniment, and bass action of the strings.

Beyond these conventional fabrics, of course, imaginative composers create personal conventions for each piece and movement that they write.

Contributions of Sound to Movement

The effects of timbres, dynamics, and textures on Movement are usually less immediately apparent than the contribution of other elements. In general, the function of Sound seems to be secondary; the acoustical clothing of melodies, harmonies, and rhythms underlines but does not influence their Movement; the refreshment of new colors and different intensities sharpens but does not direct the action of other elements. We must not overlook, however, the possibility of a more fundamental if elusive contribution by Sound: changes of tone colors or dynamic levels—especially alternations such as antiphonal and dialogue effects—can produce waves of varying activity that profoundly affect the rhythmic infrastructure. Masked by more obvious foreground action in other elements, this background activity often escapes notice, particularly in the broader dimensions. Yet it seems likely that the large-scale pulsations of Sound, precisely because of their more primitive, less defined character, may significantly activate our deepest consciousness of Movement, responses which we often feel but can rarely explain. As a suggestive illustration of this possibility, notice that units larger than a phrase in any continuum (the consistent hierarchy of durational relationships—discussed later) become increasingly harder to feel as "beats." Though one can sense the macrometer in a 4+4+4+4 bar-structure (each group of four bars functioning like the beats in a single 4/4 bar), larger units such as paragraphs of 8+8+8+8 or 16+16+16+16 occur rarely in arithmetically perfect groupings, so that in order to recognize an underlying regularity the ear must ignore or compensate for various irregularities in details. Furthermore, our perception of rhythmic regularity in such large units is easily distracted by the multiplicity of small-dimension activity—surface rhythm, line, harmony, and so on. For just such broad purposes, therefore, changes in Sound contribute the most: they can clarify larger modules amid the confusions of other elements, maintaining the hierarchic flow of the continuum in middle and occasionally even in large dimensions. Mere changes in orchestration every sixteen bars, for example, can remind us unmistakably of a paragraph structure that could otherwise easily disappear among the welter of melodic and rhythmic details.

Performance articulations, such as bowing and tonguing to produce slurs and staccatos, relate so directly to Movement and Shape that they might with nearly equal justification be included there, rather than under the subdivision of timbre in the rubric of Sound. (To avoid confusion of the general function of articulation in Growth, these small, detailed articulations will hereafter be designated as "surface articulations.") For example, in a repeated pattern of four staccato sixteenths followed by four slurred sixteenths, the surface articulations alone produce (a) small-dimension alternations that contribute forcefully if briefly to Movement; and (b) articulation of small repetition modules as part of Shape.

Contributions of Sound to Shape

If the rhythmic functions of Sound seem rather elusive, the contributions to Shape compensate in directness, for changes in Sound create the most easily observed articulations in any musical flow. When we are uncertain about punctuations in a complex of surface rhythms or in the overlapping counterpoint of upper and lower lines, articulations in Sound, such as changes from voices to instruments or from loud to soft, can set us unequivocally straight. Obviously the more complex the other elements grow, the more decisively the clues of Sound function in determining the primary and secondary articulations of a piece.

Sound also figures prominently in formal patterning, first as a

reinforcement of thematic memory—it is easier to notice the recurrence of an idea if the tone-color also recalls an earlier appearance—
and then somewhat more subtly as a source of variety and development in presenting ideas: the totally obvious yet imperishably
effective devices of repeating a theme with a different solo instrument, with new octave doublings, or with a change of dynamic
level produced by fuller (or sparser) orchestration, all illustrate
the power of Sound to fix the progress of the musical Shape in our
minds.

Sound in Large Dimensions

Large-dimension observations force us to generalize, and for
Sound, once we have noted any different selections of media
between the movements or parts of movements in question, we
must concern ourselves mainly with fabric. In line with the principle
of consistent analytical habits recommended above, we begin by
establishing a typology of fabrics for the movement, i.e. the composer's total spectrum of acoustical choices and his characteristic
preferences within this spectrum. In a group of Classic symphonies,
for example, this first stage of large-dimension examination of movements might yield a useful if somewhat obvious conclusion that
eighteenth-century composers often omit brass instruments in slow
movements, at the same time using a somewhat narrower, less
intense dynamic range for other instruments. Next we should notice
how many types of fabric occur, and which types predominate. The
various detailed, conventional fabrics mentioned above may turn
out to be somewhat too specific to serve as classifications for large-
dimension observations: we need even more sweeping categories
at the outset. For these we can borrow an illuminating concept from
the art historian, Heinrich Wölfflin:[1] his famous distinction between
the linear and the painterly approach to art, which can be translated into musical terms as *linear* and *massive* procedures for the
construction of musical fabrics. (See Example 2-1.)

   These very broad initial categories roughly parallel the distinc-

1. See Heinrich Wölfflin, *Principles of Art History*, transl. by M. D. Hottinger, repr. New
York, 1950, especially Introduction and Chapter 1.

EXAMPLE 2-1.   Beethoven, Piano Sonata, Op. 13: I, bars 131-41.
Contrast of massive and linear textures.

Massive

tion between polyphony and homophony (or counterpoint vs. harmony), but their even greater generality makes it comparatively easier to classify the fabrics under discussion. Particularly for large-scale interpretations we must constantly remind ourselves that music, by its infinitely varied nature, forces us to make schematic, summary conclusions rather than absolute determinations. Since we will not often find consistently linear or massive fabrics, it is practical to think in terms of more flexible (but nonetheless effective and orderly) categories such as "mainly linear" and "predominantly massive." In between, of course, we need a middle choice, which for fabrics might best be represented as "mixed line and mass."

From the point of view of composers' individual attitudes toward expression we will find the frequency and degree of contrast extremely important and revealing. Some composers cast entire movements in a single tone-color or on a single dynamic level, making their major contrasts only *between* movements. Others employ higher frequency of change *within* movements, which tends to reduce the strength of contrast *between* movements. Three useful observational categories at this point would be high, medium, and low frequency of contrast.

Degrees of contrast (again high, medium, and low) may not be as easy to clarify in large-dimension impressions as frequencies of contrast. These evidences of a composer's expressive pressure-range, such as degrees of change in color and dynamics, can often be more successfully observed and interpreted in middle and small dimensions. This situation parallels language in which the highest emotional impact may occur in a pungent phrase, a poignant sentence, or a haunting paragraph. Much more rarely do we find a whole chapter of sustained intensity. The larger dimensions in music similarly tend to contain a variety of shifting expressive levels.

Sound in Middle Dimensions

Middle dimensions are the most important for the study of a composer's handling of Sound, for in these dimensions we see the most influential and expressive changes and hence the most effective contributions of Sound to Movement and Shape. While there are many ways of grouping observations, the familiar categories of Typology, Movement, and Shape again furnish a reliably comprehensive approach:

1. *Typology*

a) TIMBRE. In middle dimensions, timbre begins to exert more influence, for we notice detailed contrasts more in paragraphs and sections than in parts and wholes. It is not necessary to create rigid typologies and subtypologies for all the facets of timbre; indeed, here again we must avoid drowning in data by practicing selectivity wherever possible. The important thing to keep in mind is the principle of typology: with a complete framework in the back of our minds we then record merely the significant details that gradually fill in the stylistic portrait of the composer, point by point. The checklist for timbre should include the main headings such as choice, range, and idiom, as well as degree and frequency of contrast, to which we might add any special phenomena peculiar to the particular piece or repertory. For example, the *quilisma*, as a special effect of Sound in Gregorian Chant, would be considered in the middle- or small-dimension typology of idiom. (It might also be included as an ornament, i.e. as part of Melody.)

b) DYNAMICS. Since a relatively brief inspection can tell us the types of dynamics the composer employs (not forgetting intrinsic dynamics), our main attention should focus on the degree and frequency of dynamic contrasts. Probably we feel these effects of the composer's personal intensity most in middle dimensions, where a long crescendo can produce an almost unbearably intense climax not possible in small dimensions. The typology of dynamics must carefully record lengths of crescendos and other graduated processes, as well as the strengths of juxtapositions such as echo effects: Is the contrast f/p or ff/pp (degree)? Does it take place immediately or after a rest (frequency)?

c) FABRIC. Typology of fabrics in middle dimensions also focuses more on the degree and frequency of contrast than on textural conventions and other general points covered by large dimensions. Here are some suggestive alternatives for classifying these attributes:

thick / thin	narrow / broad	high / low
loud / soft	average / climactic	simple / complex
active / stable	abrupt / gradual	

We can obtain an appropriately detailed typology with surprisingly little ambiguity by interpolating "middling," "mixed," or "partly" between the various alternatives listed above; and the separation of observations for each type into only three subdivisions presents relatively few difficult determinations.

2. *Movement.* As we progress to smaller divisions of a piece, the rhythmic effect of Sound also increases in importance. The periodic motion produced by alternations of different timbres, dynamics, or textures definitely contributes to Movement, as do the contrasts between active and stable areas of fabric. As already mentioned in the general discussion of Sound and Movement, these alternations and contrasts often clarify larger modules in the continuum, such as eight- or sixteen-bar units, so that we can feel the rhythmic hierarchy in larger values. There is also a general parallel to surface rhythm: the sense of movement produced by alternations of approximately equal responsory groups, for example, has roughly the effect of even durations, whereas a large-to-small dialogue (as between tutti and concertino) may correspond approximately to

the effect of a dotted rhythm—not in a precise durational parallel, of course, but in the more active contribution to Movement in its underlying aspects that unequal alternations can produce. Obviously, too, the degree and frequency of contrasts in surface dynamics can also confirm or even originate these deeper if less definable rhythmic responses. With inter-elemental connections of this sort in mind, we can logically establish concepts such as textural rhythm, timbral rhythm, and the rhythm of dynamic levels. These interactions cannot always be abstracted into precise durational values, but their influences on Movement may nonetheless reveal highly personal features of a composer's style.

3. *Shape*. Nowhere does Sound contribute more to the weighting of articulations than in middle dimensions. We can probably hear the difference between successive timbres or dynamic levels a bit more immediately than we can recognize a difference in melodic or rhythmic activity—or perhaps composers generally use more obvious contrasts in Sound than in other elements. In either case, Sound contributes very directly and decisively in defining Shape by punctuations of timbral, textural, and dynamic contrast. Next, the character of continuations may be changed or confirmed by different orchestration or dynamics; for example, the statement-and-response type of theme often depends for its characteristic Shape quite as much on instrumentation and dynamics as on melodic or rhythmic features. (See Example 2-2.) Echo devices, used so effectively in many periods, can result solely from shifts in dynamic level. Thus, the general character of thematic paragraphs in any exposition of musical ideas may be either initiated or confirmed and underlined by the acoustical setting.

Sound in Small Dimensions

It would be a mistake to suggest that composers differ most in details, since some broad-gauge composers pay little attention to details, while miniaturists show strength in small dimensions but inability to conceive effective large-scale plans. Comparisons, therefore, should always take advantage of the full stylistic spectrum.

EXAMPLE 2-2.   Mozart, Symphony No. 41, K. 551: I, bars 1-4.
Statement and response clarified by contrasting orchestral textures.

Yet for composers who do pay attention to details, our appreciation of their refinements in handling of Sound contributes notably to a more general understanding of their objectives.

In small dimensions we concentrate on subtleties, i.e. not so much on instruments as on choices of register in instruments; not on block effects of staccato or legato but on favorite patterns in surface articulations; not on plateaus of dynamics but on single idiosyncratic marks, such as Haydn's *sfz*; not merely on textures, but possibly even on single notes, such as the hypnotic tolling of the horn in the slow movement of Schubert's C-major Symphony. At this closest focus, matters of timbre may slightly overshadow dynamics and fabric: notice the close attention to affective details of color found commonly throughout the Romantic period.

Though we are now studying small divisions, the typologies of timbre, dynamics, and texture will not necessarily be smaller or less complicated. We can use much the same approach as in middle dimensions, but again we must consciously avoid any overly detailed observations, recording only the most distinctive phenomena. The proper test for observation is not "Is it true?" but "Is it significant?" To spend a chapter on a single bar reveals more about the analyst's mind than about the composer's music: a tragic (or comic) lack of judgment. We cannot justify ignoring larger aspects by even the most splendid verbalization of beauties in the bar.

EXAMPLE 2-3.   Beethoven, Symphony No. 5: I, bars 195-213. *Small-dimension movement produced mainly by interchanges between winds and strings.*

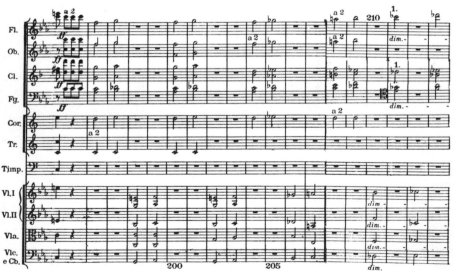

Contributions of Sound to Movement in small dimensions can be quite direct, as in the note-by-note equivalence between Sound and surface rhythm in the antiphonal exchanges between strings and winds in the first movement of Beethoven's Fifth Symphony (see Example 2-3). The sense of movement increases markedly when elements coordinate in this way. Small-dimension Sound affects Shape most by sharpening thematic distinctions, associating a particular melody or rhythm with a distinctive color or texture. The more individuality a theme possesses, the more effectively a composer can invent contrasts and formal returns to the idea. Sound can also assist in differentiating subphrases and motives, though within this restricted scope one finds less variety of articulation than in middle dimensions. (See Example 2-4.) The most useful areas of observation to bring out these functions may be tabulated as follows:

MOVEMENT	SHAPE
Rhythmic alternations of Sound	Distinctive thematic timbre /
Coordination with surface rhythm	dynamics / texture
Coordination with continuum[2] (meter, subphrase)	Articulation by timbre, dynamics, texture

Each of these points of observation may be divided into the usual three-part spectrum. Under Movement, for example, we would use the subcategories "Rhythmic," "Partly Rhythmic," and "Non-Rhythmic" for classifying any changes in Sound. Similarly, under Shape, the acoustical clothing of themes is either "Distinctive," "Somewhat Distinctive," or "Non-Distinctive"; and within these subcategories we would identify the type of distinction, whether timbral, dynamic, or textural.

2. See the chapter on Rhythm for an explanation of continuum.

EXAMPLE 2-4 (*next page*).   Mendelssohn, Overture to A *Midsummer Night's Dream*, Op. 21: bars 256-65.
Differentiation of thematic fragments by delicate timbral changes as the motive migrates downward through the string texture.

CHAPTER THREE

HARMONY

Harmony as a style-analytical element comprises not only the chordal phenomena ordinarily associated with the term but also all other relationships of successive vertical combinations, including counterpoint, less organized forms of polyphony, and dissonant procedures that do not make use of familiar chord structures or relationships. Passing the known music of the world in review, the history of western European music (and its derivatives) stands out immediately because of a central emphasis on Harmony. Whether as cause or effect, this emphasis has produced a sophistication of system in Harmony that goes far beyond the organization of other elements. We find carefully ordered spectra in Sound, subtle durational hierarchies in Rhythm, modes and scales in Melody; but each of these frames of organization is predominantly two-dimensional, dealing with simple, one-to-one relationships, which we can study and graph satisfactorily. Harmonic relationships, however (to continue a somewhat inexact analogy), are three-dimensional at the very least, dealing with numerous components, often with implications on several rhythmic levels. The intricacies of this system justify a comparison to language, with its interlocking levels of words, grammar, and syntax; the parallels may be neatly expressed in diagrams (see next page).

Precisely because of this firmly organized system, in many periods of music history we can discern rather clear conventions of harmonic behavior. These conventions help considerably with the task of style analysis, since we can make a much more knowledgeable evaluation of progressive, conventional, and regressive tendencies in any composer's harmonic style, recognizing what is common and what is rare or original in his use of chords, progressions, and

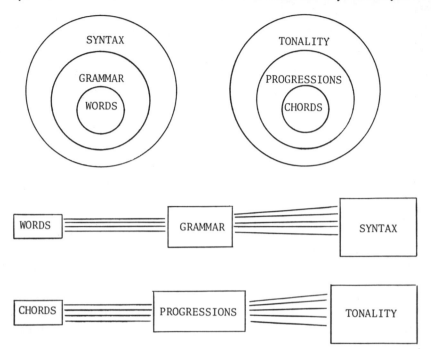

modulations. No harmonic effect can be assigned a single intrinsic stylistic value, of course, for harmony makes its impact by relationships that may vary radically between composers, schools, and eras. Notice, for example, that a diatonic passing tone that we recognize as clearly dissonant in Mozart's harmonic convention may well be the most consonant procedure observable in a passage by Richard Strauss: the conventions have changed, and where for Mozart the diatonic passing tone lies far enough outside the core of consonant procedures to sound dissonant, for Strauss the harmonic conventions have so grandly expanded that the passing tone now belongs actually to the inner, conservative circle of his devices. In Strauss's terms, then, the passing tone might even be classified as a consonance.

If we must regard harmonic procedures in the light of changing conventions, clearly we must free our minds from any single specific system. In general, harmonic analysis tends to rely far too

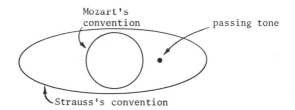

much on the conventions of the "common practice" period, in which the consistent processes of unified tonality permit an extremely refined scale of evaluation for chords, dissonances, and other harmonic or nonharmonic procedures. We must therefore go back to much more primitive and fundamental concepts of harmonic function to obtain a generality sufficient for all the requirements of style analysis. These two most basic functions of harmony are:

1. *Color.* Harmonic color is in many styles the most instantaneous affective resource of music. We are immediately conscious of changes from major to minor forms of chords; open fourths or fifths vs. triads, sevenths, or higher complexities of vertical structure; open vs. close position (partly a function of Sound, of course); various doublings; and "dark" (flat) or "light" (sharp) key relationships. Color values may also be discovered in contrasting areas of greater and lesser dissonance.

2. *Tension.* By some as yet not fully understood process, various harmonic relationships apparently have intrinsic tensional effects, so that we speak of—and obviously feel—the "resolution" of a chord or dissonance; and in larger dimensions we are conscious of areas of stability and instability in relation to a starting point. To some extent color values in harmony may also function tensionally, for example in the usually more relaxed effect of "darker" tonalities (i.e. toward the flat or subdominant side of the relevant tonal center).

Equally basic for the observation of harmonic phenomena is the need to distinguish between essentials and details, or, expressed as components of Growth, between *structural* and *ornamental* functions. We have seen above that prevailing dimensions and controlling elements generally clarify the structural functions. While we may derive some clues to structural harmonic functions by looking for confirmations in other elements, the main determinant is durational: changes of chords (or dissonant notes) of durations shorter than the prevailing unit (or the dimensions that we are examining) are ornamental, i.e. secondary in the Growth of the piece. For example, if the chord rhythm is mainly half-note, quarter-note changes will be of lesser importance. (While this axiomatic statement may seem ridiculously obvious, it keeps us from exaggerating the over-all impact of any small device, even if colorful, a surprisingly frequent difficulty in analytical writing.) Similarly, in middle dimensions a "parenthesis" modulation, such as a quick excursion in two or three bars to the relative minor and back, should not be assigned structural significance.

Owing to the extremely diversified yet highly organized nature of Harmony, however, the three standard dimensions and the prevailing beat-unit may not suffice as criteria by which to distinguish structural and ornamental functions: they may provide too coarse an analytic mesh to sort out the harmonic subtleties. To satisfy this situation and requirement, it will often be necessary to determine a dimension especially for harmonic purposes, the *harmonic module*, i.e. the characteristic unit of harmonic motion, which will not necessarily be a metrical beat. (See Example 3-1.) We will return to this concept in the discussion of small-dimension aspects of Harmony.

Another problem in a generalized view of Harmony is the whole question, "What is a chord?"—sometimes better phrased as "When is a chord?" For purposes of style analysis it is immediately necessary to expand the usual meaning of the term "chord" to include all types of concurrent sounds. Presently some writers prefer the term "simultaneity," which escapes the conventional semantic encrustations of "chord" and obviously permits a yeasty breadth of interpretations. However, "simultaneity" is a mouth-filling and sentence-clogging word, and the present discussions will show that the old, familiar term can still serve us well. In expanding the meaning of "chord," the important points to remember are (1)

EXAMPLE 3-1. Beethoven, Piano Sonata, Op. 7: III, Trio, bars 1-8.
Four-bar harmonic module defined by chord-rhythmic patterning.

that triads or other chords of superposed thirds are not necessarily
the most important vertical structures in a style; and (2) that
tension and color functions exist in all styles, even though the
vertical-horizontal relationships may be far removed from familiar
concepts of chords, progressions, and tonalities.

Dissonant Styles

If we look either forward or backward from the "common-
practice" period, we encounter uses of consonance and dissonance
that do not fit the common-practice convention. Since in order to
recognize structural and ornamental aspects of any piece we must
have some convention in mind, obviously for each style that does
not correspond to our usual conventions we must deduce or improvise a new convention. The dangers of a circular analysis here
are obvious but partly unavoidable: we will tend to say of a piece:
Chords A, B, C predominate in positions of structural importance;
then turn around and conclude that points X, Y, Z are structural
because they emphasize Chords A, B, C. Though logically incorrect,
this process actually may put us on the trail toward the new con-

vention. In recognizing the "rules" of an unfamiliar style, we must
open our minds to possibilities that may seem to overturn many of
our normal acceptances. For example, it may seem hard to accept
a style in which a normally dissonant interval (i.e. to us!) appears
to be treated as more stable than an interval that we usually consider consonant. Yet reflect for a moment that the fourth, which
both mathematically and in early music history figures as a consonance, for the common-practice period functions a dissonance.
If this can happen in our own history, there should be no difficulty
in extrapolating into a situation where the augmented fourth is
stable and the octave is unusual and transitional rather than stable
and structural. Our common-practice convention includes some
other instructive exceptions. We define normal chord structure in
terms of superposed thirds and regard notes outside this triadic
structure as dissonant, unstable, needing resolution. But what can
we say of the "added-sixth" chord so indispensable (and discour-
agingly ubiquitous) in contemporary popular music and widely
used as a stable chord in more august twentieth-century styles?
Here again is a promising avenue for extrapolation: we should be
able to adjust our analysis to differing conventions in which various
dissonances may function as consonances because they are the most
stable elements in their particular style. Consider for a moment a
Middle Eastern chant accompanied by a bowed drone of two notes
a second apart. Certainly one may begin by hearing the drone as a
dissónance, but as it persists, its stability compels the ear to recognize it as a consonance. Actually many of our habitual distinctions
between consonance and dissonance will not stand up long under
an absolutely logical scrutiny: think of the dissonant partials (to
say nothing of miscellaneous noises) in any "single" tone. But
harmony is not absolute logic; it is a pattern of relative intensities
that we should think of more as a flexible gamut between stability
and tension than as a clear-cut table of consonances and dissonances. To implement this point of view we should take three related
steps:

   1. *Find the stable harmonic structures.* The stable elements in
any harmonic system or convention can often be recognized by
inspecting areas where other elements indicate a condition of sta-

bility. In general one finds the best hints at endings, beginnings, and major points of articulation. (The style-analyst always looks first at the conclusion of a piece, not at the beginning.)

2. *Find the source of maximum tension.* While we may begin this search on the basis of conventional ideas of tension, a radical or exotic style may force us to recognize unconventional sources of tension. Here again we should use high activity and tension of other elements as clues to tensional effects in harmony.

3. *Make a gradation between stability and maximum tension.* For radical and conventional styles alike, the gamut between stability and instability will usually rest in part on familiar assumptions such as the notion that a third is more consonant than a second. Notice that seemingly abstruse styles often simply reverse normal harmonic conventions, e.g. making the augmented fourth the prime consonance while treating the unison, octave, and fifth as unstable and transitional. Thus, they actually operate according to the norm—interpreted negatively. Even in a style that never uses a simple triad one can deduce gradations. In general we can expect chords that include more dissonance to function with less stability, i.e. a chord C-F♯-B will be chosen less frequently for stable functions than a more nearly consonant chord such as C-F-G.

Whatever the convention turns out to be, once we can identify the composer's general harmonic habits, we can apply this knowledge in discovering the detailed Movement and Shape of his piece. The hints about harmonic stability that we earlier derived from melody or rhythm can now be turned to reciprocal advantage: passages that are ambiguous rhythmically or melodically may be clarified by our increasing understanding of the harmonic conventions.

Counterpoint

In early stages of listening and studying music it is useful to place Harmony and Counterpoint at opposite poles, contrasting the horizontal, linear approach with the vertical, block-chordal approach. Unfortunately, or perhaps fortunately, composers do not usually maintain such rigid distinctions. The Baroque period, for example, combines extremes in a "harmonically saturated counter-point," to use Bukofzer's succulent phrase. Even considered as polar alternatives, then, Harmony and Counterpoint form the two ends of a single continuous spectrum, and we will quickly find that discussions of one aspect tend to overlap the other. Since for practical purposes one needs a single term to subsume this whole area of analytical consideration, and since the word "harmony" already has rather broad connotations, it has seemed the most natural choice as the term for the second general style element. If we thus expand and reserve the word "harmony" for this categorical meaning, we can substitute "chordal" as a suitable alternative to "contrapuntal." We must then find ways of defining the interpenetrations of the two divergent textural approaches.

The occasional use of contrapuntal procedures, e.g. fugato within predominantly chordal styles, such as those of the later eighteenth and nineteenth centuries, makes it desirable to have some clear way of distinguishing a genuinely contrapuntal style. The chief ingredients of a fundamentally horizontal, linear orientation are:

1. *Approximately equal activity of concurrent lines.* As a sample problem, consider the so-called canon in the finale of César Franck's piano and violin sonata: it does not qualify as true counterpoint, since one part holds a single, long note while the other part moves. There is point but insufficient counter.

2. *Overlapping articulation.* Genuinely contrapuntal styles give an impression of smooth continuity because one part bridges over the articulations in other parts. In a Palestrina cadence, for example, one or two voices may already have begun the points of imitation of the following phrase. These noncoordinated articulations result naturally from the linear independence characteristic of Renaissance works. A typical illustration of the contrary influence of coordinated articulation may be seen in passages of apparently contrapuntal nature that occur in many Classic symphonies, notably in development sections of Sammartini, Haydn, and Mozart; here the coordination of articulations approximately every two or four bars undermines the contrapuntal effect: we may find considerable melodic and rhythmic individuality in the lines, yet if they phrase

EXAMPLE 3-2. Haydn, String Quartet, Op. 20, No. 2: IV, bars 99-119. *Coordinated articulations within a contrapuntal section: see bars 107, 114, 118-19.*

and cadence together, they obviously lose much of both their independence and total continuity. Similarly, the most striking reason that fugal finales in the Classic period usually do not sound like Baroque fugues may be traced to the overly frequent use of coordinated rather than overlapping articulations. (See Example 3-2.)

For classifying various degrees of contrapuntal organization it is helpful to postulate some general framework, such as the following levels of increasingly rigorous control: polyphonic, contrapuntal, imitative, canonic, complex. At the outset it is well to reserve the term *polyphonic* as the most general category for all music with more than one part (hence opposed to monophonic), without any necessary implications of conspicuously independent activity. A fabric of two or more lines that give some evidence of interdependence, though not necessarily with melodic relationship, can be described as *contrapuntal*; a degree of unity attained by interchange of similar material between voices raises the process to the next level, *imitative*; strict, systematic imitation produces a *canonic* fabric; and if one or more parts of the canon contain additionally specialized devices such as stretto, inversion, augmentation, diminution, or retrograde, the term *complex* is appropriate.

Contributions of Harmony to Movement

The contributions of Harmony to Movement are particularly direct, owing to the obvious forward motion implicit in every contrast of harmonic tension and stability, an immediate kinetic impact quite different from potential motion that may gradually develop from changes in Sound, for example. As a result of the greater systematization of Harmony as an element, this harmonic motion also exhibits a relatively high degree of organization, which may be summarized by the general term *harmonic rhythm*, the rate of harmonic change. In small dimensions the chief harmonic changes result from chord action, which can logically be described as *chord rhythm*. At the other extreme, in large dimensions we are conscious of movement between tonalities, or *key rhythm*. In between these two main dimensions of harmonic rhythm lie a great variety of small- and middle-dimension effects that are difficult to pin down with a single term. For example, at times the patterns for resolution of dissonances create rhythms of their own that must be taken into account when determining chord rhythms. (See Example 3-3.) Also, small patterns of consistent harmonic progression, as in sequences

EXAMPLE 3-3.   Palestrina, *Missa L'homme armé:* Agnus I, bars 36-42.
Rhythmic flow maintained by suspensions and resolutions even though
chord rhythm slows (x = dissonance, o = consonance).

of various types, create what might be called *progression rhythm*.
Finally, in areas of swift modulation the key rhythm becomes so
rapid that another term, such as *modulatory rhythm*, may prove
to be useful. In all of these intermediate situations the *harmonic-*
rhythmic module must be determined by the progress of the individual piece. We can use this module as a consistent point of
reference in determining the ornamental and structural functions
of chords and dissonances.

Contributions of Harmony to Shape

Harmony makes equally important and definite contributions
to Shape, since it can clarify both articulations and types of continuation with a wide range of subtly but unambiguously gradual
procedures. At least five important harmonic phenomena can either
cause or strengthen an articulation: change of mode, change of key,
acceleration or deceleration in chord rhythm, intensification (or
detensification) of vertical complexity, and increase or decrease in
frequency of dissonance. These changes in harmonic "pressure"
affect us particularly strongly, probably because each vertical unit

contains several components, with numerous resulting interactions. These same changes can affect all options for continuation, from interrelationship to contrast, at times subtly, but with potentials of great force. For example, the nuance of affect in a phrase can be delicately altered by changing a single chord or progression; more decisively, a reharmonization in relative minor or with faster chord rhythm can change the entire meaning of the phrase; and each of the other degrees of interrelated development (mutation, derivation) may result from changes in harmonic treatment. Similarly, the option of response may depend as much on harmony as on melodic content for creating a convincing thematic module. We are all familiar with four-bar phrases that move to a half cadence on the dominant, followed by a response of four more bars moving back to the tonic. The option of contrast, of course, owes a special debt to harmony, since various accepted tonal relationships furnish the primary foundation of conventional forms. Among these, the functions of the middle area in the dominant, the contrast episode in the relative minor, and the coda with subdominant emphasis have established well-worn pathways in music history, expectations so normal that composers can create effective surprise merely by turning away from these usual harmonic routes. Finally, in the realm of nonsurprise, the firmest evidence of recurrence in tonal music is the return of primary material in the original tonality.

Harmony in Large Dimensions

Observations of Harmony in large dimensions begin with general impressions of whole movements. If we are dealing with a large series of movements, it may yield quite important general conclusions if we can construct a typology of impressions among the following alternatives:

> Coloristic — Tensional
> Chordal — Contrapuntal (imitative, canonic, fugal, etc.)
> Dissonant — Consonant
> Active — Stable
> Uniform — Variegated
> Major — Minor
> Diatonic — Chromatic — Modal — Quartal, Exotic, etc.

If the harmonic structures justify speaking of keys, preferences for particular keys and preferred sequences of keys in successive movements should be observed. The Baroque period, for example, makes far more use of minor keys than the Classic period. Applying this general knowledge, if an early Classic composer shows notable preference for minor keys, this conservative harmonic attitude may lead us to discover other conservative (or even regressive) characteristics in his style that might otherwise pass unnoticed. This is a good time to bring up a typical (and potentially misleading) ambiguity in the determination of old and new fashions in music: composers, like designers, tend to change style in recurrent cycles, so that effects rejected by one generation may, two generations later, suddenly come back into fashion as new discoveries. Thus, the interest in minor keys, which we have just identified as conservative in early Classic composers, for middle and late composers may be pre-Romantic, hence progressive rather than regressive.

Since harmony shows a high degree of organization, one of the important large-dimension observations will concern the relative degree or stage of systematization reached by a particular piece or repertory. The history of tonality is an enormous subject, as yet insufficiently explored and obviously much too complex to deal with here except in the most summary terms. Beginning in the Middle Ages with chords produced incidentally by polyphony, composers gradually discovered satisfactory progressions, including directional chains such as cadences, sequences, and modulations that help to control and relate broader stretches of music. By 1750 the tonic-dominant axis of unified tonality supports a whole small universe of chords in hierarchical relationships. Shortly thereafter, however, growing interest in harmonic color weakens the structural emphasis, as we can easily see by comparing two masters of harmonic effect, Beethoven and Wagner. In Beethoven's music harmonic phenomena underline an abstract structure; for Wagner harmony generates feeling controlled by changing dramatic situations. Responding to these differing requirements, Wagner's vocabulary is considerably richer but his syntax is looser. He needs color, but not a tight, independent harmonic structure, which might actually compete or conflict with the dramatic organization. As we can see from this example, harmonic evolution is a selectively developmental process. Speaking in the most general terms, structural aspects predominate before 1800, affect and color receive more attention thereafter. While all of these historical developments naturally overlap and interlock, we will find it useful to relate any style we are studying to one or more of the following stages in the evolution of tonality:

1. *Linear tonality*: the harmonic syntax of the period from the earliest polyphony to the middle of the Renaissance, in which considerations of melodic line play a dominant part in determining vertical choices. Initially the use of a derived melody as a cantus firmus obviously commits the composer to a predetermined line that may considerably restrict his vertical freedom of choice. Later the conventions of the modal system and of imitative counterpoint exercise a similar if more general restraint. The word "modality," however, is ambiguous and misleading when used as a term to describe this stage of harmonic evolution, since the modal system is a specifically melodic development, never fully or consistently applied to harmony. The opposition of the term "modality" to "tonality" is particularly confusing and undesirable, since at various stages tonality may include modal progressions.

2. *Migrant tonality*: a type of harmonic process observed mainly from the early Renaissance to the late Baroque, which passes constantly from one temporary key center to another without establishing consistent directions or any central gravitational goal. This migrant quality tends to counteract the ascendancy of any one key, though general key feeling develops strongly in the Renaissance period. In later works the gradual emergence of the circle of fifths as a characteristic modulatory highway gives evidence of tonic-dominant consciousness and a firmer sense of control than the Renaissance habit of settling at any convenient point—sometimes distinctly "wrong" for modern ears because it contradicts the cumulative tonal emphasis of the piece.

3. *Bifocal tonality*: an intermediate stage in the development toward unified tonality, encountered chiefly in the seventeenth and early eighteenth centuries, characterized by oscillation between major and relative minor, without as much other excursion as

migrant tonality. The two centers seem to be of approximately equal importance, hence the term "bifocal." This curiously ambivalent form of tonality can. be observed most clearly at structural divisions in Baroque works, where the dominant of a minor key often resolves directly to the relative major rather than to its own tonic, thus functioning in a dual or bifocal capacity.[1] (For a compact example, see the two-chord Adagio movement of *Brandenburg Concerto* No. 3.) Passages of this sort, by no means rare, show that composers conceived of the two keys as a bifocal unity.

4. *Unified tonality*, or simply *tonality*: a functioning hierarchy of chords centered around a single tonic, characteristic of music from about 1680 to about 1860 (the symmetrical inner digits have no occult significance). The tonic system represents a slow accumulation of harmonic experience, establishing gradually by endless trial and error a set of effective conventions for chord progression, resolution of dissonance, modulation, and large-scale key relationships. The two controlling ideas in this evolution were (a) *directionality*, resulting from tension and resolution, expressed most effectively in the tonic/dominant axis, and (b) *unification*, produced by relating all harmonic structures and procedures to a single center. In the developments toward and away from tonality, we can often evaluate a composer's attitude most clearly by reference to these two underlying principles. The most significant influence of tonality results not so much from its control (and later codification by Rameau and others) of harmonic vocabulary, grammar, and syntax, as from the tensional drive it imparts to musical forms when allied to thematic structure and orchestral contrast. This new concinnity suddenly made possible an enormous expansion in instrumental forms and a tangible deepening of musical expression.

5. *Expanded tonality*: composers extended harmonic resources rapidly during the nineteenth century primarily in search of affective or descriptive color. Often these expansions occurred so quickly that no grammar or syntax could be evolved to furnish a structural framework. As a result, a desirable enrichment also tended to

1. See Jan LaRue, *Bifocal Tonality, An Explanation for Ambiguous Baroque Cadences*, in *Essays on Music in Honor of A. T. Davison*, Cambridge, Mass., 1957, pp. 173–84.

decentralize or even break down the centripetal character of unified tonality. The long-persisting tradition of beginning and ending a piece in the same key or tonal area, however, shows that many composers continued to sense a basic tonal unity even in the face of radical experimentation. Some typical innovations that one may expect to encounter in works of expanded tonality are:

a) ENLARGED DIATONICISM, including larger chords of superposed thirds and free exchange of major and minor forms of the same key.

b) CHROMATICISM, including alteration of conventional chords and modulation between chromatically related keys.

c) NEOMODALITY, exploiting the antique flavor of modal progressions, particularly those of an antitonal character, such as I–♭VII, or V♭³–I, or IV–Im; exotic modality, such as the whole-tone scale, Bartók's folk modes, and the like, which produce fresh chordal possibilities.

d) STRUCTURAL DISSONANCE, beginning with the added sixth and continuing with normally dissonant chord structures, such as I⁷, accepted in cadential and other stable functions; expanding to combination chords, i.e. V/I as a continuing vertical structure rather than as an ultimately resolving polydissonance.

e) BITONALITY AND POLYTONALITY, produced by extensions of the principle of structural dissonance to middle and large dimensions, so that two keys such as C and E may proceed as parallel structures, just as in small dimensions two chords are carried along without resolution.

6. *Atonality*: the conscious avoidance of tonality by pursuit of antitonal procedures, together with the development of a nontonal, syntactical substitute, *serialism* (a more useful term than "dodecaphonism," since a serial style may not necessarily use all twelve notes, or may depend for structure on some aspect other than pitch).

Once the general harmonic milieu of a work is established, we set out to classify its tonal relationships, both between and within movements. Returning to the invaluable Rule of Three, when applied to tonality the logical classifications of relationship are *direct* (primary), *indirect* (secondary), and *remote*. For initial hypotheses we should base this typology on conventional relationships of the "common practice" convention, classifying tonalities roughly in the same manner that we classify chord relationships (discussed below among the small-dimension aspects of Harmony). Supposing the choice of chords and tonalities to be unfamiliar, exotic, or otherwise nonconventional, however, we must then discover the composer's own convention or anticonvention. At times we may be forced to broaden the concepts of key and tonality to include collections of rather loosely associated harmonic phenomena. Under such circumstances we can usually identify contexts that exert a centralizing tonic function on the basis of frequency and stability of occurrence. Here again the clues to stability may be simply durational—which chord associations persist longest—or it may be necessary to study interactions with other elements to discover which tonal effects the composer feels to be stable. If we can determine one or more tonal foci, the tracing of other, subsidiary relationships will proceed more easily.

The contribution of Harmony to Movement in large dimensions is one of the subtlest potentialities of musical response. There are two interlocking aspects that should be considered—key rhythm and tensional plan, i.e. degree of tonal change. Our general impressions of vitality and activity in a movement or series of movements undoubtedly originate partly from key rhythm, the rate or amount of change between tonal centers. Closely related is the degree of change; if the sequence of tonalities between movements includes tension relationships, particularly dominant-tonic successions, the impression of continuity will be very strong, pulling movements and parts of movements tenaciously into related or even concentric orbits, thus giving the listener both a broadly and subtly unified experience. If the over-all tonal plan lacks tensional sequences but places strongly contrasted keys in immediate succession, the impression of activity will still be strong, but the sense of unity will suffer.

In large dimensions we probably cannot often sense the total part and movement durations as rhythmic patterns; it is difficult to apprehend a succession of longer and shorter movements as a gigantic |♩ ♪|♩ ♪|♩ 𝄾| or similar alternation pattern. (Rondo forms, however, particularly those with short returns and longer episodes, may possibly be felt in durational patterns.) We do react in a general way to proportions, however, which should be thought of rhythmically and durationally, not as dead architectural masses. For this reason, if a slow movement seems disproportionately short, it may either give evidence of a composer's lack of sensitivity to large dimensions or, quite the contrary, it may result from obscure but effective linkages between movements, such as a tensional plan for key successions that related the key rhythm of the slow movement to the harmonic strategy of other movements.

As a contribution to Shape, large-dimension Harmony has somewhat the schematizing power already noticed in large-dimension Sound: amid many details of melody and rhythm, which tend to confuse the larger impressions of a piece, contrasts in tonality may serve to clarify the parts of a movement with considerable distinctness, a capacity actually broader than orchestration or other aspects of Sound can ordinarily match. Similarly, tonality can remind us of the return in a da capo aria quite as strikingly as thematic material, and we will actually do well to think of tonality as a part of thematic character, not limiting the concept or the term "theme" to melodic connotations. Contrasts in general harmonic character, as between chordal and contrapuntal fabrics, also serve to distinguish parts and movements one from another. Fugal action in a development section, for example, can effectively heighten the contrast of this part between the exposition and recapitulation in a sonata form.

Harmony in Middle Dimensions

Some of the aspects already discussed in large dimensions may also apply to middle dimensions, notably the contrasts in general procedures (chordal vs. contrapuntal, etc.) between various phrases or sections. For example, the continuous flow of a contrapuntal transition may be subtly emphasized by contrasts between a preceding chordal section and the overlapping articulations of the counterpoint. On the whole, however, harmonic action in middle dimensions concentrates on the smaller but more directly powerful

EXAMPLE 3-4.   Schubert, *Die schöne Müllerin*: VI, *Der Neugierige*, bars 23-28.

A momentary, ornamental change of mode for text expression.

effects of modulation and harmonic rhythm. Any typology of modulation should include at least three aspects: modulatory goals, Growth functions, and harmonic paths. For tonal goals the three-part classification suggested for large dimensions (direct, indirect, remote) works equally satisfactorily for middle dimensions. (See the detailed chart of small-dimension chord relationships, p. 61 below, which at least for initial hypotheses can be extrapolated to serve middle dimensions.) The functions of modulation, of course, can be either ornamental or structural, determined largely by duration and direction. Short modulations that lead immediately back to the point of departure obviously have only ornamental functions. Schubert's major-minor shifts perfectly exemplify this type. (See Example 3-4.) Not all coloristic modulations, however, are merely ornamental: in the nineteenth century the tonal relationships of large sections are often coloristic rather than tensional, yet the size and content of the contrasting key areas clearly indicate their structural importance.

   The pathways of modulation lead to some of the most significant of harmonic observations, since they reveal the composer's control of transitional processes and hence his ability to sustain musical continuity without irrelevant interruptions. Modulations that make use of direct tonic-dominant relationships or a pivot chord common to both tonalities obviously produce smooth seams, and the richness of invention that a composer shows in finding such natural pivots is a useful index to imagination. As an illustration, the *Pilgrim's March* of Berlioz's *Harold in Italy* repays study for its variety of modulation, ranging from facile common-chord transitions to shocking juxtapositions that jar the fundamental movement without any apparent purpose.

Harmonic rhythm enters into middle dimensions in two ways. First, changes in chord rhythm can create sharply effective articulations, and contrasts in general chord-rhythmic flow often differentiate whole paragraphs and sections. In the eighteenth century, for example, most transition sections settle into a slow, regular chord rhythm quite different from the more variegated activities in primary and secondary material.[2] Second, the use of drive patterns in chord rhythm (such as consistently unequal chord durations) may lend a markedly active character to a particular section, contrasting sharply with a neighboring section of sustained harmonies. This impact of chord-rhythmic functions on Movement is extremely powerful if not always easily definable. A revealing evidence of this source of control over Movement is the occasional existence of a harmonic module in middle dimensions, a phrase- or sentence-sized unit structured by chord rhythm that some composers (Mozart, Beethoven) can maintain with considerable consistency, giving a powerful sense of harmonic continuation to their music at this level, comparable to metrical control in small dimensions. Even when no complete regularity is attained, modular tendencies of middle-dimension durations are far more readily heard and felt than the comparatively vague timings produced by patterns of long duration. In an exposition with repeats, for example, if we hear twenty bars of stable, sustained rhythms on the tonic, ten bars of regular chord change during transitional modulation, and thirty bars of variegated activity centering on the dominant, this 2:1:3

2. See Jan LaRue, *Harmonic Rhythm in the Beethoven Symphonies*, in *The Music Review*, 18 (1957), 8–20; also Shelley Davis, *Harmonic Rhythm in Mozart's Sonata Form*, in *ibid.*, 27 (1966), 25–43.

relationship, especially when repeated, certainly hints at a macro-rhythmic enlargement of the pattern |♩ ♪|♪· |♩ ♪|♪· | . Actually, in large- and middle-dimension situations the arithmetical precision matters less than general effect, and a short section of high activity may balance a longer section of low activity. With suitable adjustments of interior activity, therefore, the following lengths of key areas in a long chain of modulation, 9 8 7 10 4 4 5 4 might easily be generalized by the ear as 8888 4444, or schematized in reduced values ♩♩♩♩ ♪♪♪♪ , a useful shorthand for comparing large durations. Even where no such consistent action or module can be observed, the contrast of chord rhythms and tonalities in successive middle-dimension segments can produce a far more specific sense of motion than that found in similarly irregular changes of Sound. Notice the powerful effect of chord-rhythmic acceleration in the first part of the Trio of Beethoven's First Symphony (Example 3-5).

The influence of Harmony on Shape is quite as decisive in middle as in large dimensions. In addition to the broad shaping that results from contrasts between modes or tonalities, we now experience lively if less fundamental contrasts produced by differences in chord complexity, frequency of dissonance, and patterning in chord rhythm, all of which affect both the articulations and the internal character of sentences, paragraphs, and sections.

Harmony in Small Dimensions

Small-dimensional aspects of harmony are the most familiar, since conventional harmonic instruction, both in writing and analysis, concentrates on small problems. Piston, Tovey, and others classify chords in typologies that are only partly useful to style analysis, owing to a natural concentration on the "common practice" period, which too rigidly circumscribes the sphere of direct

EXAMPLE 3-5.   Beethoven, Symphony No. 1: III, Trio, bars 88-103.
Chord-rhythmic acceleration.

relationships to accomplish the broader purposes of style analysis. Nevertheless, since the late eighteenth century brings all style elements into the closest concinnity of any period, its core of common practice furnishes the most satisfactory point of departure for a general typology of chord functions:

1. *Primary chords*: the directly related vocabulary within a tonality.

2. *Secondary chords*: those related indirectly through a primary chord, such as secondary dominants and altered chords.

3. *Remote chords*: those related through secondary chords or not functionally related at all.

The force of any harmonic effect, of course, can be strengthened or weakened by orchestration, dynamics, position in the range, textural arrangement, rhythmic accentuation, raw duration, thematic function, and functional (i.e. phrase or sectional) location—to mention only a few of the possibilities. Hence, the table below is merely a general scheme that will require constant adjustment to take account of local circumstances.

HARMONIC RELATIONSHIPS
IN MAJOR KEYS

Primary (Direct)	Secondary (Indirect)	Tertiary (Remote)
Chords of tonic scale.	Chords from scales built on degrees of tonic scale: V of V, IV of IV, etc.	Chords related through secondaries: ♭iii, ♭vi, etc.
Tonic minor.	Altered chords: raised ii and vi, V with altered fifth, etc.	Roots chromatically related to I, if not "explained" by primaries, i.e. ♭V when not approached through Neapolitan ♭II.
♭II (Neapolitan).		
A⁶ (Augmented sixth).		
Stabilized alterations: tonic with added sixth.	Borrowing from tonic minor: ♭VI, ♭III. Parallels of primaries: II, III, iv, v, VI.	Complex and dissonant alterations.

While the general division of the typology into primary, secondary, and remote relationships serves for all periods, the chords included will change as these classifications themselves expand, contract, and alter in various ways to describe styles that fall outside the conventions of "common practice." Bearing in mind the changing position of the passing tone in the conventions of Mozart and Strauss, we can see clearly that some chords that function as primary structures for Strauss would be on the remote perimeter of Mozart's vocabulary. To take another illustration, in early forms of expanded tonality, such as Schubert's vocabulary, secondary chords borrowed from the minor mode, notably ♭III and ♭VI, occur so frequently and flexibly that we obviously must consider them as part of Schubert's primary—not secondary—vocabulary. Looking backward, in bifocal tonality the constant fluctuation between major and relative minor brings ♭VII in the minor into primary importance as dominant of the relative major, at the same time giving the major chord on III, a secondary dominant in the "common practice" period, primary status because of its frequent progression to the major tonic as well as its primary function in relation to the relative minor. In the period of "common practice" these chords would achieve only secondary status.

The situation in styles that do not have a consistent harmonic grammar and syntax may at first seem impenetrable—and indeed, this may be the final conclusion, since individual composers, once they stray off the paths of common practice, may not be able to devise consistent harmonic networks of their own. To test any style for harmony consistency in small dimensions, it is helpful to follow the same general plan recommended for treatment of dissonant styles; in attempting to construct a chord typology, therefore, we tentatively place in the primary category the most frequent and stable structures; as secondary effects we collect the less frequent and apparently transitional combinations; and to the remote category we consign the rare and functionally isolated verticals.

The last typology in small dimensions is the vocabulary of dissonance. Simply by arranging non-chord tones and other forms of dissonance into a frequent/average/rare typology, perhaps making exact statistics for one or two pieces, we uncover the composer's preferences in a revealingly expressive area: a dissonance is like a descriptive adjective, and the composer's choice of these non-chordal "adjectives" closely reflects his creative personality. For the most detailed studies of harmony we may wish to examine the length of dissonances and their control with respect to chord rhythm, thus relating them indirectly to Movement. Also in small-dimension dissonance we include more complex concepts such as appoggiatura chords and structural dissonances that never resolve.

The contribution of small-dimension Harmony to Movement can be analyzed with considerable refinement through the inter-actions of chord rhythm. While it is possible to use a broad typology for chord rhythm, such as sustained/varied/driving, it is likely that we will also want to notice the types of chord-rhythmic patterns and the degree to which the activity determines or confirms the structure of motives, subphrases, and phrases.

The element of subjective interpretation affects the analysis of chord rhythm, particularly in dealing with changes that are momentary ornaments rather than fundamental progressions in the harmonic scheme. In making analytical distinctions, factors of tempo, melodic line, and rhythmic accentuation play a considerable part. Let us examine a few synthetic examples:

EXAMPLE 3-6.

Should one analyze progression (a) simply as a bar of ornamented tonic harmony (o) or as a progression of three chords (♩♩♩)? Certainly in a quick tempo the former solution would prevail; and even in Adagio the fact that both moving notes return to their original position emphasizes the purely ornamental nature of this progression. In (b), however, the sense of progression is a little stronger because of the change in chord position and the stress on the V chord produced by the melodic skips in the moving voices. If we add rhythmic accentuation, as in (c), the feeling of harmonic motion becomes still more tangible. Yet all three cases are fundamentally static if compared to (d), where the chords progress to new roots. On the other hand, there is no question that even example (a) gives us more feeling of harmonic motion than a sustained C-major harmony, as in (e). From this we can see that the subjective difficulties arise chiefly in trying to decide between degrees of ornamental change. We can avoid most of these subjective pitfalls by concentrating our analysis of the music in terms of the three conditions of chord rhythm that are most nearly self-evident: sustained harmony, ornamental change, and root change, without attempting to establish subcategories among the elusive ornamental changes. In the notation of analyses, sustained harmonies may be indicated by ties or brackets *above* the notes and ornamental changes may be shown by ties or brackets *below* the notes, while root changes appear as unencumbered individual notes. Thus the chord-rhythmic analysis of the examples above would be as follows:

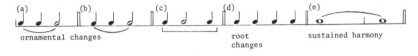

Shelley Davis[3] has added some useful modifications to the symbols for sustained effects. Where harmonies oscillate between tonic and dominant, one may use a wavy line (d) rather than a straight pedal-point bracket (a). Interior and upper pedal-points can be symbolized by inverted and special brackets (b and c). Pedal points merely implied by recurrent brief notes or chords can be suggested by a bracket with broken lines (e).

TYPES OF SUSTAINED CHORD RHYTHM

a) └─────────────────┘ pedal-point

b) ┌─────────────────┐ upper pedal-point

c) ├─────────────────┤ interior pedal-point

d) ┌──∿∿∿∿∿──┤ oscillation (usually I-V-I-V . . .)

e) └ _ _ _ _ _ _ _ _ ┘ implied pedal

3. Davis, *op. cit.*, p. 26.

Passages in unison offer a special problem: although they usually imply harmonies, the sense of harmonic movement obviously cannot entirely equal a clear chordal progression. Furthermore, any interpretation of implied harmonies contains possibilities for subjective disagreement. For example, how should one analyze the following passage?

EXAMPLE 3-7.

The constantly vital first question in HR (harmonic-rhythmic) analysis is: What is the tempo? In an extremely quick tempo one might hear the first two sixteenths as double appoggiaturas to the A-C-E triad. In successively slower tempos we arrive at the versions (b), (c), and (d), though (d) is probably too fussy, since the neighbor notes (*) deflect the line less than the chromatic G♯ and A♯. Fortunately, as in many other determinations for style analysis, the subjective error, so critical for any absolute evaluation, greatly decreases in a comparative situation, providing only that we can maintain a consistent method.

A more refined and subjective contribution to Movement comes from the relative tension of chords and dissonances. While this subject requires much further research, both from the historical and psychological points of view, some generally accepted principles will help us to organize our observations of what composers do. For example, the effect of a V–I resolution is strongly propulsive; progressions toward the sharp side increase tension, those toward the flat side decrease tension, both creating motion; and dissonances in positions of rhythmic stress also increase the fundamental Movement. A composer's responses to these situations reveal a great deal about the control and sophistication of his style, since interaction of two elements, harmony and rhythm, requires a higher order of stylistic integration.

The contribution of small-dimension Harmony to Shape takes several forms. In the first place, a single progression may have such an original and hypnotic character that it alone functions thematically, scarcely requiring support of melody or rhythm. A singularly pure example is the chord alternation that begins the Coronation

EXAMPLE 3-8. Mussorgsky, *Boris Godunov*: Coronation Scene.
A striking harmonic oscillation creates a thematic effect.

Scene from *Boris Godunov*. (See Example 3-8.) Equally memorable is the ♭VI⁷–I progression in the motive near the beginning of Tchaikovsky's *Swan Lake*, sometimes considered the motive of the Black Swan. Sensitivity to harmonic color (but rather less to harmonic tension) apparently characterizes the Russian approach: Scriabin's mystic chord (C-F♯-B♭-E-A-D) furnishes another example of Harmony used in a highly concentrated thematic function.

EXAMPLE 3-9. Mozart, Symphony No. 39, K. 543: I, bars 26-40. *Balance of harmonic movement and stability.*

Chord rhythm, in addition to its effect on flow within the phrase, exercises a shaping function in two respects. As in middle dimensions, contrasts in chord rhythm produce admirably clear articulations. Also, differences in chord-rhythmic activity can create a sense of interdependence between subphrases, or even between phrases in a sentence, as we can see in the finely wrought balances of the opening sentence of the Allegro of Mozart's E♭ Symphony (K.543; see Example 3-9). The exquisite counterpoising of articulation and continuity begins with the very first articulation at the end of bar 4, where the break in the sustained chord rhythm lightly

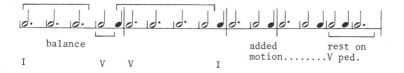

punctuates but does not break the continuity: Mozart safeguards the flow by tying the V harmony across the articulation. Few composers have understood so fully and exploited so subtly the secrets of interaction between Harmony and Rhythm.

CHAPTER FOUR

MELODY

The average person probably responds more knowledgeably to melody than to any other musical element, partly because it reaches us early in the form of cradlesong and continues in adult singing of bathtub or barroom ditties. This welcome familiarity may work against analysis, however, since it emphasizes only one small facet of melody. And while thinking of melody mostly in terms of song and theme, we may easily overlook various fundamental aspects. For purposes of style analysis Melody refers to the profile formed by any collection of pitches. To be sure, the experiments of late twentieth-century composers have considerably expanded the idea of pitch to include variable types of pitch previously considered nonmusical. Also, the active pursuit of discontinuity obviously complicates the problem of identifying a series. Nevertheless, we cannot escape the larger articulative effect of changing intensities of all sorts, which in turn define segments of Movement and Shape in which we can study melodic formations. Fortunately also, for previous centuries a simpler concept of melodic profile yields significant evidence for the understanding of style.

Melody in Large Dimensions

Melody is unusual among the musical elements for one rather special reason: the possibility that it may depend or derive to some extent from pre-existent material, such as plainsong, folksong, chorale tunes, material quoted from earlier compositions, or entirely exterior components, such as sound effects taped from human activity or nature. Style analysis thus must take account both of the characteristics of pre-existent material and the treatment it receives. At the outset the composer's attitude can be gauged in part from sheerly literal considerations, by comparing source and quotation for omissions, alterations, additions, variants, and even mistakes. Articulations in the original may not coincide with the later matrix. Total length may be either strictly related to a cantus firmus, for example, or nearly independent, as in the case of Bach chorale-preludes that submerge the chorale almost completely in a self-sufficient flow of music before, between, and after the phrase quotations. In earlier periods, even if no direct quotations are found, the modal unity of a mass or motet governs and therefore partly limits the melodic style. In a slightly more detailed way, differentiated terminations in modal music such as final and co-final cadences of Gregorian chant may help to indicate points of greater and lesser articulation. Going beyond church modes, any special scale must be regarded as a melodic precondition. For example, Debussy's use of the whole-tone scale or Liszt's use of the so-called "Hungarian minor" show the attractions and limitations of any such predeterminations. We must remember that pre-existent material creates opportunities at the same time that it imposes limitations, and the degree to which the composer responds to these opportunities may reflect in a revealing manner the traits of his melodic character. Pursuing the same logic, the major-minor system of scales could also be considered as pre-existent material, but obviously any basis that is so widely shared cannot in itself furnish many stylistic differentials (except between ethnologically different musics); such broad preconditions tend to unify rather than diversify the stylistic landscape, helping us to understand the largest chronological unities in Western music, perhaps, but not illuminating the personal idioms of individual composers.

The large-dimension typology of Melody results partly from the circumstances mentioned just above, which lead us to apply extremely general descriptive terms to characterize Melody of a whole movement, such as modal, diatonic, chromatic, exotic, and the like. We may feel justified in classifying the total melodic impression as cantabile, instrumental, stepwise, leaping, and so on, though distinctions of this nature become more meaningful in middle and small dimensions. Considerations of range and tessitura,

however, contribute vitally to large-dimension impressions of a
style. These two considerations largely parallel the analogous aspects in Sound, so that in both observing and describing a style
we will often think of these parts of Sound and Melody together.
The distinction between the two perspectives in range and tessitura,
if we need to make such a separation, is between a generality
(Sound) and a contributing particularity (Melody). For example,
it would be possible to compose a movement of high general
tessitura by using sustained string harmonics; yet at the same time
all significant melodic action might take place in the middle octaves
of the woodwinds. Tessitura for Sound, then, would be high; for
Melody it would be central. (See Example 4-1.)

The large-dimension contribution of Melody to Movement
results from two functions: profile and density. Owing to our own
experience with tunes, we will tend to sense profile mainly in
middle and small dimensions; but there is also a mountain-top survey that can be made for many works by establishing the pattern
of peaks and lows, a macropattern that enhances Movement in an
Olympian dimension—if we can sense such a gradual progression.
For example, Brahms's First Symphony soars to Bb^3 after only
three bars of the first movement, then underlining modulatory tension at the end of the exposition with an intense octave, $Cb^{2\text{-}3}$. In
the slow movement the climax rises to B^3, but Brahms saves C^4 for
the coda of the finale (bar 431, insistently confirmed in bars 450–
53). Who can say whether he intended this macroline Bb-Cb-$B\natural$-C?
This question of intent, though biographically important, is stylistically irrelevant: regardless of intention, the line exists, and there
is a special zest in trying to hear this music broadly enough to
respond to the grand dimension of the four peaks. The sense of
direction developed by peaks in Wagner's Prelude to *Tristan* can
be felt more easily because of the shorter time span involved. Large-
dimension organization of lows occurs much more rarely, but
Beethoven, for example, clearly planned lows as well as peaks, and
the coordination of these two potentialities of profile may have a
strong, even climactic effect on Movement. The possibility of consistent progression of peaks and lows between movements of a
large work affords a composer extremely subtle opportunities for
unification and climax.

EXAMPLE 4-1.   Debussy, *Ibéria*: II, *Les Parfums de la nuit*, opening.
High tessitura for Sound simultaneous with central tessitura for Melody.

In determining peaks and lows we must be careful to identify
the significant thematic register rather than just the highest or
lowest notes, possibly mere doublings. Register duplications can
create genuinely climactic tessituras for Sound without necessarily
similar effects on Melody. True peaks and lows affect the main
structural line itself, which we trace in the register that yields the
greatest continuity of general impression rather than by hopping
wildly between registers as the orchestration changes.

The second influence of Melody on Movement, melodic density (the degree of melodic activity), also applies more tangibly in smaller dimensions. Yet we should keep the potentiality in mind even for our broadest responses: since melodic perception probably exceeds all other musical response in keenness, we are justified in providing analytic framework for sophisticated reactions. As an illustration of large-dimension possibility we need only think of a chain of variations of rising melodic density, each segment adding an increment of intensity to the melodic activity.

To understand the full effects of different levels of melodic density we will most often turn to Shape rather than to Movement. A sudden impression of change in melodic activity, for example, may give the listener his first hint of phrase articulation (Ex. 4-2).

EXAMPLE 4-2.   Bach, *The Well-Tempered Clavier*, Book I: Prelude No. 3, opening.
Articulative effect of increased melodic density.

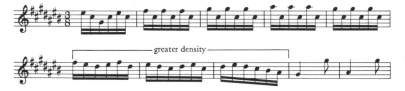

And by gradual changes, levels of melodic activity can create or confirm many other patterns of continuation. The clearest demonstration of large-scale planning of melodic Shape, however, is found in thematic relationship between movements, a subject that has been badly contaminated by the irresponsible conclusions of tune detectives. (A tune detective is a musician of rich imagination but poor judgment who proclaims that whenever two passages contain similar pitch-patterns the passages are related.) Any determination of thematic relationship requires convincing evidence and impartial judgment to distinguish significant from coincidental relationships. To reach firm conclusions we should apply the following tests:

1. *Frame of reference.* Does the historical and statistical background justify the possibility of relationship? Historically we are justified in seeking exceedingly complex thematic relationships in

isorhythmic motets, for example, in which elaborate devices of inversion, augmentation, and the like were common occurrences; in the eighteenth century, however, composers' minds ran in much less complex melodic channels; and if we find the first two notes of the main theme later occurring inverted as long notes in the bass, it is more likely an accident of harmonic progression than an evidence of inversion plus augmentation. A cadential mannerism used by hundreds of composers, for example, cannot usually function as a significantly relating thematic tag. And in a single composer's style, a melodic profile occurring in dozens of sonatas can hardly be regarded as evidence of significant relationship between two movements of a single sonata—we might with equal justice conclude that all the sonatas are so related.[1]

2. *Melodic contour.* A convincing relationship results in most cases from similarity between whole melodic contexts—not merely the coincidences of a few places, but the functionally similar details of profile in a generally analogous situation. If the similarity affects only part of the contour, we should be proportionately cautious in attributing significance to the supposed but possibly coincidental relationship. In most cases composers attempt to make their intentions clear—there is no artistic profit gained by fooling the listener. A convincing relationship must be clearly recognizable, "proven" to the listener by actual hearing rather than by minute eye comparisons out of context.

3. *Rhythmic function.* To affirm a relationship, the corresponding notes in two similar lines must occupy similar rhythmic positions in relation to the main outlines of stress. Rhythmic displacement alone can sometimes so weaken a melodic similarity as to threaten patterns of relationship otherwise apparently intended by the composer.

4. *Harmonic background.* Both the supporting progressions and larger harmonic implications should confirm melodic and rhythmic features shared by supposedly related material. Ear memory responds strongly to colorful harmony, a potent force for relating—and differentiating—thematic areas.

To sum up: significant thematic relationship depends upon a

---

1. See Jan LaRue, *Significant and Coincidental Resemblances Between Classical Themes,* in *Journal of the American Musicological Society,* XIV (1961), 224–34.

concinnity of stylistic similarities unified by strong, undistorted similarity in at least one element. (See Example 4-3.) Historical and statistical plausibilities should support this similarity with enough force so that the relationship can "explain itself" to the listener rather than emerge from elaborate "proofs." These general guidelines apply with equal justice to the recognition of thematic relationships in middle dimensions, such as the potential connection between primary and secondary themes in sonata form.

Melody in Middle Dimensions

Middle dimensions are the most important for Melody, since it is in these dimensions that we recognize tunes and themes, one of our most immediate and definable musical responses. Also, middle-dimension considerations embrace an extremely large range of structural possibilities for Melody, approximating large-dimension effects in the profiling of paragraphs and sections, yet at times also evaluating the character of sub-phrases as components of sentences and paragraphs. It is exactly here that some flexibility in the concept of middle dimensions must be allowed, if we are to develop meaningful comparisons either between works or between composers. For example, structure of subphrases would ordinarily fall into the category of small dimensions; yet obviously any rigid boundary here could leave a blank area of discontinuity in understanding the interaction of dimensions—precisely the reason for the intentional overlap in the diagram of dimensions in the first chapter. As a matter of analytical "common sense," therefore, the student of style analysis will seek to discover and understand the *significant module of movement* in any dimensions, including whatever incursions upon neighboring dimensions may be relevant to this process. If it is important to the understanding of large paragraphs to study tiny subphrases, by all means they should be included, not in and for themselves—which is a small-dimension concern—but for their contribution to middle-dimension structures.

The typology of middle-dimension Melody can be approached by two avenues. First, we may find it illuminating to take an over-

EXAMPLE 4-3.   Brahms, Symphony
No. 3:
(a) I, ending (*left*);
(b) IV, ending (*right and following
page*).
Significant thematic relationship.

view of parts, sections, and paragraphs as profiles, both upper and lower, to determine general characteristics rather like those observed in the typology of large dimensions: active/stable, cantabile/instrumental, articulated/continuous, climactic/level, and the like. Second, since this dimension includes most thematic aspects of Melody, a detailed study of thematic typology obviously will reveal important traits of a composer's style. Thematic functions, however, are most logically grouped among the contributions of middle-dimension Melody to Shape, discussed below.

Profile and density again furnish the main contributions to Movement, much as in large dimensions. For example, the characteristically directional feeling of transitions of all sorts generally results from a clearly rising or falling macroline, accompanied by increasing density of melodic action. Sonata forms often confirm a modulation to the dominant with a rising line; coda sections typically signal the terminal area of a piece by a stabilization or descent. Furthermore, in middle dimensions we can at times feel a rhythmic effect from recurrent peaks, lows, or other recognizable patterning. This *contour rhythm*, which may be confirmed by parallel changes in melodic density as well, forms one of the special types of rhythmic interactions between elements, analogous to harmonic rhythm and textural rhythm. Like so many of the interconnections of musical style, it can be considered either as an aspect of Melody or as a layer of Rhythm, depending upon the proportion of its function that is applied in one direction or another. As part of an initial hypothesis for analysis, however, its function tends more toward the area of Rhythm, where it will be discussed in more detail.

Middle-dimension Melody contributes very significantly to Shape by the melodic ramifications of thematic design. Although a theme may occasionally consist merely of a single isolated sound, harmony, or rhythm, thematic design is usually more highly organized in Melody than in other elements, possibly because composers' and listeners' experience of Melody is more direct and deeply rooted—we can sing a tune for ourselves. Thus, while we should begin by examining middle dimensions for long-range profile and changing densities, our chief impressions will center upon the thematic design of phrases, sentences, and paragraphs. The diversity

of possibilities in thematic design seems at first to be nearly overwhelming, so at this point the pathway to greater understanding
requires not so much refined discriminations as the ability to discern
general trends and family relationships between procedures. To
train our thinking toward this generalizing capacity and to control
the myriad of potentialities we should bear in mind that at any
point of articulation a composer has four basic options: recurrence,
development, response, and contrast. These options appear in the
outline of the first chapter under Growth, and they can apply to all
elements, of course, as procedures that contribute to Shape. Yet
since thematic design owes so much to varieties of melodic treatment, the basic discussion of options for continuation occurs most
appropriately here.

The terms applied here to the various options for continuation
should not pose undue semantic problems if we understand the
general objective: to set up effective divisions within a spectrum
between similarity and difference—a polarity that can also be
expressed as continuity/discontinuity or relationship/contrast. For
specific composers and pieces, the analyst may require special subcategories that better express and define a particular style; for general purposes, however, the following categories will serve as solid
points of departure:

1. *Recurrence*, including both immediate repetition, the simplest form of continuation ($a\ a$), and also return after change
($a\ b\ a$), potentially one of the most highly developed procedures
of Shape.

2. *Development* (interrelationship), which includes all changes
that clearly derive from preceding material, such as variation,
mutation, sequence or other less exact forms of parallelism, and the
cantus-firmus techniques of augmentation, diminution, inversion,
and retrograde: $a\ a^1\ a^2$. . . . (See Example 4-4.)

3. *Response* (interdependence), which includes continuations
that give an antecedent-consequent effect, even though not specifically derived from preceding material, e.g. symmetries between
authentic and plagal tessituras in successive incises of plainsong,
and other types of partially homogeneous continuation ($ax,\ ay$).
(See Example 4-5, p. 82.) The opening of Mozart's "Jupiter" Sym-

EXAMPLE 4-4.   Beethoven, Violin Concerto: II, opening.
Recurrence and development (variation/mutation, sequence) in the treatment of an opening thematic motive.

EXAMPLE 4-5. Kyrie X (*Alme Pater*). (From *Liber Usualis*, Tournai, 1938, p. 43.)
Continuation by response: authentic (normal) tessitura in the first incise is balanced by plagal (lower) tessitura in the second incise.

phony furnishes a typical example of antecedent-consequent response. (See Example 2-2, p. 35.)

4. *Contrast*, a complete change (*a; b*), usually following (and confirming) a heavy articulation by cadences and rests. (See Example 4-6.)

The boundary line between the categories of Development and Response is not always easy to fix; but it helps to think of Development as a continuation closely related by Melody while less related or even unrelated by other elements. Response then simply reverses this situation: it includes continuations unrelated melodically but

EXAMPLE 4-6.   Mozart, Piano Sonata, K. 331: I, opening.
Varied recurrence, development, and contrast in a chain of thematic phrases.

perceptibly related by other elements. For most styles a melodic relationship will outweigh dissimilarities in other elements; hence, the categories above are arranged to reflect our stronger response to Melody. For a greater generality that would cover less familiar styles, however, it may be desirable to fix the boundary in some other manner; for example, we might define Development as a continuation related by several elements, Response as a continuation related by only a single element. As another possibility, we might define Development to include only ornamental changes, leaving structural changes as characteristic of Response. Whatever the decision in refining these definitions, we will quickly become aware that nothing reveals the true orientation of a composer more clearly than the mix of related and unrelated elements in his processes of continuation.

Melody in Small Dimensions

Intervals and motivic patterns are the words and phrases of Melody. While musicological comment on Melody often includes tables of intervals, this rather clinical approach reminds one of a list of words without any explanation of meanings. We do not gain much insight from the comment "The piece contains many augmented fourths and major sevenths," a mere enumeration of components without real illumination of function. The analyst should take a further step toward understanding by attempting to show musical meaning: "The piece contains many expressively dissonant intervals, such as augmented fourths and major sevenths." Here the words "expressively dissonant" suggest both affect and function of the intervals. (In a quarter-tone style, of course, augmented fourths and sevenths might sound relatively consonant.) While a small-dimension typology should list intervals, therefore, it is desirable to place them in functional groupings, such as the conventional dichotomy between steps and skips, to which we should add, for purposes of style analysis, a useful further category—leaps. The utility of this third grouping will be immediately apparent if we consider for a moment the problem of describing an opening phrase that consists entirely of steps and small skips, followed by a passage of consistently large intervals. To reflect the different character of the continuation we are immediately forced to speak of "large skips," which in effect sets up a third category of motion that can be much more distinctly and graphically represented by the word "leaps."

All such categories must be related to a particular style, of course, and for most styles the conventional definition of steps and skips as seconds and more-than-seconds will serve us well. Leaps are exceptional skips, exceptional by size or chromaticism, typically anything larger than a fifth up or a fourth down, each of which, despite the large intervals, do not necessarily give a sense of leaping, probably because they can be readily anticipated by the ear as part of an implied triad structure. In a strongly active style, with intervals averaging well above an octave, a simple third or fourth might be included functionally in the "stepwise" category, which we should not necessarily define as literally scalewise motion, but rather as small motion in a relative sense. The three groups of actions, therefore—steps, skips, and leaps—will define almost any melodic style if we think of them flexibly as relatively small, middle, and large melodic motions.

EXAMPLE 4-7.

Going beyond intervals, we may find it useful to investigate the range and tessitura of phrases, though this type of analysis more usually relates to middle dimensions. A handy summary of *melodic excursion* in a phrase or subphrase can be made by representing the beginning and end with whole notes, then showing peak and low as stemless quarters in between.

EXAMPLE 4-8.

More important is some method for generalizing about the melodic flow, and particularly the general character of motives, subphrases, and phrases. To establish a typology of small-dimension contours we can represent motion by a scheme of shorthand, abbreviating the adjectives *rising, falling, level,* and *wave-form* as R, F, L, and W. Then by combining letters to symbolize the relevant contours, we can describe almost any melodic action in a simple and easily remembered alphabetic code. Furthermore, by using upper- and lower-case letters we can even give some notion of the magnitude of the melodic actions, either spatially or durationally. If greater precision seems appropriate, the Wave-form category can be sub-divided into *sawtooth* and *undulating* (S and U).

EXAMPLE 4-9.

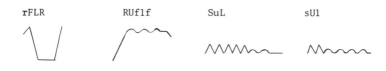

rFLR   RUflf   SuL   sUl

As soon as we become aware of structural units within a melodic flow, the need for typologies becomes obvious. Like Harmony, Melody tends to crystallize first at points of articulation, notably those that have a strong cadential function. The limited choice of motion to final notes obviously encourages the development of formulae. Terminations of psalm tones, cadences of incises, and melodic rime all illustrate this potentiality. Within the phrase, we must study the types of recurrent motives and every other sort of patterning. Here also the RFLW shorthand can be used to advantage.

The small-dimension contributions to Movement are often rather obvious, such as the rhythmic effect of repeating patterns, which can create a powerful continuum. As a specific example, a repeating, broken-chord pattern of four sixteenth notes clearly yields a continuous quarter-note pulse (except in slow tempos). Larger contour rhythms, produced by recurrent peaks and lows rather than

by exactly repeated patterns, also affect the sense of Movement.
More subtly, any contrast between patterning and random flow or
between greater and lesser density of melodic action tends to produce a wavelike alternation of action and rest with strong if underlying rhythmic implications. Finally, in studying melodic action in
small detail we can sometimes attain unexpected insight into Movement by the simple means of taking a *flection count*, i.e. adding up
the total number of changes in melodic direction between relevant
articulations.

EXAMPLE 4-10.

Each of these "simple" methods, however, reveals only a small part
of the enormously complex nature of Melody. There is nothing
simple about even the smallest melodic actions, since no interval
can be regarded as an absolute value, but must be weighted according to its durations, accentual circumstances, position in the
range, location in the phrase, relationship to critical notes such as
dominants and finals, and function in the contour or pattern as
peak, low, turning point, pivot, and so on.

The small-dimension contributions of Melody to Shape closely
resemble the situation for middle dimensions: we can directly transfer the four options for continuation as a basis for studying relationships between subphrase and phrase, or between motive and subphrase. At this detailed level, however, we may occasionally note a
new concentration in emphasis. Development and response, particularly, seem to acquire greater connective power. For example,
a complementation between dense and thin melodic activity in two

subphrases may give a stronger sense of interdependence than it produces between larger units such as successive phrases or sentences.

Clearly each of these perspectives on Melody cannot produce more than a narrow angle of insight on this seemingly most familiar and accessible, yet actually quite elusive and ambiguous—even mysterious—of musical elements. It seems likely that in relation to this element familiarity has bred not contempt but complexity: Melody has reached beyond itself to borrow subtle influences from Rhythm, Harmony, and even from Sound that make each progression a source of analytical danger as well as esthetic delight.

CHAPTER FIVE

RHYTHM

Faced with the many fascinating but often frustrating inscrutabilities of music, it is tempting to identify Rhythm as the arch-ambiguity, the single most mysterious and problematical of musical elements. Aware as we are now, however, of the nearly total interconnectedness of the elements—how observations of contour may suddenly reveal a macrorhythmic pattern, how a series of orchestral contrasts can develop implications for Movement—we may at most conclude that the puzzling aspects of rhythm illustrate with particular sharpness a general, fundamental ambiguity that is characteristic of music. If the present chapter fails to solve all rhythmic questions, it is right in step with previous attempts, none of which have shed universal light on these elusive problems. By recognition of two axiomatic conditions, however—again interconnected—the discussion that follows seems to make a promising beginning and a convincing indication of new directions for potential clarification.

1. *Rhythm is a layered phenomenon.* To a large extent Rhythm results from changes in Sound, Harmony, and Melody, in this respect relating closely to the Movement function in Growth, which accomplishes an expansion of Rhythm on a large scale, just as Rhythm controls the details of Movement on a small scale. For this reason R and G are placed together at the end of the analytical plan, and they would be joined under a single heading were it not for the circumstance that small-scale Rhythm contains a larger proportion of specifically durational rhythmic effects (patterns of surface rhythm and hierarchy of units in a continuum, for example) while Movement contains more of the generalized resultants (broad, less definable interactions such as contour rhythm and textural rhythm). While recognizing a general family unity between Rhythm

and Movement, therefore, we will nevertheless find it instructive to separate them for purposes of study. The ambivalent or actually conflicting stresses that so often arise in music show that the whole nature of stress must be conceived as a stratification in which contributions of other elements may not always confirm durational stresses; furthermore, a large- or middle-dimension emphasis in Movement will not necessarily coincide with small-dimension rhythmic accents. In understanding Rhythm we cannot always resolve these conflicting stresses into a single, oversimplified pattern —nor should we: the composer may have contrapuntal or otherwise complex intentions. Instead, we should attempt to trace the sources of complication back to the elements in which they originate, evaluating the contribution of each element.

2. *Stress is variable in duration.* Release of tension is not necessarily instantaneous, and as a result, durations of stress will tend to reflect the dimension affected: a motivic accent in Vivaldi may highlight only a single sixteenth, whereas Beethoven may prolong a phrase stress for several beats by successive injections of his special musical adrenalin (sforzando). Similarly in larger dimension, a sectional emphasis obviously requires an extended area of high activity and tension.

These differing qualities and quantities within Rhythm deeply influence the processes of Growth, with a consequent dividend of individuality in musical styles. In tune with the comprehensive approach of style analysis, the two points above expand the concept of Rhythm to embrace all dimensions of Movement, at the same time showing the significantly rhythmic aspects of other musical elements.

No attempt will be made in this abbreviated presentation of style analysis to review earlier theories of Rhythm except to mention that they have generally suffered from two limitations: (1) attempts to relate musical rhythm to poetic prosody, which lacks the many-layered resources of musical stress and therefore supplies a much too rigidly metrical framework to be illuminating or genuinely relevant for music; (2) concentration on small-dimension patterning, with a consequent neglect of irregular but often directional arrangements in all dimensions that may actually make more significant contributions to fundamental Movement. The following discussion proceeds from a definition of Rhythm that emphasizes the multiplicity of its sources and dimensions: *Rhythm results from changing combinations of duration and intensity within all elements and dimensions of Growth.*

The Layers of Rhythm

Explanations of Rhythm commonly include only immediate durational aspects and the concept of meter. For purposes of style analysis both of these approaches must be considerably expanded and a further category added to account for rhythmic influences contributed by other elements. According to this view, the rhythmic impression of a particular passage may result from any or all of three layers of action: the *continuum* or metrical hierarchy, the durational arrangements or surface rhythm, and the interactions with Sound, Harmony, and Melody.

1. *Continuum* goes beyond meter to represent the whole hierarchy of expectation and implication in rhythm, the consciousness of a continuing pulse from which we infer a multidimensional structure of motion that carries through sustained notes or intervals of silence. The center of this hierarchy is the individual pulse and the grouping of pulses into a consistent meter that we feel as a rhythmic basis underlying many styles, even when neither pulse nor meter is consistently expressed in any single line. The persistence of this core of continuous expectation can be neatly demonstrated by the phenomenon of syncopation, which continues to be felt as a rhythmic dissonance even when no part reaffirms the continuum against it (see the end of the exposition in the first movement of the "Eroica," Example 5-1). The continuum may also establish larger expectations, such as recurrent phrasing of 4+4+4 bars, and in the other direction, smaller assumptions such as consistently duple or triple fractures of the pulse into a subhierarchy of microcomponents.

Tempo is the speed of operation of the continuum, typically

EXAMPLE 5-1. Beethoven, Symphony No. 3: I, bars 124-31.
Rhythmic dissonance produced by all parts playing against the continuum.

governed by the speed of the controlling pulse. Changes in tempo indications obviously influence Rhythm in all dimensions. (Fluctuations in actual performance tempo cannot be adequately considered within the necessarily general and abbreviated scope of these *Guidelines.*)

2. *Surface rhythm* includes all relationships of durations, assumed to be approximately as represented by the symbols of notation.

3. *Interactions* result when the events in other elements approach a condition of regularity that can be felt either as reinforcement of the continuum or as patterning related to surface rhythms. It is important to remember here that rhythmic properties can be recognized in arrangements that may not be absolutely regular; very few performances, for example, attain absolute equality of pulses in a meter (fortunately!); yet the listener receives a perfectly clear impression of the meter, nonetheless. Similarly, we tend to discover rhythmic effects in any structure of Sound, Melody, and Harmony that approximates a familiar module. These effects apply most directly in small dimensions, since our consciousness of Rhythm is more immediate than in middle and large dimensions. The importance of these interactions is that they can give stress

and directional movement to situations that are rhythmically un-differentiated, i.e. that contain activity without direction.

The rhythmic flow produced by alternations of tutti and solo in concertos has already been mentioned: frequent literal repetitions of material in Corelli's concerti grossi, for example, would be nearly static except for the fact that his simple, striking exchanges in fabric produce intermittent stresses without changing a single pitch. A repeated succession that might give a boringly undifferentiated impression (*aaaaaa*) thus becomes by alternation of forces a differentiated pattern, *Aa Aa Aa*, which confirms and strengthens the metrical level of the continuum. Explained by converting to rhythmic terms, a series of otherwise undifferentiated half notes (𝅗𝅥 𝅗𝅥 𝅗𝅥 𝅗𝅥 𝅗𝅥 𝅗𝅥), when presented in two alternating textures can be perceived as metrical groups of 2/2: 𝅗𝅥 𝅗𝅥 | 𝅗𝅥 𝅗𝅥 | 𝅗𝅥 𝅗𝅥 . (See Example 5-2.)

EXAMPLE 5-2.   Corelli, Concerto Grosso, Op. 6, No. 8: I, bars 141-47. *Textural rhythm: metrical movement created by alternation of textures.*

Another common interaction between S and R is the tendency of composers to apply "extracurricular" accents in the form of sforzandos. A simple 3/4 pattern that alternates halves and quarters, for example, takes on new and more complex rhythmic meaning if the quarters are marked *sfz*. Descending to very primitive interactions, a single sustained tone can become a phrase, rhythmically, by the addition of a crescendo and diminuendo in performance.

We can approach melodic interactions by thinking first of a series of sixteenth notes, CCCCCCCCCCCCCCCC. The series attains motion only at the lowest level, the sixteenth unit itself, with no sense of direction whatever. Yet if we add a melodic pattern CDCB CDCB CDCB CDCB, the sixteenth notes suddenly flow also in quarter-note units; and how much more lively this becomes if we use a larger melodic differentiation, adding a third among the second, ECBC ECBC ECBC ECBC. Furthermore, we can expand the dimension of controlled flow merely by creating *contour rhythms* of whatever durations are required, such as halves (ECBC DCBC ECBC DCBC) or full bars (DCBC ECBC FCBC GCBC | DCBC ECBC FCBC GCBC). (See Example 5-3.) The retention

EXAMPLE 5-3.
Rhythmic differentiation by recurrent contours.

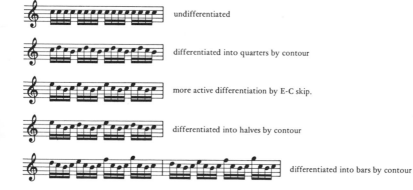

of strict patterning in larger dimensions would give an undesirable rigidity, of course, but good composers clearly exploit contour rhythms of much larger size by use of recurrent peaks and lows, as well as by modular (approximately regular) placement of characteristic motives or strong contrasts in type of melodic activity.

Harmonic rhythm, especially in small dimensions (chord rhythms), furnishes somewhat more easily observable interactions, since there is no need to convert or schematize in order to compare durations—we simply observe that one harmony extends for a half, the next two harmonies last a quarter each, and so on, after which all of the familiar analytical considerations of surface rhythm can be applied. In middle and possibly even in large dimensions there are at least two significant sources of harmonic interaction. First, any changes that articulate chord rhythm into patterns may produce a macrorhythm of phrase or section dimensions. The following arrangements of chord rhythm, for example, would give a four-bar swing:

Second, the durations of successive tonalities (or thinking in largest terms, even of unified groups of tonal areas) produce underlying key rhythms (the rhythms of key succession) whose effect is difficult to measure but which undoubtedly contribute something to Movement.

The Component States of Rhythm

It seems likely that much of the difficulty in understanding rhythm arises from a failure to appreciate the many and various sources from which the changing intensities that generate Movement can emerge. An accent that seems inconsistent with existing small-dimension patterns may "explain itself" with perfect consistency on a higher level, i.e. according to middle-dimension considerations. A stress in chord rhythm may confirm metrical regularities, yet conflict with peak rhythms of the particular section taken as a whole. Furthermore, the whole idea of thesis and arsis (downbeat and upbeat) borrowed from prosody is confusingly irrelevant to music, because the processes of musical stress, lull, and transition are so infinitely more complex and variable. What analogy, for example, can poetry offer as a parallel to harmony or counterpoint?

Or, for that matter, surface duration? The changing intensities that give rise to rhythm cannot possibly be thought of as clear-cut, regularized, consistent functions: an upbeat preparation may last a whole bar; a downbeat effect may spread over most of a phrase.

EXAMPLE 5-4.   Beethoven, Piano Sonata, Op. 81a: I, bars 62-66. *An extended downbeat.*

Regular recurrence is only one aspect of Rhythm and Movement, possibly not even the most important. As a basis for understanding rhythm, therefore, we should first postulate a spectrum of intensity, ranging from comparatively low to comparatively high activity. Rhythmic functions are not fixed but relative, and we should be prepared to recognize active and relatively inactive stresses as well as stable and relatively unstable lulls. The spectrum for each composer and style will be different, and we will be able to understand the specifics of a composer's rhythmic style only when we have begun to comprehend the full spectrum of his activity. As a general hypothesis we should distinguish three states of rhythm within any spectrum:

1. *Stress.* High levels of activity *from any source* may produce a stress of *any duration.* To describe this variety in durations of rhythmic intensification by consistent terms, it is convenient to use *accent* for brief intensifications mainly within the bar; *stress* as the categorical term and also for middle durations, such as phrase stress; and *emphasis* for broad areas of intensified activity. While very primitive or rigidly conventionalized music may proceed so regularly that metrical accents seem entirely consistent and measurable, most music moves by extremely varied stresses that are correspondingly difficult to define. Apart from the ever possible conflict of accents resulting from uncoordinated interactions, the differing dimensions of rhythmic activity produce dimensional conflicts as

EXAMPLE 5-5.   Beethoven, Piano Sonata, Op. 31, No. 2: I, bars 1-24.
Simultaneous accent, stress, and emphasis (bar 21).

well. For this reason a particular bar may at times serve a three-fold function: as the location of a metrical accent, as a phrase stress, and as a sectional emphasis. Furthermore, each of these stress functions, although coinciding initially at the focal point of high activity, may differ in duration: the metrical accent may last only one pulse, the phrase stress may require half a bar or more, and the sectional emphasis may consist of a plateau of generally intense activity lasting through several phrases. (See Example 5-5.)

In making a detailed study of stress one would set up not only a typology of stress durations but also a typology for the character of stress—how active, resulting from which elements, and so on. It is no surprise that in attempting to analyze such complex conditions we experience a multitude of difficulties in defining rhythm. Since we have defined stress as a state of high activity, it may on first thought seem contradictory that we can feel a long note following a rising preparation of short notes as a heavy downbeat stress, even though it appears stable, compared to the activity of the preparation. A full exploration of this ambivalent situation must be left to a future essay, but in briefest summary, it seems likely that the long note begins with an apex of stress that is extremely short, and the strength of this stress results from the high contrast in the rapid release of tension: the lull immediately succeeds the stress, without transition, magnifying the stress effect in a manner analogous to the apparently magnified sound of a forte followed by a piano, as compared to a forte followed by mezzoforte. Stress should be understood, therefore, as the impact felt at the critical point of change in activity; in small dimensions this produces an explosive peak detonated by momentarily concinnous forces of activity, not unlike the spark generated between two terminals when their difference in potential becomes sufficiently great.

2. *Lull.* At the opposite end of the spectrum, a condition of relative stability or rest obviously results from low levels of rhythmic activity. (As a matter of terminology, the word "lull" is more effective than "rest," which conflicts with notational meanings. Furthermore, "lull" connotes a merely temporary stability that more accurately reflects the continuing flow of varying intensities.) A particularly attractive potentiality of rhythm is the condition of relative calm produced when one element stabilizes, even though other elements continue in full swing. In this way Beethoven can signal an important articulation by the preparatory stability of a long dominant pedal, even though all other musical elements create an increasingly intense barrage of activity. (See Example 5-6.)

EXAMPLE 5-6 (*following pages*). Beethoven, Symphony No. 4: IV, bars 141-75.
Chord rhythm stabilizes from a mixture of ♩ and ♩ to one change every four bars (bars 149-60) and finally to a long dominant pedal, reducing activity to signal the recapitulation, though in other respects there is more activity (pp, cresc. to ff and sf; expansion of instrumentation; more surface rhythmic action).

Guidelines for Style Analysis

3. *Transition.* In coasting smoothly to rest or preparing for a situation of stress we encounter many transitional states of rhythmic activity. For the more familiar parts of the repertory—i.e. the last two centuries—these transitions are mainly preparations, often carefully graded intensifications, in the form of upbeats of various sizes; in still earlier and later centuries, however, we encounter both less and more highly structured situations that make proportionately greater use of receding transitions. For different styles of music we may decide to individualize the terms for these rising and falling types of transition as intensification/detensification, preparation/ recovery, activation/relaxation, impulse/recoil. (See Example 5-7.)

EXAMPLE 5-7.   Beethoven, Piano Sonatas, (a) Op. 57: I; (b) Op. 13: I. *Rising and falling transitions.*

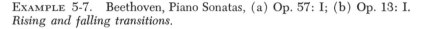

The shades of semantic difference can suggest differences in rhythmic effect exposed by analysis. A further important point for the analyst to remember is that transitions, like stresses and lulls, adhere to no rigid, necessary length—they can be of widely varying durations.

Rhythmic Typology

Unlike Sound and Harmony, for which single phenomena (timbres, chords) can be compiled into vocabularies, Rhythm is more like Melody, in requiring several events in conjunction before we can sense the happening of movement. In both Melody and Rhythm this concentrates our attention on patterning, which at the motivic or phrase level can be discovered and typed quite readily, for the simple reason that melodic patterns tend to coincide with rhythmic patterns (and vice versa—a double check); and where they do not fully coincide, durations and contours each give strong clues to the functional groupings of the related element. When rhythmic arrangements become too complex or irregular to be treated as patterns, we must then devise a more flexible typology that will nonetheless reveal the sources of Rhythm as they produce conditions of stress, lull, and transition. In many styles this will result in near-patterns and other characteristic dispositions based on the familiar options for continuation. These identifications of procedure go far to explain a composer's fundamental Movement. Hence, in seeking to understand rhythmic procedures, it is usually effective to follow a consistent routine such as the following:

1. Locate the articulations relevant to the dimension of observation. Many difficulties in the study of Rhythm originate in confusions between dimensions and sources of stress. As we have seen above, a middle-dimension stress may conflict in principle with a small-dimension accent, just as melodic stresses do not necessarily coincide with points of highest harmonic activity.

2. Between articulations, find the stresses for each rhythmic layer (continuum, surface rhythm, interactions); establish if possible a controlling stress; then identify the neighboring areas of lull and transition associated with this controlling stress. The borderlines between stress, lull, and transition are notably among the most elusive articulations in music. Apparently we sense any alteration in rhythmic function largely by some change in direction, whether sonic, harmonic, rhythmic, melodic, or interactive. While the point in change of direction may often seem quite obvious—a turn in contour, for example—the influence of other elements may expand this apex of stress in either direction, or set up conflicting stresses. From this wider perspective it is clear that the normal accents of the continuum represent only one among many determinants of stress.

3. Sort out consistent types of rhythmic arrangement according to the relative duration of the three states of Rhythm. For Haydn there is never much lull, and his characteristically kinetic phrases include a higher proportion of transitional intensification than

stress, a categorical type that can be symbolized conveniently as
Ts (long transition, short stress). (This may partly explain his
fondness for reinforcing stresses with *sfz* indications, possibly to
compensate for the shortness of the stresses.) Mozart, on the other
hand, tends more toward balance, with shorter preparations and
more lull: *tSL* or *tSl*. The elegance of the typological approach, as
opposed to the systematic, can be seen now in the provisions for
confusion and indeterminacy. If we consistently find phrases in
which contour rhythm conflicts with continuum, for example, with
no convincing way of determining the victor, then "conflict" is our
conclusion, and "conflict = contour vs. continuum" becomes part
of the composer's rhythmic typology. Composers are not perfect!
Their communications contain quite as many unintentional ambiguities as any other form of human expression.

Instead of attempting to force clarity upon such passages, we
should attempt to understand the sources of confusion, deciding
if possible which elements cause the most consistent difficulty. In
a disorganized style we may not even be able to find any prevailing
types of confusion; perhaps at best the pieces contain merely an
inconsistent assortment of various confusions that can hardly be
fashioned into any logical sort of range or spectrum. A total indeterminacy of rhythmic procedure thus finally emerges as the composer's characteristic approach, a conclusion quite as valuable for
style analysis (even if musically rather uninteresting) as a finding
of high concinnity in organization.

Rhythmic Contributions to Shape

Since Rhythm is Movement in microcosm, there is need only
to comment on its contributions to Shape, which are unexpectedly
varied. In the first place, merely by itself a rhythm can act as a
theme; and memorable rhythmic motives not only help to bind a
piece together but can strongly reinforce the impact of melodic
and other recurrences important to Shape. Changes in the level of
rhythmic activity exercise a significant influence on both articulation and phrase formation. In small dimensions a controlled rhythmic

acceleration and deceleration (*rhythmic contours*) such as the following series:

can create a satisfying phrase, though some coordination with melody and harmony, of course, will add greatly to the effect. (See Example 5-8.) In middle and large dimensions both the level of

EXAMPLE 5-8.   Mozart, Minuet, K. 1: bars 1-4.
Rhythmic contour produced by steady acceleration in mid-phrase and deceleration at end: quarters, eighths, sixteenths, thirty-seconds, and back to quarters.

activity and grouping of rhythmic functions (the relative proportions of stress, lull, and transition) contribute markedly to the manner of continuation, notably as reinforcement of sectional contrast.

Rhythm in Large Dimensions

Large dimension considerations begin easily enough with the typology of tempos and meters. Checkpoints to bring out the style contributions of general tempo indications should include at least the following:

1. Total spectrum of tempos.

2. Preferred tempos within the general groups of slow, moderate, and fast movements.

3. Preferred associations with particular movements, i.e. do fast first movements differ in tempo preference from fast finales?

4. Tempo planning between movements: contrast, speed-up, slow-down, alternation, balance.

5. Internal alterations of tempo that affect the relationship of parts. The answers to these questions, both direct and implied, will often reveal surprising individualities in composers.

Meters obviously cannot tell us quite as much—with fewer choices there is less opportunity for individualized expression. Yet how essential is Berlioz' choice of 3/8 rather than 3/4 in the *Ballet of the Sylphs (Damnation of Faust)*. Similarly important, if we know that for eighteenth-century symphonic first movements, duple meters outweigh triple by about 5 to 1, we become pointedly aware of the personality of Haydn in using triple meter for nearly half of his output. Also, to make a stronger stylistic differentiation we can adapt the five-part typology above to study correlations between tempos and meters as follows:

1. Range of tempos in a particular meter.

2. Range of meters in a particular tempo.

3. Consistent treatment of specific types of movements, e.g. presto 3/8 minuets rather than moderate 3/4.

4. Evidence of planning such an alternation, intensification, and the like.

5. Significant correlations between internal changes in tempo and meter.

To look at whole movements as rhythmic quantities may seem at first so vague as to be entirely pointless. Yet the evidence of musical literature itself, i.e. the fairly consistent preferences that composers have demonstrated in associating particular tempos and lengths of movements in groupings such as the suite, sonata, and symphony, suggest that underlying rhythmic responses exist even in the largest dimensions. Within the present style-analytical approach, the attempt to explain these largest responses must first reject any rhythmic theory that demands regularity, adhering rather to the view that Movement results from variations in activity, whether regular or irregular. Any view of rhythm dependent on regularity overlooks the often more vital sense of motion produced by unequal activities; in fact, regularity quickly develops cyclic responses that we have already identified as a limited, localized form of activity, i.e. motion in equilibrium that is incapable of producing the fundamental directionality that an effective composition requires.

Any study of rhythmic proportions must obviously involve comparisons between lengths of movements, at some point converting numbers of bars into estimates of actual elapsed time, using tempos indicated by the composer, or a consistent predetermined association of beats per minute with whatever tempo indications may exist. The raw total lengths may not tell us much; however, composers definitely consider the proportional lengths of compositions—how else can we explain the steady enlargement of symphony finales, relative to first movements, during the eighteenth century? Another, more specific example: when Bach added long preludes to the English Suites and Partitas, the neighboring allemandes were not only enlarged, but proportionally more enlarged than the following movements. This probably reflects a feeling that the usual small allemandes, such as those in the French Suites, would seem too brief after the large preludes. The whole question of relative lengths of movements or parts is plagued with ambiguities such as variations in performance times and perceptual confusions of listeners who feel "slow" and "fast" passage of time (and resultant "long" and "short" durations) of supposedly equivalent segments in the same composition. Presumably these contradictory impressions result from differing density of events within two passages of supposedly equivalent length. Until further research has clarified this whole immensely complicated area we would make a great mistake to look for either very exact or very involved ratios between large musical spans, instead organizing our observations broadly and simply according to the following generalized relationships:

1. Equivalent, similar, or congruent lengths.
2. Significantly greater length of one movement or part.
3. One member twice as large as the other. (A middle articulation in the larger member will often help us to recognize this double proportion.)

By this extremely general method we may be able to regard larger movements or longer parts as stresses, perhaps even as enormous downbeats. And by a reciprocal extension of this underlying rhythmic feeling in the other direction, a smaller movement or segment may be felt as a transition, preparation, or even as a gigantic upbeat. With these possibilities in mind we should inspect any series of potentially associated movements for signs of quickening, slowing, symmetry, or simple alternation of contrasting sizes. The lengths of songs in a cycle, or of instrumental movements in a long suite, may activate broad rhythms such as long-short-long-short-long or long-short-short-long-short-short-long, which as an exercise and aid to long-range response we can represent abstractly as $| \, d \quad \text{♩} \, | \, d \quad \text{♩} \, | \, d \, |$ or $| \, d \quad \text{♩ ♩} \, | d \quad \text{♩ ♩} \, | d \, |$.

Rhythm in Middle Dimensions

As we descend in size of dimensions, rhythmic properties become more specifiable and demonstrable, though not necessarily more important. Nearly all of the considerations just discussed in large dimensions apply to middle dimensions as well, but with a more evident relevance. Yet as a concomitant we also begin to notice more possibilities of layered ambiguity. In large dimensions the mere perception of rhythm is such a vague and tenuous response that the very existence of the response—of any true consciousness of large-scale rhythmic relationship—depends on diverse subjective interpretations. Within a framework that is itself ambiguous, it is patently difficult to isolate or define ambiguity: we need points of stability and certainty as baselines. Hence, even as we become more securely aware of rhythmic functions in middle dimensions we also perceive more clearly the potentials of conflict and resultant ambiguity.

The typology of meters and tempos now becomes a spectrum of metrical and tempo changes, and also of frequencies of change within the movement, verbally a bit confusing if described as rate of change of change (better: rate of change *in* change). The function of these changes in determining articulation and continuation should be studied as phenomena of Growth (see next chapter); but subtler nuances of tempo, such as accelerando and ritardando (rubato mainly affects small dimensions), should be studied as typologies and functions by means of questions such as these: How extensive or how brief are these nuances? Can we deduce any plan that controls their occurrence or any resulting pattern of motion?

Also, particularly in contemporary music, we must be prepared to deal with extremely subtle exploitations of tempo and meter, involving concepts such as tempo contour (Bartók's exactly prescribed limits of tempo fluctuations), "curved tempos,"[1] and "metric modulation."[2] These sophisticated controls on tempo contribute a novel resource of rhythmic development in which the tempo itself may become a primary thematic idea. Some earlier music also reaches a high degree of organization without going beyond the standard options for continuation, e.g. Mozart's operatic act-finales, which build tempo contrasts into a broad pattern of irresistible acceleration.

Length of sections becomes more directly significant in middle dimensions, since we can be reasonably sure, within a part of a movement, that composers intend some relationship of section and paragraph durations. The three main classifications of relationship already suggested for large dimensions—equal, longer, twice as long—also represent the commonest possibilities for middle dimensions, now further pointed up and reinforced by thematic content. (Here as always, "thematic" must be understood broadly to include all SHMRG possibilities, not merely Melody.) For example, if an exposition introduces events P, T, S, and K, a recapitulation that includes all these events will be heard as approximately equal, even if in actuality it is slightly longer or shorter. On the other hand, the moment any additions, substitutions, or subtractions are underlined by fresh thematic events, the listener's consciousness of length relationships receives an appropriate cue, and he pays more effective attention. Along with relationships of length we also become more conscious of changes in the general rhythmic character of sections and smaller divisions, particularly the differing densities of rhythmic texture and fabric, the aggregate sense of activity generated by the number of impacts per phrase, per sentence, and so on. Except for the most preliminary of statistical purposes, note impacts cannot be considered equal in force: all of the layers of rhythm influence the relative strength of notes so significantly, yet indefinably, that

1. See Whitney Balliett writing about Charlie Mingus in *The New Yorker*, June 13, 1964, p. 135.
2. See Richard F. Goldman, *The Music of Elliott Carter*, in *The Musical Quarterly*, XLIII (1957), 161.

one despairs of reaching an adequate approach to the problem of rhythmic density except by way of broad summaries. Nevertheless, as we have seen so often before, style-analytical observations attain a collective power and validity by correlation and confirmation. In this way even general observations of rhythmic density may add tangibly to the growing insights obtained in middle dimensions.

Seeking Shape in middle dimensions and often reaching across the border into small dimensions, we must attempt to determine a composer's *characteristic rhythmic module*, the size of gesture or idea that seems most often to occur. Because of hierarchic expectations, the continuum normally implies modules in every dimension, of course, but not all of these possibilities reach full realization in a particular piece. On the other hand, some very highly organized composers (Beethoven, Bartók) exploit modular structure (and evasions of it) in all dimensions. In most music, however, composers have concentrated their organizational power on one or two dimensional levels. We can identify these characteristic modules by looking for controlled differentiation, i.e. a richness of change (SHMRG) that nevertheless exhibits order and direction. Differentiation gives profile to the music, while control articulates and emphasizes a particular dimension. This question of characteristic modules relates also to Growth, under which topic some further aspects will be discussed.

If a module can be isolated, we next attempt to generalize about its Shape. Since rhythmic aspects of articulation tend to confirm and interact with functions of other elements, the most individual contribution of Rhythm to Shape lies in the varied relationships of stress, lull, and transition. Following the steps listed above under "Rhythmic Typology," we can find a variety of modular types. This stress analysis requires comparative evaluation of all three rhythmic layers, which we can represent on a three-level timeline that offers a simple yet accurate graph of rhythmic functions (see Example 5-9).

Using another variant of the Rule of Three, we can distinguish the following types of modular profiles (see Example 5-10):

1. Early stress: SLT (Stress, Lull, Transition); also SL or ST.
2. Middle stress: TSL.
3. Late stress: TS or LTS.

EXAMPLE 5-9.   Haydn, Symphony No. 102: I.

			s			S
Surface Rhythm						
Continuum	S	s	S	s	S	s	S
Interactions { Harmonic Rhythm			S			S
Contour Rhythm		S				S
Articulation and Dynamic Texture				s	S	S
	S					

Surface Rhythm. The first rest gives a light stress, since in effect it extends
   the single eighth into a quarter, a longer note that naturally receives
   a stress after a long chain of shorter, undifferentiated durations.
Continuum. If we assume a one-bar module, beat 1 normally receives the
   main stress, beat 3 a smaller stress. One might also feel a two-bar
   module, however, which would produce main stresses on bars 2 and 4,
   lighter stresses on bars 1 and 3. (This second possibility does not
   appear on the timeline.)
Interactions: Harmonic Rhythm. The chord rhythm produces stresses on the
   longer notes:

Contour Rhythm. Stresses will be felt at the turning points of the contour.
Surface Articulation and Dynamics. Starting with four-note groups in bar
   1, the articulation intensifies by reduction to a two-note group and
   staccato single notes, an activity crescendo leading neatly to the *sf*
   in bar 2. It seems likely that Haydn indicated this *sf* to prevent a
   pedestrian stress on the first beat of bar 3.
Texture. The tutti chords in bars 1 and 2 create a middle-dimension
   stress that does not entirely overpower the small-dimension stresses
   because we feel its broader implications rather than compare it
   directly to the subtle stresses that other elements produce in the
   small dimension.

To make a slightly more refined discrimination of types we
can roughly parallel the duration of the stress-lull-transition functions with upper- and lower-case letters, e.g. Ts = long Transition,
short stress. While this typology is adequate as a description of
stylistic events, it is by no means certain that small-dimension
rhythm actually should be grouped in this manner. There is some
doubt in the present writer's mind, for example, as to whether any
pattern can be "beginning-stressed," since all stresses require some
preparation, such as intake of breath, raised bow, or other transition
toward the apex of stress.[3] Further research is badly needed to

3. For a short introduction to Hugo Riemann's valuable but exaggerated "Auftakt" theory,
see the article *Auftakt* in *Riemann Musik-Lexikon*, 12th ed., *Sachteil* (Mainz, 1967), p. 63.

EXAMPLE 5-10.   Mozart, Piano Sonatas, K. 457, 545, 332.
Early, middle, and late stress in phrases.

clarify this fascinating ambiguity, although ambivalence of stress (what Cooper and Meyer[4] call "latent stress") is probably a fundamental property of rhythm, not to be explained entirely away. Pending such clarifications, providing we consistently use a fixed set of criteria for sorting types of rhythmic profiles, we will arrive at satisfactory distinctions, relative if not absolute, between works and composers.

Rhythm in Small Dimensions

The smaller the dimension of rhythmic analysis, the more we will find its typology tending to merge with the functions of Movement and Shape. To cite an illuminating analogy in physics, various subatomic particles are known only by their actions. Somewhat similarly, pulses and pulse fractions can hardly be examined and typed in themselves (except as part of a spectrum of durations), though their actions create both Movement and Shape. In attempting to understand this small-dimension activity we should study three aspects: the internal nature of stress, the character of surface rhythm, and the operation of the continuum. In some pieces the nature of stress could with equal reason be studied as a middle-dimension question; but since it is clearly a subsidiary detail of the

4. Grosvenor Cooper and Leonard Meyer, *The Rhythmic Structure of Music*, Chicago, 1960, p. 13.

larger stress-lull-transition states, it is procedurally appropriate to consider it here, in a smaller dimension. Like a good many other style-analytical levels, in actual operation these dimensional laminations will often telescope together; yet as part of a comprehensive theory, we gain clarity of understanding from this partly artificial separation. As we have seen, the three-level timeline analysis provides an effective identification of the sources of stress, though at times the determination of the predominant source may require a subjective decision. A further important question concerns the actual duration of stresses, lulls, and transitions. While the criteria for exact determination of these durations are much too complicated to discuss in this preliminary survey, we can easily notice whether the apex of a stress is sustained in some way, either as an extended melodic peak, a long highpoint of dynamic force, or a plateau of climactic activity in chord rhythm. The exact position of the stress (or lull or transition) in relation to the continuum is also stylistically revealing: does it perhaps anticipate a continuum accent, does it coincide, or is it delayed?

The contributions of surface rhythm to Movement are more easily understood, since we have only one element to examine, Rhythm itself. Here we can still create a typology of patterns arranged first according to sizes, i.e. cumulative durations, and then, more important, according to their formations, with particular regard to the degree of contrast, which strongly affects our sense of Movement. Within a steady quarter-note pulse of the continuum, a distinct rhythmic crescendo can result from progressions such as this: even eighths; triplets; eighth and two sixteenths; dotted eighth and sixteenth; double-dotted eighth and thirty-second. The degree of contrast mounts from 1:1 to an extreme of 1:4.

The relationship of surface rhythm to continuum, particularly the degree to which they coincide, also affects the strength of small-dimension rhythm very critically. The continuum itself may be extremely active (highly stressed) or rather passive (undifferentiated, beat-marking), depending upon the reinforcements it receives from surface rhythm and interactions. It may contain metric complications such as polymetric and polyrhythmic textures as well as rhythmic dissonances such as syncopations, which can exist only if the infrastructure of the continuum either persists in another part or has accumulated sufficient momentum to withstand the momentary challenge of the dissonance.

Surface rhythm contributes to Shape in two ways: first, contrasts in durations produce or confirm articulations and rhythmic profiles; second, patterns such as rhythmic motives are small shapes themselves, of course, and they enrich the typology of subphrases. Rhythmic interactions also play a significant part in small-dimension Shape; chord rhythm creates articulation and patterns; contour rhythm can reinforce the formations of phrases and subphrases; and textural rhythm initiated by loud-soft and tutti-solo alternations constitutes one of the main resources for individualizing phrases and subphrases. One final aspect, rhythmic texture and fabric (not to be confused with textural rhythm), neatly illustrates the close and complex interconnection of all these functions: How do we classify homorhythmic and contrapuntal textures—as contributions to Movement or to Shape? The answer, so typical of musical ambivalence, is: either or both. Contrasts between homorhythm and counterpoint in successive subphrases can activate an alternation pattern that definitely contributes to Movement. Quite as clearly, however, this same alternation can define modules that belong in the typology of Shape. With all these dualities and ambiguities, it is no wonder that we have ears on both sides of our heads.

CHAPTER SIX

THE GROWTH PROCESS

The style-analytical view of musical form as a resultant and combining element requires a fresh, stimulating term to express the vitality and immediacy of a functional approach as well as to dissolve the rigidities suggested by the unfortunately static word "form." Happily the word "Growth" admirably fulfills these needs, since its connotations include both the feeling of expansive continuation so characteristic of music and also a parallel sense of achieving something permanent. These coterminous aspects of Growth, though both delicately and decisively interactive, can be separated for analytical purposes into two parallel functions: Movement and Shape. Yet in making any such useful if artificial separations we must always somehow remain continuously aware of this indispensable unity-plus-duality: *musical Shape is the memory of Movement.* Fortunately the two aspects constantly remind us of their relationships in the recurrent process of articulation, a uniquely ambivalent transaction in music that both marks a node of change and yet maintains sufficient continuity to preserve and sometimes even to enhance the fundamental Movement. Only by a cumulation of articulations can we recognize a growing Shape; and only by responding differently to the expressive entities that articulation bonds together (yet also partly segregates) can we sense the changes that govern musical flow. If the *Guidelines* have accomplished anything thus far, they should have instilled a settled habit of regarding music first as a process of growth, then attempting to understand this growth by an analysis that fully reflects the character of musical flow. The fluidity of music must always be perceived as a stream (whether a spring, brook, or river) with tributaries of many sizes from many directions, never as a scattering of ponds and lakes, or worse still, as buckets and boxes into which a composer pours his thoughts.

The Morphology of Growth

Although the history of musical style cannot be viewed as a straight-line evolution, despite occasional circlings and false directions a steady morphological development can be traced along two general lines: enlargement of dimensions and functional specialization of material. Much like geographical explorers, composers discover new lands and sample their novelties long before the new country is fully settled. The history of style repeats over and over this cycle of discovery and gradual control of new dimensions and fresh effects, a process that one colleague has humorously dubbed the *Drang nach Kontrolle*. Already in early periods composers felt the need of purely musical methods of organization and integration, even though the primary structure might be furnished by a religious or secular text. The recurrence of melodic formulae in plainsong, independent of text recurrence; the complex schemata of isorhythm; the elaborate canonic and rhythmic manipulations of the cantus-firmus technique—all these show instinctive drives toward purely musical expansion and coordination.

Throughout the history of music the sources of control shift and sometimes conflict. The early centuries of polyphony, for example, give evidence of either harmonic *or* rhythmic control, but not both: even in Machaut, an elegant isorhythmic design will not be matched by equally satisfactory harmonic progressions. The idea of patterning, brought to such a height in isorhythm, next takes effect in the melodic aspect, producing various stages of imitation, from simple *Stimmtausch* to highly involved canonic devices. This melodic emphasis, however, at first drew interest away from rhythm and harmony: in early works one must frequently endure neutral or deficient harmonic and rhythmic treatment to savor the arcane joys of retrograde devices. These difficulties of complementary control, then, furnish us with yet another yardstick to measure a composer's technical mastery. We should also begin to look upon contrapuntal sophistication partly as a problem in dimensional control. In early periods we applaud composers for achieving a reasonable degree of consonance at the start of each large rhythmic unit, such as a perfection; and the smooth effects achieved by a composer such as Landini may be traced in part to his consistent distribution of consonance and dissonance within the tactus, avoiding both indigestible clusters and sudden textural vacuum. (See Example 6-1.) In the High Renaissance, the control of dissonance begins to

EXAMPLE 6-1. Landini, *Che cosa è quest' amor*: bars 1-7. (From Leo Schrade, ed., *Polyphonic Music of the 14th Century*, IV, Monaco: L'Oiseau-Lyre, 1958, p. 164.)

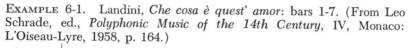

expand to a metrical level: the consistent placement of dissonant impacts on beats one and three of a quaternary meter multiplies the dimension of control by two: we no longer think in terms of a single tactus. In some composers the differentiation of the first from the third beat in various ways (not only by dissonance but also by chord tension, linear activity, spacing, and so on) raises the dimension to four beats, by implication an entire bar. Not until the decisive expansion in amount of instrumental composition during the sixteenth century, however, did composers squarely face the problem of creating a convincing musical flow without external aids such as texts and dance routines. For example, an early instrumental favorite, the keyboard variation, makes little conceptual advance on techniques of cantus-firmus compositions: in both genres Growth remains on a leash, as it were, bound by the implications of an initial gesture. In early sonatas, such as the violin publications of Marini and Fontana, the struggles of the composers to cope with formal freedom are almost comically evident. Structure does not arrive all at once: some composers control melodic lines nicely but flounder dismally among their harmonies; others discover the power of dominant tension but cannot match it with any parallel melodic logic. The melodic sequence occurs before the harmonic sequence, and the joint melodic-harmonic sequence that serves as the workhorse of Baroque music comes somewhat later. Still later, alert composers realized that eight good bars could become thirty-two merely by making three appropriate modulations—moving, for example, from tonic to dominant, submediant or subdominant, and back to tonic, transposed recurrences that led to the modulating ritornello plan. At this point S and H were more organized—more controlled in Movement and Shape—than M and R, since the modulations created tonal-textural spans of considerable length, whereas the melodic and rhythmic action may not extend beyond bar size, with a strong and confining emphasis on the motivic beat. To escape these limitations the emergence of large instrumental forms in the eighteenth century depended on the expansion and increasing coordination of all SHMRG elements, i.e. their organization into articulated patterns of controlled relationship.

Apart from expansion of modules in Movement, the stages of this long development in controlling musical expression may be traced in a clear if somewhat generalized way by studying the functional character of the musical material itself, which passes through four phases of increasing relevancy to the delineation of Shape:

1. *Heterogeneity*: a continuous proliferation of ideas unified mainly by a consistent medium. These loosely segmented proce-

EXAMPLE 6-2.   Leonin, *Sederunt principes*: opening. (From William
G. Waite, *The Rhythm of 12th-Century Polyphony*, New Haven: Yale,
1954, transcription p. 82.)
Heterogeneity of style.

dures are characteristic of early music and continue into the Renaissance. (See Example 6-2.)

   2. *Homogeneity*: the common state of Renaissance and Baroque
materials, which vary in S and H but remain largely constant in
melodic and rhythmic character. (See Example 6-3, next page.)

   3. *Differentiation*: as control increases and M and R phase into
concinnity with S and H (mainly an achievement of early Baroque
music), the sense of continuation increases to the point where we
become markedly aware of contrasting material, i.e. areas of greater
and lesser Movement and clearer or more obscure Shape. With the
aid of matching articulation, these areas gradually evolve into
progressively differentiated (not merely contrasting) materials that
finally achieve the detailed organization of themes.

   4. *Specialization*: the growing sophistication of formal control,
reflected in imaginative ramifications of the options for continuation, apparently led to a realization that certain types of themes
fitted into certain formal functions particularly well. In sonata form
the primary section typically demands forceful themes that establish
tonality and set the continuum strongly in motion, easily recognizable, too, so that one will note both development and recapitulation. Transition sections, charged with the responsibility of
modulation, need short, motivic material that can be flexibly per-
muted through quick-moving key changes (to which larger, more

EXAMPLE 6-3. Bach, *Brandenburg Concerto* No. 3: I, bars 17-20.
Homogeneity of style.

stable material could not so easily be fitted). Secondary themes, coasting on a successful establishment of both rhythmic flow and dominant key, often produce an admirable contrast to preceding sections, particularly if they exploit cantabile possibilities. Finally, to end the exposition we require decisive, repeated cadencing combined with high rhythmic activity to secure a dual objective, the powerful stability of a major articulation without loss of fundamental movement. Attempts to satisfy this double requirement led to specialized features in closing themes. (See Ex. 6-4, pp 122-23.)

The greatly oversimplified morphology suggested above gives us an initial framework within which to evaluate comparative historical achievements of composers as well as a general method of establishing evolutionary progress within a single style. For the latter purpose, however, considerable caution must be exercised in using size as a criterion of advancement: on the basis of size alone, how would we date Beethoven's F-minor Quartet, Op. 95? Looking merely at first movements, its 151 bars of 4/4 are briefer than most of the quartets in Op. 18. Measured for its dimension of contrast and control of musical elements, however, this quartet could never be mistaken for an early work. We should never underestimate composers' consciousness of their own technical and expressive problems and achievements. Though much of creative effort is spontaneous, we should not conclude that it is unsystematic— consciously or unconsciously, the music itself constantly demonstrates composers' awareness and struggles to control SHMRG. In Mozart's letters we find many probing comments of a style-analytical nature, showing that he identified weakness in other composers (more frequently than strengths!) directly by reference to specific musical elements. These hints from the workshop show that considerable insight can be gained from the evolutionary and morphological approach.

Style Stratification

As we have just seen above, schools and composers control different elements of style at different times. In between epochs of control we find periods that music historians tend to lump in an undifferentiated way as "transitional." Yet a great deal can be learned about the nature of any transition by regarding its style as a many-layered fabric with some layers well-controlled, others in a primitive state of development, or even in disorder. This explains the puzzling phenomenon of a composer to whom we respond strongly as far as his melody is concerned, yet about whom in other respects we feel strangely blocked and frustrated. If we then look closely at his Harmony, Rhythm, Sound, and Growth, each in isolation, we will discover various inconsistencies, incompletenesses, and unresolved conflicts that prevent these elements from communicating any clearer expression. This stratified view of style opens up immensely intriguing possibilities of identifying the stylistic elements that change first in a particular historical transition, as well as making clear precisely in which directions a composer was advanced or retarded by comparison with his peers. (See Example 6-5, p. 124.)

EXAMPLE 6-4. Sammartini, (below) Symphony No. 2: I, exposition; (facing page) Overture to *Memet* (1732), exposition. (From Bathia Churgin, *The Symphonies of G. B. Sammartini*, Cambridge: Harvard University Press, 1968, pp. 69, 207.)
Two stages of differentiation, the first still rather homogeneous (recurrent dotted figure), the second clarified by more contrasting rhythms and profiles.

EXAMPLE 6-5.   Leopold Mozart, *Sinfonia di camera* (1755): I, bars 1-4.
(After *Ausgewählte Werke*, ed. Max Seiffert, in *Denkmäler der Tonkunst in Bayern*, 9/2, Leipzig, 1903, p. 83.

*Style stratification, combining (1) Baroque aspects: motivic dimensions
in rhythm and melody (sixteenth triplets); beat-marking repetitions of
undifferentiated rhythms (eighths in viola and bass); small-dimension
alternations of timbre (half-bar of solo horn vs. half-bar of solo violin); and
(2) Classic aspects: motivic dimensions superseded by inclusion of motives
in a two-bar phrase balanced by its variant, so that we can even sense
a four-bar superstructure, clued by the heavier articulation when the
cadence texture shifts from the solos to the violas in bar 4—the solo
texture had continued in bar 2; slow chord rhythm (opening D chord
stabilizes for five beats in each phrase).*

Typology of Growth

The typology and subtypologies of Growth are much more
variegated and complex than those of other elements; exactly be-

cause Growth is a resultant, emergent, or combination of other elements, its typologies must reflect multiple interactions. For example, in isolating middle-dimension contributions to Movement of Melody alone we might investigate only four aspects (possibly: contour, patterning, peaks and lows, and density). In considering middle-dimension phenomena of Growth, however, we would again have to review these four melodic aspects to discover possible interactions with as many or more aspects in each of the other elements, with a consequent proliferation of observational possibilities. Lest this whole categorical structure seem unendurably procedural and rigid, it should once more be emphasized that the experienced analyst uses this framework only as a conceptual background, not as a horrendous bank of pigeonholes, each of which must be inspected and reinspected at every turn of the music. It is the task of any *Guidelines* to show the full theoretical matrix of style analysis, not as an objective in itself, but rather as a means of broadening and sharpening our power to make significant observations, to recognize the important sources of Movement and Shape rather than clicking through a detailed checklist like a data-processing machine.

Typologies of Growth will for the most part reflect interactions and concinnities in the music. While these functional types of categories are particularly revealing and instructive about the nature of a musical style, we may occasionally find reason to refer to various conventional forms, whether derived from poetry (rondeau, virelai, etc.) or fixed by consistent practices in various periods (da capo aria, sonata form, etc.). Since we are seeking to establish each composer's idiosyncratic solutions to problems of Growth, however, in most cases it is more illuminating to derive typologies from these individual preferences and practices rather than from the unavoidably generalized categories of conventional forms. Reflecting this lesser relevance, therefore, the conventional forms will be relegated to the following chapter.

Articulation

Having defined articulation partly as an indicator or symptom of change, we will recognize in turn that every change can produce its own articulation. Seen in the smallest dimension, when a first sound is succeeded by a second sound, the ending of the first and the beginning of the second is an articulative process, and the control of this process in surface articulations such as staccatos and slurs is the most familiar type of articulation. Among the millions of articulations, large, middle, and small, which music thus involves, we tend to make instinctive selections, responding significantly only to articulations of greater duration, or to those confirmed by change in more than one element. As a microcosm of the phenomena of Movement and articulation, compare two rhythmic patterns: eighth + two sixteenths vs. dotted eighth + one sixteenth. In each pattern, apart from the microscopic articulation that occurs between any two notes, for the just slightly larger dimension produced by the two-note grouping there is an articulation by change in duration. This inequality places a stress on the longer notes, at the same time generating a very small sense of Movement, somewhat more active in the second pattern, since the durational ratio there is higher (eighth/sixteenth = 2:1, dotted eighth/sixteenth = 3:1). In the course of a piece our ears naturally pass over such tiny, detailed articulations in responding to larger gestures, but the principles of articulative change and of flow generated by inequalities of all sorts can be applied to every dimension and element of music. Hence, as preparation for the style-analytical routine (Typology, Movement, Shape) we must always begin—partly instinctively—by identifying the location and relative weight of articulations. In well-organized composers the weight of articulations gives reliable clues to the relative importance of the division thus marked off. In particular Mozart[1] and Beethoven use differential articulations as clear as commas, semicolons, and periods to indicate the punctuations of Growth.

Since the chief requirement for evaluating articulation is a comprehensive awareness of its complexity, it is worthwhile to begin by reviewing potential sources of articulation available in SHMRG:

S. Changes of: combination, handling of texture; textural rhythm; dynamic level; dynamic pattern, e.g. from a stable treat-

---

1. See Marian W. Cobin, *Aspects of Stylistic Evolution in Two Mozart Concertos: K. 271 and K. 482,* in *The Music Review,* 31 (1970), 10ff.

ment to an active treatment.

H. Changes of: complexity of chord type or vocabulary; chord rhythm; cadencing; modulation; key rhythm; type, duration, and frequency of dissonances; type and intensity of fabric, e.g. from chordal to contrapuntal to stretto.

M. Changes of: range or tessitura; density of melodic action; thematic style, e.g. from mainly interrelated continuations to contrasting continuations; size of pattern or recurrent module of contour determined by peaks and lows.

R. Changes of: general state (stable, locally active, directional); continuum, either of unit, fractional basis (two or three), or metrical grouping; surface rhythmic patterns; surface rhythmic density; frequency of rhythmic dissonance; polyrhythmic complexity; proportion of stress, lull, and transition in all dimensions; source of prevailing dimension or control among the interactions.

G. Changes of: module in any dimension; degree of confirmation or concinnity between sources of change; choice of coordinated elements.

In addition, of course, *the frequency of change itself may change*, so we must consider the possibility that any of the types of change mentioned above may create an articulation by an abrupt rise or fall in the frequency as well as the degree of change.

The manifold potentials above associate to produce articulations of varying weight, to which three separate aspects contribute: duration, number of contributing elements, and concinnity between elements. As we have seen, ideally the weight of an articulation should correspond to the importance of the section that it defines. Let us consider an illustration of differential articulation in an eight-bar sentence consisting of two four-bar phrases. Here the articulations at the end of the fourth and eighth bars should reflect the lesser importance of the phrase as compared with the sentence. The simplest device would be a longer note in bar 4, leading up to the longest note in bar 8, defining the phrase/sentence hierarchy by relative rhythmic stability. Equally effective are distinctions in the length of rests: notice the articulation that introduces the secondary section of the first movement of Mozart's C-major Sonata, K. 545 (bars 12–13) by five beats of rest in the right hand, which is so much more decisive than earlier phrase articulations by quarter

EXAMPLE 6-6.   Mozart, Piano Sonata, K. 545: I, bars 11-14.
Heavy articulation produced by rests, new dynamic level, and changes in texture and register.

rests. (See Example 6-6.) Shifting to the harmonic area, a pattern of chord rhythm such as the following would clearly "explain" the hierarchic relationship of articulations (a) and (b) by the longer duration at the end:

Articulation by Melody brings up the other factors in weighting articulation, since melodic articulations are particularly elusive: most of the articulations that we may at first interpret as exclusively melodic actually become noticeable because of confirming changes in surface rhythm, continuum, or chord rhythm. It is only in styles with strong melodic orientation that we can distinguish phrase from sentence articulations merely because the composer consistently gives tiny clues of stability, such as smaller intervals or none at all, to indicate heavier punctuation. When elements coordinate to produce articulation, the articulative weight usually increases, and a close concinnity of timing produces the most convincing joints. In the Mozart example mentioned just above, the section articulation produced by the long rest is confirmed by a quarter rest in the left hand, which has just completed a bar of high activity; and after building increasingly broad sweeps to the climactic long scale, d^1 to c^3 (bars 9–10), the whole texture tapers abruptly from a melody-plus-accompaniment structure to open octaves, while the surface rhythm decreases successively from sixteenth- to eighth- to quarter-note action, and the chord rhythm stabilizes over a two-bar implied pedal. Even if no rest were present, these concinnous interactions would create a line of demarcation between sections, further highlighted by the beginning of the S theme on an entirely fresh, untouched note after the largest interval yet used (g^1 to d^3, bars 12–14) with a faster surface rhythm in the accompaniment: sixteenths as compared to eighths at the beginning.

With such examples in mind, the possibilities for creating typologies of articulation according to participating elements is obvious; but more significant to Growth, perhaps, is the typology of tensile strength ranging from open, homophonic punctuations to various special sorts of tightly knit contrapuntal articulations that composers of high kinetic sensibilities have developed. These more closely interlocking articulations can be divided into four types:

1. *Stratifications*, including both anticipations such as *upbeats* at the beginning of phrases and *overlaps* at the end of phrases. The distinguishing feature of overlaps is that they are layered or even contrapuntal: one or more parts actually reach over the articulative boundary established by the other parts. A fine example that shows simultaneous anticipation and overlap—possibly the most effective complex articulation ever written—occurs in bars 34–35 of the first movement of Beethoven's Ninth Symphony, where the articulative boundary is the barline, the sextolets in the second violins and cellos anticipate, and the sweeping descent of the thirty-seconds in the first violins and violas hangs over into the new phrase. (See Example 6-7.)

EXAMPLE 6-7.   Beethoven, Symphony No. 9: I, bars 31-39.
Stratified articulation, with anticipation of D minor tonic in bar 34 by second violins and cellos, followed by the overlapping continuation of the scale in first violins and violas.

EXAMPLE 6-8.   Beethoven, Piano Sonata, Op. 10, No. 1: I, bars 17-26.
*Elided articulation: the asterisked partial bar functions doubly as the
end of one phrase and the beginning of the next.*

2. *Elision* refers to the articulative situation in which a single
bar can serve either as the concluding bar (often only part of the
bar) of one phrase or as the beginning bar of a following phrase.
This type of articulation is not contrapuntal, however; the connective bar sounds at first like a conclusion, and only in retrospect do
we realize that it has also functioned as a beginning. This double
function dispenses with one bar in any regular patterning, turning
4+4, for example, into 3+4 or 4+3, depending on whether the
elided bar seems more closely bound to the preceding or following
phrase. The resultant compression produces an extremely well-knit
Growth. (See Example 6-8.)

3. *Truncation* describes the complete elimination of the final
bar of a phrase by too early intrusion of a following phrase. Here
the sense of compression is more complete than in elision, since
the first bar in the following phrase cannot be heard as a completion of the phrase. Both elision and truncation involve the dis-
appearance of one bar, but the impression of loss (and heightened
tensile connection that results) is more complete in truncation than
in elision. The astonishingly complex example from the Ninth Sym-

EXAMPLE 6-9.   Mozart: Piano Sonata, K. 332: I, bars 76-85.
Truncated articulation (for full context, see Example 7-3).

phony cited above contains a further complication in its articulation:
the harmonic progression is truncated, passing from I_4^6 immediately to I in D minor, without the expected dominant between.[2]
(See also Example 6-9.)

4. *Lamination.* In all of the articulations above, the interruption or disruption of the phrase module lasts at most a single bar.
At times, however, even in basically homophonic styles, the disagreement of articulations between two strata of the texture may continue
for some time, giving an effect of lamination going considerably
beyond anticipation and overlap. This type of lamination, of course,
results naturally within any imitative texture such as a canon, or
the entry points of imitation in motets. Conversely, while a continuing offset of articulations inevitably produces a polyphonic im-

2. The C# in bar 35, though immediately neutralized by a C♮ , possibly represents a
vestige of the missing dominant.

EXAMPLE 6-10.   Beethoven, Piano Sonata, Op. 10, No. 1: III, bars
20-26.
Laminated articulation.

pression in the texture, the word "lamination" is more broadly useful
to describe a miscellaneous spectrum of layered effects, not all of
which fall clearly under such categorical terms as "polyphonic" or
"contrapuntal." (See Example 6-10.)

These categories represent merely the most generalized types of
articulations; and owing to the ambiguities of contrapuntal or stratified fabrics that we so frequently encounter, many articulations fall
between the categories, particularly between elision and truncation, where continuity of accompaniment figures may make it difficult to decide whether the articulative bar is double-action or not.
If one can extend the concept of dissonance beyond harmony to
include any conflict with a prevailing norm of materials or structure, it is not difficult to see that three of the types of articulation
noted above represent examples of *modular dissonance,* i.e. situations in which a momentary conflict develops in the normal flow
and then resolves.

As we have seen, the idea of morphological dissonance can also
apply to Rhythm (conflict with the continuum), Melody (conflict

EXAMPLE 6-11. Johann Stamitz, Symphony (DTB/Wolf Op. 4, No. 6): I, bars 9-16. (From *Denkmäler der Tonkunst in Bayern*, 7/2; repr. in *Mannheim Symphonists*, I, 107.)
Dimensional stratification in which rhythm, melody, and sound emphasize compatible modules of different sizes.

with a prevailing melodic basis: in a diatonic style a chromatic is a melodic dissonance), or Sound (a forceful short interjection of a new texture into a prevailing fabric). Clearly each of these types of dissonance may contribute to modular dissonance. Equally important are the potential conflicts with articulations in other dimensions, what we might call *dimensional stratification*. A well-crafted piece owes much of the conviction of its flow to the confirmation of articulations in different dimensions. A short syncopation between strata can stimulate new vigor in the Movement, but too frequent conflict runs a danger of disintegration. As an early example of unusually skillful control of three-dimensional strata we can examine a passage near the opening of Johann Stamitz's Symphony in E-flat (DTB/Wolf E♭-5). Here surface rhythm creates a half-plus-quarter bar rhythm; a melodic parabola treated as a tethered sequence yields a two-bar module; and the octave repetition of this sequence establishes a repeating four-bar sentence, the last stratum partly confirmed by slow harmonic change. (See Example 6-11.) A particular fascination of this example is the variety of musical elements— R, M, and H—that produce the three strata of Movement.

Growth in Large Dimensions

There is no doubt that it is difficult to analyze or even to describe sensations of Movement in large dimensions. Yet, like Movement of smaller, more perceptible types such as surface rhythm, the largest motions, though extended on a grand scale, must also be infinitely diverse compounds of action and rest, of tension and stability, or whatever names we may give to these poles of change and nonchange. Beginning with the obvious, the estimated timing of parts or movements clearly furnishes a relatively unambiguous if primitive durational emphasis. More important in the exploration of large-scale Movement, we then attempt to recognize which of a series of movements (or parts of a movement) leave impressions of greater activity. These areas exert stress in large dimensions, so that between the parts or movements we can observe arrangements of relative stress and lull or transition. An impression of strong Movement in large dimensions apparently derives also in large part from the degree and frequency of contrast between the three states of rhythm. Within these basic categories of fundamental Movement we can go on to determine the sources of observed activity. At times the discontinuous or disorganized character of musical activity may go so far that we are scarcely conscious of activity at all. Under such conditions we simply remind ourselves of the parent category, change, which is activity in the most broadly generalized sense. No piece can exist without some form of change that we can observe and study.

The process of subtypology should begin with a collection of large-dimension contributions to Movement by all the elements, particularly as they combine and coordinate to produce the concinnity of Growth. For any piece or composer it is our objective to discover the *characteristic modules of activity* and the *prevailing or controlling combinations of elements*. These considerations apply much more to middle than to large dimensions, since few composers have a consistently long span of thought. In styles that have not reached a high degree of organization we may occasionally experience difficulty in finding any significant module of coordinated Movement at all. Conversely, a highly organized composer may be able to control characteristic modules in large, middle, and small dimensions simultaneously, a sophistication slowly developed since the Renaissance, gradually progressing from beat control to bar control and on to phrases, parts, and movements. It should perhaps again be emphasized here that exact durational equality is by no means required or indispensable in creating a modular structure. Since varying intensities of activity between articulations obviously prevent exact equality anyway, clearly music operates on a principle of *modular equivalency* rather than equality. Hence, owing to the fortunate elasticity of human perception, a pattern of 4+4+5+4 +3+4 bars may often be perceived as regular four-bar modules, despite the inequalities. The cause for this discrepancy between musical actuality and perceived effect cannot easily be clarified, but we can at least discover some clues to the situation. For example, the same duration will be perceived as shorter if it is played with rising intensity, but seems longer if played with falling intensity. As a possible confirmation for this, notice that almost all performers accelerate at least slightly in loud or crescendo passages, decelerate in soft or diminuendo passages.

In constructing typologies of Movement we obviously must take account of the three aspects of change: stability, local activity, and directional motion. And, in evaluating various observed phenomena of activity, it now becomes particularly important to make sure that we analyze musical events consistently in one dimension at a time, so that our identification of structural and ornamental functions do not become confused. For example, what we perceive in large dimensions as merely local activity, when studied in middle dimensions may become directional motion, just as what we perceive as a tiny rivulet of rain may seem to an ant to be a veritable Mississippi.

While on the subject of modular structure, it is perhaps worthwhile to review one slightly puzzling aspect of Growth mentioned earlier, namely the idea that Shape can contribute to itself, which at first seems paradoxical. The paradox disappears when we realize that Shape includes both contributing and combining functions. The contributing functions have to do mainly with modular expectations and preconceptions of all sorts and in all dimensions, including modular articulation (e.g. a middle-dimension continuum of 4+4+4 . . .) and conventional forms (e.g. ABA, rondo, etc.). Any externally derived scheme must take its place as but one of the many features contributing to Growth, not necessarily as a controlling function. As we shall see below, a good composer may seem to carry a general convention such as sonata form vaguely in mind, but the reality of the Shape emerges freely as he invents and develops each fresh combination of elements, typically superseding, evading, or frustrating any conventional structures that a rigid preconception might impose. Carrying the notion of formal preconception to a possibly extreme length, the very idea of structural hierarchy and musical syntax is to some extent an external preconception, and as such, one of the contributions of Shape rather than a natural emergent of combining functions.

For Growth as for other elements, in the process of stimulating fundamental Movement by juxtaposing areas of varying activity, composers simultaneously create profiles of permanent Shape, which when converted to graphic values are jagged for movements with many changes, plateau-like for movements with slower change. The potentialities of graphs as a method for identifying the large-dimension character of a style are considerable. The next step involves observation and typology of the controlling element or elements. With a group of five songs we might notice the following pattern of controlling elements:

I	II	III	IV	V
MH	SR	M	SR	MH

Here the composer obtains sharp contrasts between songs I and II as well as between IV and V. The central song, which clearly emphasizes lyrical values without other activity, serves as a resting point; and the large-dimension Growth achieves a partial symmetry by the recurrence of MH emphasis in I and V, enclosing a parallel recurrence of SR emphasis in II and IV. The hypothetical composer, we might conclude, has reached a nice balance between unity and variety. For all typologies such as these, the four standard options for continuation obviously furnish an effective and convenient point of departure.

Particularly appropriate for consideration in large dimensions

is the possibility of climax, which lies somewhere between Movement and Shape, since it not only results from an intensification of
motion but also acts as a definitive peak, setting the scale for the
profile of a piece. If we can assume that a composer's moments of
deepest emotion and highest excitement are his most characteristic
expressions, then the stylistic components of these critical moments
(which may not always be climaxes, of course) give us the fullest
insight into his creative personality. Can we speak of one movement as the climax of a cycle? Do we find more than one climax
in a movement, possibly a hierarchy of climaxes within a well-
developed profile of intensity? What is the degree of contrast between these highest points and the lowest ebb? These are some of
the questions that we must ask; and in the process of answering,
the piece itself will lead us to other observations that add relevant
details of understanding.

As we have already seen in the discussion of Melody, thematic
design does not generally affect large dimensions, but movements
and parts do exhibit general procedural traits that can be described
in broad terms such as thematic or diffuse; expositional or transitional; developmental or recurrent; intermediate or final in stabilization. The wide perspective of Growth adds to our depth of response
in relating parts or movements, since we learn to view every element
as potentially thematic. This open-minded and open-eared approach
circumvents the danger of relying too much on the conventions of
any particular period for our clues to Shape and its thematic
processes. For example, from the late seventeenth century through
the eighteenth, composers signal a secondary subject by stabilizing
a tensionally related key-area, typically the dominant or major
mediant. In some Romantic compositions, however, since the clue
to significant new material may come more reliably from changes
in orchestral color, Romantic complications and refinements in
harmony make it far more difficult to sense a controlling opposition between two keys, and in compensation composers set up
thematic polarities by means of other elements.

Thematic Relationship

Although thematic design can be observed typically more in middle than in large dimensions, thematic relationship is potentially of great importance to large-dimension Shape since it furnishes a major source of relationship between parts. In the chapter on Melody we have already derived some rules of thumb for admitting and excluding thematic relationships. Since these relationships become even more influential as they apply to Growth, we need to place our criteria for determining significant relationships—as opposed to coincidence—on even deeper foundations. Looking back over the history of music, one of the most important caveats for us to keep in mind concerns the attitudes of composers. Relatively few, before the nineteenth century, can be said to have had a strong sense of personal identity: they did not typically regard their works with obsessive possessiveness, nor did they strive for labels or personality tags that would specifically identify their products. Attitudes vary from time to time, however, and the first commandment of the analyst requires him to investigate the frame of reference, the prevailing norms of any style, school, or period. In general, in order to contribute significant relationships of Shape, a resemblance must connect two ideas within a piece by a sufficient number of aspects and elements so that we may sense a specific familial thread binding the material within this one specific piece or movement. If we can trace approximately as many facets of relationship between one of these themes and analogous material in other works, perhaps even by other composers, clearly the familial character includes so many pieces that it cannot exclusively and significantly relate the themes of a particular movement. In a village of all blue-eyed people, it would not occur to us to identify families by looking at eyes. Similarly for music, in looking at plainsong, for example, we must be careful that we do not give undue thematic weight within a single chant to a formula that may be endemic in the whole repertory.

Passing from the general frame of reference to the composer

himself, we should check his prevailing habits in two ways. First, most composers emphasize one or two of the stylistic elements more than others. As a consequence, these elements will be more important to us as bases for identifying significant relationships. Haydn, for example, places more stress on rhythm than on melody. Applied to evaluations of potential thematic relationships in Haydn, this means that rhythmic similarity outweighs melodic similarity as a criterion. Second, we must attempt to establish a range of probability (and credibility) within which the composer operates. How radically does Tchaikovsky generally alter an idea? Does he vary only one element, or several? The clues to composers' typical practices will be found in the morphological positions where variational procedures most commonly occur, such as the immediate small variants of primary material that are often used as a bridge to transition or even as a transition itself; development sections, which naturally tend to explore more remote derivants and mutations; and recapitulations which, since they are intended to be exact or nearly exact parallels to the exposition, furnish important evidence of limitations from another point of view, i.e. of the degree of variation a composer considers possible without obscuring formal parallels. And variation form itself, though not fully analogous to forms with more complex thematic interbalances, nevertheless adds significantly to our bases for judging whether an observed relationship is functional, i.e. justifiably heard as relationship in a given style. Putting the results of this background into practice, if we find that a composer characteristically turns to Melody when he wishes to produce a variant, changing the interval pattern, perhaps even inverting, but rarely tampering with surface rhythm or harmony, clearly we may more confidently attribute thematic relationships to his melodically variant materials than to passages with patent rhythmic or harmonic differences: in the latter situations the potential relationship falls outside of the range of normal probability for this composer's style. Even though we may be able to point out some apparently related aspects, the composer himself in effect does *not* point these out; hence, following his lead, we should regard them as coincidences rather than significant formal ties. Remember that a clever analyst can relate anything to anything—on his own terms. But sensible style analysis must adhere to the composer's terms, quite a different matter.

We can summarize the discussion above in two general principles for determining significant thematic relationship within a single piece or movement: the themes in question must possess:

1. A statistical similarity appreciably higher than partial, coincidental resemblances to themes in other works;

2. A structural similarity consistent with the spectrum of variation found in the composer's style: two themes for which we claim relationship should neither vary more than the composer's normal degree of mutation nor vary in elements other than those which the composer typically exploits in making variants.

This brings up a recurrent problem in musicological analysis and writing: Must one leave out all ideas that fall below the "confidence level" in probability? On the contrary, phrased with appropriate limitations, one may often include observations and tentative conclusions of potential utility to later researchers. A work of musical art makes its place in a culture by the multiplicity of responses it evokes from listeners. Accordingly, analyses that attempt to furnish insights for music will draw strength from similarly collective, cumulative processes, each researcher sharing and borrowing as he attempts to advance our agglomerative search for wisdom. The basic rule is one of attitude: do not pervert any observation or conclusion by elevating it to the level of dogma or Divine Truth. A proper analysis exposes its methods and its conclusions fully, ready for later researchers to make their own judgments and adopt the aspects that they find convincing or helpful.

With so much talk of themes, it is perhaps time to paraphrase once more the ancient warning about horses and animals: all melodies can act as themes, but all themes are not necessarily melodies. Nothing weakens Growth analysis more than astigmatic views taken merely from point M. The nineteenth century, with its search for striking, highly characteristic ideas, often used a single galvanic rhythm, a perfumed chord, or a shimmering timbre as a central thematic idea; and in all periods, when studying Growth, we should remain open to conviction by any or all the elements: the wellsprings of Growth may emerge from unexpected directions.

Growth in Middle Dimensions

As in discussions of other elements we will find it much easier to discover the sources of Movement and the outlines of Shape in middle than in large dimensions, and for a very good reason: it is also easier for the composer to control a less extended creative span. Since for intermediate dimensions we do not have so many overtly typographic clues to articulation, such as double bars and tempo changes, it immediately becomes important to observe the differing sources and weights of articulations, beginning with obvious aids such as rests of all sizes and changes in texture or register, then proceeding to indicators of more subtlety though not necessarily of lesser effect, such as chord rhythm and flection count. The typologies for any piece or composer simply ramify and expand the two basic categories for observing articulation—source and weight. As we have seen, in well-organized pieces differential articulation will tend to signal the relative importance of corresponding sections, paragraphs, or phrases. But we cannot rely upon such hints; not all composers can control their material, and many able composers have been born into situations of stylistic conflict between obsolescent and emergent idioms, or in a time when a newly established style has not yet matured to the point of full control. Very few composers manage to exceed the general accomplishments of their eras: they profit from existing controls and suffer from conventional inconcinnities.

Within segments established by articulations we now seek to discover areas of activity, stress, and climax as the first clues to Movement, during these initial stages allowing lulls and transitions to emerge somewhat as confirmations and reminders. To achieve flow within a bar we must have beats of different weight; and flow in middle dimensions seems to be similarly dependent on differing stresses and emphases. If a composer wishes to write a series of four-bar phrases or sixteen-bar paragraphs that really move, he must carefully provide not merely variety but some perceptible directional principle to generate flow, such as alternately stressed and unstressed areas, or cumulation of interest over a whole section.

(Symmetrical balancing tends toward stability rather than flow; to give it Movement these stabilized phrases must be part of a larger, sentence-sized alternation pattern of stability and activity.) Consistent four- or sixteen-bar groups produce merely a continuum of Movement, within which we must look to dynamics, orchestration, melodic curve, harmonic activity, and other nonregular elements for the patterns of stress and lull that assure a fundamental sense of Movement. Listening to the opening of the "Jupiter" Symphony, for example, we might notice first a balance between the subphrases: an aggressive, annunciatory opening followed by a softer, more lyric answer. On closer inspection we would see that the opening is stable both harmonically and melodically: a single sustained harmony and an exactly repeating motive. The answering subphrase, however, makes decisive moves in the very same two elements: the harmony changes and the melodic motive moves upward. Though softer and less impressive, the answer actually initiates the flow of the movement both in itself and in its lull/transition function as part of an alternation pattern with the opening subphrase. To understand a composer's sentence structure we must now study the interrelationships of component phrases, applying at the next higher Growth level the same analytical approaches that we have just used to appreciate the internal operation of a phrase. The opening theme of the Andante in a piano concerto of J. C. Bach (Op. 7, No. 5) neatly illustrates concinnous treatment of five aspects to secure an effective flow throughout a relatively long sentence. (See Example 6-12.)

EXAMPLE 6-12.   J. C. Bach, Piano Concerto, Op. 7, No. 5: II (Andante), opening primary theme.
Concinnous treatment of several elements to produce continuous flow.

1. Gradual increase in variety and activity of surface rhythm, from a predominantly eighth-note motion to triplet sixteenths at the end.

2. Successive peaks (marked "x") matching growing and quickening flections (ranges of sixth, seventh, and octave) in the melodic line.

3. Stronger continuity in the second phrase (bars 5–12) produced by longer subphrases (two bars as compared with single bars earlier), confirmed by

4. Tighter articulations—no rests in the second phrase—and

5. Larger dimensions of contrast in the second phrase: after two subphrases of rather stable character (owing to the recurrent lower G under a rising sequential design) the line opens out with sudden freedom of excursion, creating a contrast pattern—stable to active—within this second phrase quite different from the consistent, repetitious figures of the subphrases in the first phrase.

Bach's subphrase in the second phrase deserves special comment: the subtle variety in surface rhythm offered by shifting the position of the quick notes from the beginning of the first beat to the end of the first beat in the following bar (compare bars 5 and 6) relieves the danger of too much patterning threatened by the repetitions in the opening phrase. Also, by alternating syncopated and normal bars Bach expands to a two-bar pattern of rhythmic dissonance followed by resolution. The articulation confirms this larger dimension, since the end of the syncopated bar is active, whereas the end of the normal bar is stabilized not only by the undifferentiated note values (successive eighths) but also by the pitch repetitions on D and G.

Expanding still further, the analytical process next concentrates on sentences and paragraphs in their relationship to sections, and finally on sections as they join and interrelate to form parts. For the larger segments of music we need to go beyond the four usual options and add a further consideration in the realm of continuation: *cumulative effect*. Except for the option of recurrence, the standard situations include mainly neighbor relationships, A:B:C. As a piece grows, however, we must increasingly look for long-range relationships such as A:M:Z or B:F:S (e.g. the recurrence of a motive from the primary theme, first as part of the closing section and later as the basis of an episode in the development). In middle dimensions the most important possibilities are extended intensifications and detensifications, crescendo and diminuendo effects, expansions or compressions, and progressive tempo alterations. These may result from any or all of the SHMRG elements, a typical example being the gradual intrinsic crescendo in the first-movement coda of the *Eroica Symphony*, produced by cumulative orchestral additions, new complexities of fabric, and increased rhythmic activity—a concinnous rise in excitement far more powerful than the parallel intensification of surface dynamics. The length and degree of contrast in such cumulative effects contributes a particularly revealing measure of a composer's style.

Growth in Small Dimensions

The typology of Growth in small dimensions largely repeats the observations for middle dimensions, again using the options for continuation as the primary framework for understanding Movement and Shape, but considering the contributing elements, and particularly their correlations and concinnities, at a much closer focus. The recognition of functions in very small dimensions may actually require more acuity because, just as an atom is less specialized than a molecule, so the character of motives is less individual than that of phrases, and we are more likely to disagree about the location of a subarticulation than of a whole recapitulation. The smaller the dimension, the fewer and less clear the directional clues. With this generalizing tendency of small dimensions to counteract, we must be correspondingly alert to discover the characterizing possibilities of interactions and concinnities as they confirm stresses, contrasts, and directional motion. Compare, for example, a motive of one eighth and two sixteenths applied to each of the following patterns:

/ C BC D CB C BC D CB / C   and   / C DE D EF E FG F GA / G

The first pattern attains only local activity, since the melodic line cycles back to its starting point; the second pattern, however, produces clearly directional motion by reason of the consistently rising line. Yet, as we study intensification and detensification of the various elements at these close quarters, we will often notice conflicting cues, one element apparently rising in activity while another rests or falls. This conflict itself, however, is a change and source of activity, a dissonance in the flow of the piece; and the contrast in effect between the disagreement (instability) and the surrounding concinnity (stability) of elements may contribute in extremely subtle ways to a deeper flow, which absorbs momentum from temporary whirlpools on the surface. Furthermore, the expectations set in motion by various modular arrangements contribute ambiguously to Movement, since expectation is a sort of psychological dissonance or tension, and its resolution when a change takes place as expected produces an added increment of stress or weight of articulation; yet also, quite the opposite, if an expectation is frustrated, evaded, or delayed, we experience an added increment of tension. Viewing the situation just slightly more broadly, we can see that any phrase will have slightly different intensity profiles when heard from the different perspectives of SHMR, with perhaps even a fifth, modular perspective (G) to be considered. The cumulative sense of small-dimension Movement results from the conflicts and resolutions of these profiles, and the elemental sources of controlling or prevailing profiles indicate the deepest creative instincts of the composer. Yet just at this vital point of potential discovery we will strike the most serious disagreements among musicians. Since we have recognized the possibility of ambiguity repeatedly in the study of single elements, in looking at the combining functions of Growth we must expect more, not less ambiguity —a veritable multiplication of ambivalence, because we must take account of all previous sources of ambiguity in combination—a buzzing beehive of interambiguities! This seems an impossible task until we stumble upon the second most characteristic fact of music: *reversibility, the power of one element to trigger effects of other elements in opposite directions of intensity.* While the possession of this elusive but utterly simple insight can by no means resolve all the complex potentialities of ambiguity we have just noted, it defines the nature of the problem in a revealing way that opens new avenues to better understanding.

To give an example that I hesitate to label "clear" (how can an example of ambiguity and reversibility be entirely clear?), the rhythmic pattern:

represents an unmistakeable rise in rhythmic intensity. If performed with a slight retard and a barely perceptible diminuendo, however (pulling triggers of R and S), the same pattern that produced a feeling of crescendo now exerts a powerful cumulative drag. The RS triggers have reversed the normal effect of the pattern, and the final four sixteenths affect us much like the divided beat a conductor uses to control a retard at the very end of a piece. (See also Example 6-13.)

With the potential of reversibility lurking in many phenomena of musical intensity, it is no wonder that musicians often disagree about the profile of a phrase. Typically, even when looking at the same notes on paper, we may be hearing different things. Hence, a disagreement about stress or crescendo may arise not so much from actual differences in principle of interpretation as from differing responses to the musical notation itself: one performer may insist on a particular stress because in his own ear he is emphasizing a latent harmonic implication that does not appear overtly on paper. His colleague may disagree simply because he has not considered the harmonic interactions, feeling different stresses according to surface rhythm and line only. The beauty of the situation—and the special attraction of music—is that both are right, according to the version of the music that they hear; and in well-crafted music the reversibility of individual contributions to Movement does not change the basic Shape any more than the change between photographic negatives and positives alters the basic contours of a picture. The problem of performance, then, really centers as much on understanding the whole of a score in all its implications as on expressing a sensitive, cultivated reaction to any single implication. To this end, the contribution of style analysis in sharpening perceptions of all elements in all dimensions is nearly unlimited.

EXAMPLE 6-13.   Brahms, Trio for Clarinet, Viola, and Piano, Op. 114:
II, bars 26-31.
*Reversibility: rising tension in surface rhythm and chord rhythm out-
weighed by falling tension in textural activity, dynamics, and the implied
6/4 bars.*

The Influence of Texts

In view of the large part of the musical literature that involves words, a comprehensive stylistic survey obviously must take into account the influence of texts. Although this influence undoubtedly affects Shape more than any other aspect of style, in line with previous efforts to develop a consistent routine of observation it seems worthwhile to maintain the SHMRG order of comment in the discussion below.

At the most fundamental conceptual level, the text affects a composer's choice of vocal and instrumental combinations. A delicate lyric suggests a solo voice with a chamber combination of instruments; a violent declamatory poem requires a massive chorus and orchestral setting. The sensitivity of a composer's response to the affect of the text thus may be one of the first and most impressive features of his style and one of the sharpest continuing challenges to his imagination. Supposing that we were to make a study of the works of Méhul and come across his opera *Uthal* (1806), which lacks violins, apparently in attempt to create a murky "Fingal's Cave" atmosphere. Here the evident interest of the composer in projecting the mood of the text suggests a major point of attack for further observations: to see whether color responses to text characterize all of Méhul's works, not only in a general way such as the basic scoring but also in details such as the coloring of a particular affective word or phrase.

Merely the sound of words themselves often can project mood and atmosphere, and, noticeably beginning in the 19th century, composers exploit this aspect of texts. Vowels and consonants may also create pitfalls for the unwary: any composer attempting to make a choral setting of a text including the word "Sisyphus" should be alert to the possibilities of unintended humor in such a situation. More usefully, words can enhance textures and contrapuntal layering: imagine, for example, the lower voices of a chorus repeating the word "boom" slowly, while above this sustained sonorous effect the remaining voices rapidly chant "fight right, fight right."

Of all the elements, probably none has been exploited more

thoroughly for text expression than Harmony, because of the power of chords and tonalities to change a mood almost instantaneously. Schubert used this power magically for characterization in *Erlkönig*, in which Death calls to the dying boy in a falsely sweet major tonality. In *Der Lindenbaum*, he makes the reverse tonal change: the entrance of the tonic minor clearly marks the "winter" sections of the song. Equally striking are the effects of harmony in small dimensions, notably the use of a single chord or progression as a motif (see the opening of Schubert's *Am Meer*, where the slow, enigmatic rocking from augmented sixth to tonic suggests a mysterious, deep-lying power in the ocean). Often a single chord or characteristic dissonance can underline a specific word with telling appropriateness, for example, the clanging augmented triad on the name "Nothung" as Siegfried forges his sword in Act I, Scene 3 of Wagner's *Siegfried*.

In contrapuntal styles the specific sounds of the words themselves may add greatly to linear clarity. Hard consonants such as t, g, or k, in particular, can project a series of imitative entries with higher definition. And, in the opposite direction, inventive and experimental composers like Charles Ives have shown that the dissonance of conflicting words followed by homorhythmic consonance of syllables furnishes a whole new resource of contrast in expression.

The relationship between text and Melody brings in a good many subjective elements. Can we be sure that our reactions will be useful to others? For the present writer, Schumann's song *Im wunderschönen Monat Mai* is a perfect melodic expression of full springtide. Yet while this observation may remind the reader of a marvelous burst of lyricism and stimulate his agreement—or disagreement—it does not add much to his understanding of how this text-melody relationship contributes to Movement or Shape. A potentially more revealing area of observation concerns the direct relationship of sentence intonation and musical line. When in *Die Zauberflöte* Tamino finds Pamina's portrait and begins his aria with the enthusiastic phrase, "Dies Bildnis ist bezaubernd schön," the vaulting and descending musical line seems to reflect exactly the fervent way he would have spoken the words. Many composers have shared this gift for finding a startlingly exact translation of a word or phrase into melody, a reinforcement and concinnity that adds tangibly to Movement at that point. The confusion resulting from inappropriate matching of words and tones has the opposite effect, impeding or stagnating the flow, creating not so much a dissonance as a momentary deadlock. In a smaller dimension, the placement of individual vowels or consonants in the text may impose severe problems on the composer, and the intrusion of awkward vocables at the peak of a melody may ruin the effect of a whole phrase. Low vowels can be equally dangerous. Notwithstanding Verdi's normally infallible instinct for vocal effects, when the assassin Sparafucile sings his own name in the first act of *Rigoletto*, the setting of the syllable "cil", leaping down an octave to low F, creates so much difficulty that some singers alter the vowel toward a more open and relaxed sound such as "chawl" or "chahl".

The sensitivity or indifference of a composer to detailed problems of texts such as these may indicate a major emphasis of his style. We realize that Beethoven is primarily an instrumental composer after a single hearing of the Dungeon Scene from *Fidelio*, in which his setting requires Florestan to repeat the word "Freiheit" so often and so rapidly that we can easily confuse the illusion of delirium with a more pragmatic conclusion that the tenor is out of breath.

The most obvious influence of text rhythm can be seen in the patterns of individual words, and careful composers have usually tried to match notes to the stress and length of syllables as naturally as possible. Composers whose native language is English, unfortunately, must deal with the somewhat anti-musical predilection of English words for the combination of a short, stressed syllable with a longer, unstressed syllable, as in the word "never," which many composers, from Purcell to Britten, have set as a ♩♩. pattern. The frequency of such syncopated words in English texts, however, vastly exceeds the number of syncopes that can gracefully be absorbed in music, so that the setting of an English text can be regarded as a major test of any composer's imagination and ingenuity. Sometimes a text phrase will suggest a special rhythmic atmosphere for a section, as in Stravinsky's discovery of staccato implications in the ancient Latin adjuration "Laudate DOMINUM" from the finale of the *Symphony of Psalms*:

Lau-da-te DO-MI-NUM

In a larger dimension, word rhythms produce consistent meters that often influence the musical meter of a whole piece. The 6/8 swing of the text of Schubert's *Die Post* is unmistakable:

Von der Strasse her ein Posthorn klingt,

Was hat es,dass es so hoch aufspringt,Mein Herz?

Equally clear though in another language is the duple implication of *Sur le pont d'Avignon*:

Sur le pont d'Avignon l'on y danse, l'on y danse

We can feel the differing influence of the two texts in comparison: the 6/8 that produced such a fine swing in *Die Post* would create merely a pallid sing-song in *Sur le pont*, so crisp and natural in duple:

Sur le pont d'A - vi-gnon l'on y dan - se, l'on y dan - se

Where the metrical pattern of words is less strong or more varied, however, the rhythmic expression tends to range more widely, as we can see in the varying meters of five different settings of

Erlkönig: by Reichardt (3/8), Klein (6/8), Zelter (6/8), Schubert (4/4-12/8), Loewe (9/8).

The influence of texts on Shape can be seen most directly in stereotypes such as the *formes fixes* of early periods and the da capo aria (see Chapter 7). Even where the text is freer, however, the word arrangement may largely determine the length of the piece and the position of major articulations. Surprisingly often composers make rearrangements in the poetic material, or request alterations of a libretto in progress, as we can read in the correspondence between Mozart and Da Ponte, or between Strauss and Hofmannsthal. More important for style, the composer can repeat part of a text, giving special emphasis to particular points; and by extended introductions, intercalations, and codas he can completely surround the text with a musical design, so that we can no longer think of text as a prime determinant, but only as a condition to which the composer reacts in creating a predominantly musical solution.

The frequent changes of meaning in some texts pose a different problem for the composer, since musical movement typically acts in a different way: though music can make one or two sharp changes in direction, it cannot alter mood in every new line, like Hamlet, without losing its basic unity. Texts, therefore, tend not so much to support the movement of music as to create problems of too much movement.

For a full evaluation of the influence of texts, the style analyst must become to some extent a critic of poetry. Only when he understands the structure and content of the text in all its subtleties can he evaluate the success of the composer in bringing these features to full expression. Yet the fullest expression of poetic implications may actually threaten the musical design. The ultimate measure of a composer's achievement takes the text realization into account, but the degree of control of musical movement and shape remains the final standard.

CHAPTER SEVEN

SYMBOLS FOR ANALYSIS
AND STEREOTYPES OF SHAPE

The exclusion of conventional forms from the chapter on Growth was intentional: we must learn to regard each piece first as a unique expression and only later as a member of some general category of Growth-types: cumulated experience with style analysis shows that the identification of any Growth process with one of the formal stereotypes (sonata form, two-part form, and the like) not only tells us comparatively little about a particular piece but also, more dangerously, may give us a tidy but false impression that we have in some measure discharged our analytic responsibilities. For, as we can quickly see, placing a piece in one of the categories of conventional form is almost the least that one can do, analytically: comprehensive observation can only make a beginning with this identification as a crude first step. All of the individualities of a composer occur as refinements, improvements, mutations, perhaps even as evasions of a stereotype. Although the final Shape may correspond fairly closely to a conventional type, only a full discovery of the sources of Movement and Shape can give us genuine understanding of a composer's style.

Since all discussions of Shape can be speeded and clarified by the use of appropriate symbols as a form of shorthand for musical notation, it is useful from the beginning to have in mind a hierarchic dimensional framework of symbols with provision of suitable opportunities for expansion. At all times we must keep carefully before us the proper objective of any system of symbols: to abstract and simplify the original complexities so that we gain potentially instructive overviews, unencumbered by detail. The moment a symbolic representation goes beyond what can be taken in at a glance—to be sure, a careful glance—we may often be better off with the original symbols: the musical notation itself, supplied with suitable labels.

All of us have experienced the frustration of analyzing a complicated piece and running out of symbols. The original motivation of the system below was utterly simple: to end this embarrassing sense of coming to the end of a cul-de-sac. The second objective was a system of symbols that represented widely applicable functions of Growth, chosen as far as possible mnemonically, so that the alphabetic graph would easily recall the musical functions. The final requirement was typographic: the symbols should be available on the ordinary typewriter keyboard, so that all preparation, from fair copy to final printing, can be accomplished without recourse to special fonts or handwork. This requirement also assures compatibility with various input devices for computers. (The Greek letters so dear to the hearts of some analysts add quite unnecessary complications exactly where the objective should be simplicity.) Fortunately these fairly complex demands can be satisfied within the normal typewriter alphabet with relatively few compromises; and the avoidance of more special symbols is well worth a few small adjustments, such as the use of *K* instead of *C* for closing functions (*C* is needed as part of an *a, b, c* . . . series). The general framework of symbols can be summarized as follows:

1. *Main symbols that indicate the chief Growth functions.*
   O — Introductory material, or primitive version of other functions.
   P — Primary materials.
   T — Transitional or other episodic, unstable functions.
   S — Secondary or contrasting functions.
   K — Closing, articulative functions.

If there are two or more themes of similar function, appropriate numbers should precede the function: *1P, 2P, 3P,* and so on. Similar numeration can be applied to all other functions as required: *4T, 2S, 3K, 2N.* Numbers following a letter, however, have a different meaning, to be explained under "variation" below.

2. *Less definite functions.*

N — New material, occurring *after* the expositional phase of *P*, *T*, *S*, and *K* material; for example, unrelated themes appearing in the development section can be suitably labelled *1N*, *2N*, and so forth. Episodic material in rondo or other ritornello growths usually performs a secondary or contrasting function, so that *S* represents such material better than *N*; but where (as in the case of a sonata-rondo form) the contrasting episode goes beyond expositional ideas, *N* symbolizes this relationship nicely. For the somewhat rare situation in which a new theme occurs in a recapitulation, *N* also can suggest the exceptional function clearly; in this way *N4P* can symbolize a fourth primary function that appears for the first time in the recapitulation.

Q — Questionable functions, too ambiguous in character to justify a more precise symbol. One must fight the temptation to use this symbol as a means of sweeping Shape problems under the rug! Remember that you are accusing the composer of disorganization. It is better to make a partly unsatisfactory assignment of function, using *Q* only as a last resort.

$(\ )$ — Parentheses indicate the original source of an idea: *S(P)* represents a secondary theme derived from a primary theme.

Important: *each theme should be symbolized according to its immediate, current function* rather than in terms of any previous service. For example, when Haydn repeats a primary theme in the dominant key (see Symphony No. 104), this new appearance functions now as a secondary theme, no longer as a primary theme; it should therefore be labeled *S(P)*, the parentheses showing the derivation. Composers sometimes set up a chain of internal derivations that may be important to record on the timeline. For this purpose a familiar etymological symbol for derivation (>), though it has the disadvantage of not being found on most typewriter keyboards, is conveniently self-explanatory: *K(2S>P)* refers to a closing theme based on a secondary theme derived in turn from the initial primary material. Symbols of this complexity, of course, should be regarded as special indicators, not everyday vocabulary. Because such expressions cannot be understood quickly by the scanning eye—they are not readily "scannable" (*übersichtlich*, the useful German term, seems to have no proper equivalent in English)—they are less suitable for comprehensive timelines than for special-purpose timeline segments constructed specifically to illustrate a composer's progressive derivations, or to emphasize some other detailed thematic point.

3. *Component elements within a thematic function may be indicated by modifying with lower-case letters.*

Ph — Harmonic, textural, or accompanimental aspects of a primary theme: in symbolizing variants and derivatives, it is often useful to be able to show the specific origin of the material. Thus, *1S(Ph)* describes a secondary theme derived from the accompaniment of the primary section.

r — Rhythm of a theme: this provides for a common need to isolate the rhythmic aspect of a theme from other elements, e.g. to show relationships by means of a recurrent rhythmic motive. In this way, *1Pr* can indicate the primary material's rhythm, and *1Sa(1Pr)* then shows that the first subphrase of the secondary theme derives from a rhythm of the primary theme.

/P — A slash preceding any symbol indicates location in the lower part of the texture: *P . . . /P* shows that in a repetition, *P* has been transferred to the bass. For special purposes, one can elaborate this textural shorthand, using */P/* (enclosed by slashes) to symbolize primary material embedded in the middle of the texture; thus *1S/Pr* refers to a secondary theme with lower parts based on a primary rhythm (see bars 51 and 85 of Example 7-2), but *S/Pr/* shows that the primary rhythm activates the middle textural components.

For certain styles or types of pieces, letters could be chosen outside the system above, to relate mnemonically more closely to a particular function. For example, in a study of ritornello forms, *R* would be a sensible choice to symbolize the returning function, though this removes the possibility of using *r* for "rhythm of a theme." *V* for variation and *S, A, CS* for subject, answer, and countersubject are other possibilities. In symbolizing functions within a Kyrie, *K* and *C* (Christe) would be useful mnemonically, but unfortunately this results in a double loss to the system of symbols: the closing function *K* and the component subfunction *c* (in the *a . . . g* series—see 6. *Subfunctions* below). Any obvious mnemonic gains by the use of special-purpose symbols, therefore, should be carefully weighed against less obvious but ultimately important losses in efficiency of communication that result from inventing and making the reader learn a second, merely temporary system. Experience suggests that we do well to adhere as closely as practicable to a single system. On the other hand, the *PTSK* symbols imply a degree of functional specialization that the music may not always support. Under these conditions, since a detailed hierarchy will probably not be required, the best solution is to use *ABCDEFG* in upper-case letters for main ideas: these letters carry no implication of particular differentiated function, since they are reserved in the system for subfunctions.

4. *Mixed Functions.* In periods such as the early Classic, when some contrasting functions begin to appear but composers do not consistently specialize any particular thematic types, we may wish to reflect this lack of differentiation by mixing the symbols: *SK*, for example, aptly describes the ambivalent nature of many themes on the borderline between secondary and closing sections that have not yet developed a consistently differentiated character. These ambiguities arise as a symptom of primitive technique, but later composers exploit indeterminate functions for continuity: in a number of Haydn symphonies the transitional material spins out of the primary section in such a way that *PT* accurately represents the relationship. Extending this principle, preliminary or embryonic versions of a primary theme can be suggested by *OP¹, OP²*, etc.

5. *Misplaced or Displaced Functions.* The more highly developed the Shape of a piece, the more the possibility of thematic miscalculation. Thus, for sonata form, particularly in early stages, we may encounter material with every stereotyped characteristic of a secondary theme, yet occurring in the primary section. A suitable representation for this apparent misplacement would be *(P)S*. We must also be prepared for displacements caused by complexity —by no means miscalculations.

Commonly in styles other than the Classic we may find more than one transition, typically in the form of transition-like, unstable, connective material occurring within a contrast area. For example, a secondary section based on two stable new ideas *(1S, 2S)* might still include an episodic transition between these two, even though a main transition *(1T)* had occurred before *1S*. *(S)T* symbolizes this type of transition within a secondary section; similarly, an interior transition of the *K* section would be *(K)T*, i.e. the transition inside the closing section.

6. *Subfunctions.* Where Growth analysis requires more detailed symbols than those for main thematic functions, single melodic phrases can be symbolized by attaching the letters *a . . . g* (*h* is already used above) to the main functions: *Pa, Pb, . . . Pg*. For differentiating subphrases we can use the series *x, y, z, v, w*, producing the following combinations, *Pax, ay, . . . aw*. Since one rarely needs more than three symbols for subphrases, it is preferable to use the familiar *x,y,z* as symbols first, before resorting, unalphabetically, to *v* and *w*—usually only in emergency. (See Example 7-3, bars 5-12.) Finally, in case we must deal with small recurring motives, the useful mnemonic series *m, 2m, 3m . . .* provides an unlimited string of symbols: for example, two motives in the last subphrase of a closing theme would be *Kgm, Kg2m*. (See Example 7-3, bars 11-12, 19-20, 22-23.) Particularly for the motivic proliferations of Baroque instrumental music, this unlimited series is a boon. We can summarize all these relationships in a chart of descending hierarchy:

Main function   *1P*
Component phrases   *1Pa, 1Pb, 1Pc, 1Pd, 1Pe, 1Pf, 1Pg*

Subphrases	$1Pax, ay, az, av, aw$
Motives	$1Paxm, x2m, x3m, \ldots$

To avoid unnecessary repetition of symbols, within any functional area we need only repeat the relevant identifying level of the hierarchy. For example, at the motivic level, we only need to identify motives m and $2m$ as belonging to the parent subphrase x, so we label them xm, $x2m$, and so on; and if only one subphrase (the x level) is developed at a time, we can even omit the second x. Similarly with regard to component phrases of main functions, once we indicate the principal function, we need not reidentify at this level until there is a change to another main function. Any redundant symbols detract from the clarity of overview, our chief objective in symbolization. In a typical situation, therefore, component subphrases of $1P$ and $1T$ would appear on a timeline as $1Pax \ldots y \ldots 1Tax \ldots y \ldots$ (not $1Pax \ldots 1Pay \ldots 1Tax \ldots 1Tay \ldots$).

On a timeline, where horizontal placement implies position in time, to show derivation of a theme from previous material, the source should be indicated in parentheses above rather than after the new theme. Thus, in the discussion of h in section 1 just above, when we transfer the expression $S(Ph)$ to a timeline, it should be

$$(Ph)$$

repositioned vertically as follows: S. This avoids the potentially confusing impression that Ph is occurring in the bar following S.

Having provided "names" for functions at their original point of entry, we must now furnish a system to represent ensuing changes in the material. To keep the logic clear, we should reserve letters entirely for functions, then use modifying numerical superscripts placed after the functions like exponents, to indicate variants, derivatives, and mutants. (We can now understand why the chronological number of the function must be placed in front of the letter symbol.) Small variants can be symbolized as superscript numbers in parentheses; larger changes as superscripts without parentheses; and variants of variants as decimals following the superscripts. While superscripts, if available, make the symbolic combinations easier to read and understand, for elementary data processing and rapid typing the numbers can appear at the same level as the letters without producing serious ambiguity. (Acceptable: $Pa \ldots Pa1 \ldots$; better: $Pa \ldots Pa^1. \ldots$) Here are some typical expressions printed in the preferred style with superscripts:

$2Pa^1$ = significant first variant: ^{1}
     of first component: a
     of second primary theme: $2P$
$2Pa^{(2)}$ = relatively unimportant second variant: $^{(2)}$
     of the original component phrase: $2Pa$
$(2Pa)$
$1Tb$ = second component phrase: b
     of first transition theme: $1T$
     derived from first phrase of second primary theme: $(2Pa)$

Occasionally, if we wish to make rather detailed studies of tiny interrelationships, such as variants of variants, we can use a decimal system following the exponent of the original variant:

$2Pa^{1.1}$ = significant first subvariant: $^{.1}$
     of a significant variant: ^{1}
$2Pa^{1.02}$ = relatively unimportant second subvariant: $^{.02}$
     of a significant variant: ^{1}

This degree of complexity in symbols, of course, should be avoided except for unusually detailed studies designed to emphasize a special point of a particular style.

In densely motivic styles, small motives often function as primary thematic material. As a consequence, symbols such as Pax, Pay, etc., not only produce unnecessary complexity, but they actually misrepresent the functional dimension: they suggest that somewhere we will find a large, complete primary theme, of which Pax, Pay are merely preliminary fragments. A more appropriate level of symbols would be $1M$, $2M$, etc. (upper case, to emphasize the motives' primary thematic function). (See Ex. 7-1, pp. 162-63.)

The superscript of "O" used alone can represent the Original version of any material, particularly useful in a chain of symbols representing variation form, where one may wish to distinguish slight alterations from substantial changes. For example, Haydn's variation schemes often suggest a rondo within the variations by returning a slightly altered version of the theme in between more substantially changed versions. Interrelationships between variations can always be symbolized by appropriate decimals. Thus, a theme followed by two interrelated variations and a return slightly varied by new orchestration would be symbolized as follows:

Theme   Var. 1   Var. 2 (rel. to 1)   Return of Theme (new orch.)

$$P^0 \qquad P^1 \qquad \overset{(1.1)}{P^2} \qquad\qquad\qquad P^{0.1}$$

Since degree of change is an important stylistic criterion, in most cases the symbolization of a series of variants should proceed in normal arithmetic order. This permits us to see at a glance how many variants a composer has managed to derive, while any interrelationships can then be shown in parentheses above or following. Thus the clearest coding of a chain of interrelated subphrase variants would take a form somewhat as follows:

$$Pax \ x^1 \ x^2 \ x^{3(1.1)} \ x^{4(1.2)}$$

Even by rapid scanning we can recognize the two important points: the original idea gives rise to four variants and three of these variants (x^1, x^3, x^4) are interrelated. No matter where the symbol x^4 appears on a timeline we immediately know that it represents a considerable evolution from the initial idea. If instead, however, we pay attention in coding first to interrelationships, a less satisfactory set of symbols results:

$$Pax \ x^1 \ x^2 \ x^{1.1} \ x^{1.2}$$

By this method, when one encounters $x^{1.2}$ anywhere other than in direct chain of x variants, there is no way one can know that this is the fourth variant, except by tracing backward along the timeline, counting all previous variants.

For further practice in the principles and problems of this system of symbolization we can turn to Haydn's Symphony No. 88, first movement, which compactly illustrates that composer's ingenuity in conceiving subtle derivations.

Typically he introduces many variants and mutants even in the exposition, providing us with an instructive exercise for sym-

EXAMPLE 7-1.   Bach, Brandenburg Concerto No. 1: I, bars 1-6.
*Motivic evolutions represented by the use of variants of 1M, 2M, etc.,
avoiding overly complex symbols.*

[R derived]

bolization. Using the system described above, several valid analyses could be made for the theme of the opening Allegro, depending upon which of several aspects or dimensions one wishes to bring out. (See Example 7-2.)

As part of a concise overview of the complete movement, $1P$ alone might suffice to represent the first eight bars. If we wish to emphasize internal relationships within the theme itself, $1Pa \ldots a^1$ shows the linkage of subphrases in a general way, and $1Pa \ldots a \ldots a^1 \ldots a^2$ gives a more detailed representation. Since the latter symbols already use exponents for the theme itself, later derivations from these subphrases will require decimals—a mutation of a^1 would be $a^{1.1}$—leading at times to considerable complications. Hence, this particular way of symbolizing bars 16–23 would be efficient mainly for discussions of the theme alone rather than its permutations during the course of the whole movement.

If instead of the interrelationship of subphrases one wishes to stress differences, the variant aspects in the third and fourth subphrases can be brought out by the symbols $1Pa \ldots b$, or in more detail, $1Pax \ldots ax^{(1)} \ldots bx \ldots bx^{(1)}$. So that we do not entirely lose sight of the internal derivations, however, it is advisable to put (a) and (ax) above b and bx, the parentheses indicating origins. Of the choices above, for most purposes the best is
$$(a)$$
$1Pa \ldots b$, since this symbolization permits reference to two elements of P for later derivations, yet it does not weight the analysis with unnecessary detail.

At times it may be desirable to keep count of the number of derivations from a given theme or motive. In the movement above, for example, since $2T$ (bars 51 ff.), $2S$ (bars 71 ff.), and $2Kb$ (bars 97 ff.) all derive from $1Pah$, the explanatory parentheses above these functions might read $1Pah^2$, $1Pah^3$, $1Pah^4$. This degree of preciseness, however, produces more clutter than clarity on the timelines: if one wishes to concentrate on such small details, it is often better simply to extract the musical motives themselves. Furthermore, once we reach the end of the exposition, each new variant of $1Pah$ has several possible intermediate ancestors, thematically speaking. The system of symbols has sufficient logical power and

EXAMPLE 7-2.   Haydn, Symphony No. 88: I.

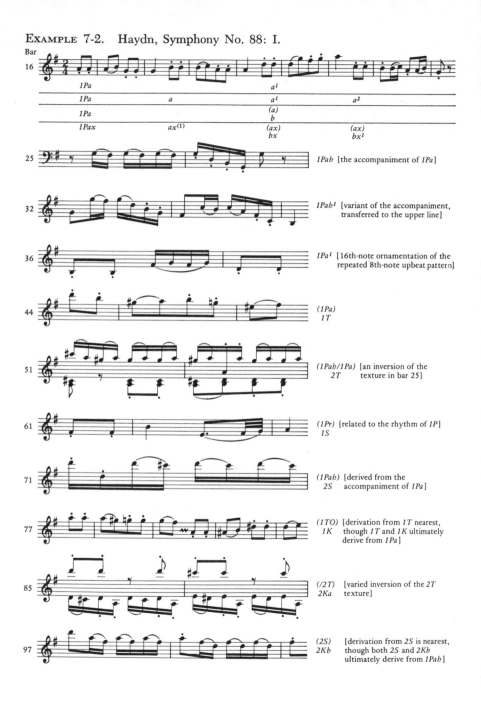

naming potential to describe all such permutations—but is this clearer than the musical notation itself? We should remember that symbols are abbreviations made to facilitate broad comparisons, mere mnemonic skeletons. If the alphanumeric code even remotely approaches musical notation in complexity, it loses its point. The more involved aspects of analysis, of course, usually belong in the workshop, where the musical anatomist can experiment with all sorts of devices and inventions of his own. For illustrating the final conclusions of any investigation, however, all charts and diagrams should aim for absolute clarity and as much simplicity as possible, not forgetting that the musical notes themselves may give the clearest demonstration, if properly arranged.

Even when employed without any surrounding context of time relationship, these alphanumeric symbols greatly simplify style-analytical discussions of various kinds; their most significant application, however, comes in the fuller representation of a piece by means of a two-level timeline on which thematic symbols occur in their chronological positions, on an upper line parallel to a second level that contains chord rhythm, with the chief harmonic and tonal events appearing underneath. (See Example 7-3.) Note that even in this short expositional section Mozart differentiates the weight of articulation between phrases and subphrases, a distinction that the system of symbols can reflect in shorter and longer verticals. For less familiar styles, where the location and weight of articulations seems more doubtful, a simple two-step process will help: (a) the magnitude of the articulations may be calibrated from 1 to 5 according to the number of elements contributing, and (b) the sources of articulation can be recorded with reference to a preliminary, "workshop" timeline during the process of establishing relative importance between articulations:

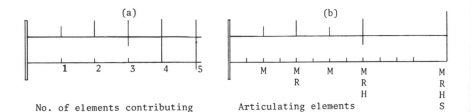

(a)   (b)

1   2   3   4   5   M   M   M   M   M
                                    R   R   R
                                              H   H
No. of elements contributing   Articulating elements   S

EXAMPLE 7-3.   Mozart, Piano Sonata, K. 332: I.

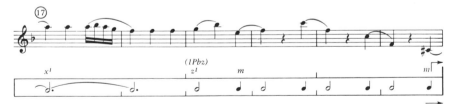

(elision)

Purely as a matter of technical know-how it should be mentioned here that timelines are easily produced on the typewriter by placing a ball-point pen in a fixed position on the ribbon shield and running the carriage across—many typewriters have a special hole or slot for this purpose; the bar divisions can then be produced by rolling the carriage one half line vertically upward, then typing apostrophes to mark bars of whatever size may be required. (This easy method of drawing parallel lines can also be useful in producing a staff for musical examples in a typed manuscript without pasting in music paper.)

Such elaborate graphings of articulations, of course, would normally be required only for an intensive study of articulative factors; but even in routine timeline analysis one should always attempt to approximate the relative strengths of articulations by the lengths of vertical division-marks. One practical problem arises in the representation of upbeats and other overlapping articulations. To avoid graphic overcomplication and consequent loss of "scannability," verticals representing articulations should generally coincide with the bar marks on the lower level of the timeline, ignoring upbeats, rests, and similar details, for two reasons. First, the ear tends to absorb these accessories into the nearest phrase, largely without reacting to them as bar fractions: we hear a four-bar phrase with a rest, not a three-and-one-half-bar phrase. Similarly, we do not reckon an upbeat as part of a four-and-one-quarter-bar phrase. Unless some prominent change disrupts the whole texture, our hearing process schematizes according to a prevailing module. Second, we must be sure that we have identified the significant— not merely the true—phenomena in a musical situation. For example, if a sentence of sixteen bars divides into four phrases of four, three and a half, four and a half, and four bars, the observation that the phrases are irregular (which is true) may not be as important as the perception that the composer has given a special middle emphasis to the sentence by displacement of the interior articulations.

Where upbeats and overlaps appear sufficiently characteristic of a style to warrant representation on the timeline, brackets with dotted lines make a suitable graphic record:

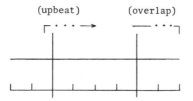

Where details of fabric are important, additional lines can be added above the basic timeline, just as we have done in illustrating the rhythmic layering of a Haydn symphony. Similarly, in a four-part vocal fugue we might schematize the texture, symbolizing two parts on each of the upper lines, with the basic lower line containing the barring, bar numbers, harmonic rhythm, modulations and so on; a simple fugue with subject, countersubject, and a recurrent motivic figure could be represented as follows:

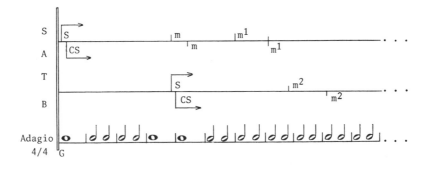

Added upper lines can also be used to map exchanges between a soloist (or solo group) and an accompanying orchestra, chorus, or other tutti combination. For example, in the first movement of Mozart's Piano Concerto in E♭, K. 271, the opening dialogue occurs in reverse order in the recapitulation. By using an asterisk to identify material introduced by the soloist (mnemonic: a "star" for the star!), we can trace the migration of ideas from solo to orchestra, while the asterisks remind us of the original source of the themes:

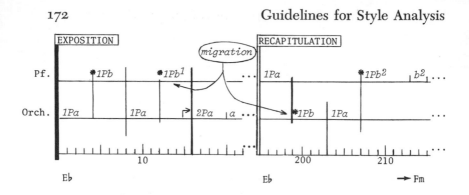

As musical style analysis develops, a number of aspects doubtless will be studied by means of data processing. For this purpose the timeline system, with its detailed hierarchy of thematic functions displayed on a consistent time scale, provides an ideal reference structure to which all other analysis and comment can be related. Used as a core structure, the timeline device thus simplifies the programming of correlations between diverse other phenomena.

Stereotypes of Shape

Even the most useful of the terms commonly applied to stereotyped growths, such as sonata form, represent abstractions more than actualities, convenient oversimplifications rather than compositional procedures. It has been pointed out by several scholars that the specific term *sonata form* does not appear in musical literature before about 1840.[1] Apparently composers of the preceding period—the ones who actually perfected various species of the sonata type—mostly did not consciously identify their products as examples of particular molds, despite various "recipes" for composing. And when we look for examples that perfectly illustrate a stereotype, we often find excrescent features that must be explained away. A good "textbook rondo," i.e. one that docilely follows prescriptions such as ABACA, occurs much less commonly than growths with the endless tiny variants that can confuse a beginning listener.

1. A. B. Marx, *Die Lehre von der musikalischen Komposition*, Leipzig, 1837.

Despite all of these objectionable aspects, however, stereotypes offer not only sound initial hypotheses of how a design may grow, but also useful general categories within which to collect designs that share important large-scale features. For these reasons it is worthwhile to review the stereotypes in concrete if brief detail.

The stereotypes of shape below all represent enlargements and combinations of the standard options for continuation. Variation form, for example, simply treats an initial thematic sentence to a succession of alterations or transformations (often surface-rhythmic), each consistently applied to the whole sentence. Fugue form consists mainly of contrapuntal variations following a conventionalized exposition, although there may be some recurrences and—to whatever extent the fugue is *not* tightly unified and consistently contrapuntal—some contrast areas. Two- and three-part forms obviously combine areas of variation, contrast, and recurrence, while rondo form simply multiplies alternating procedures into a chain of returns and contrasts. Sonata form, which particularly in its concerto subtype reaches the greatest organizational complexity of any stereotype, necessarily calls upon many types of continuation in highly evolved versions, not only in the generalized functions that we sense in large sections such as expositions, developments, and recapitulations, but also for highly specialized interior relationships as well.

In several different contexts above we have noted the fascinating changes in direction that emerge historically in the evolution of form, reflecting the impact of new elements that temporarily dominate style in different periods. During the tonal period (roughly 1680–1900) melody and harmony tend to control the standard options for continuation: we more easily identify recurrences by melodic and harmonic similarity than by other means (perhaps only because of greater familiarity with the procedures of tonal music). Skilled composers, of course, have always exploited a greater variety of elements, thereby achieving more distinct and individual personalities than their less talented colleagues. Looking back further, however, we find periods and areas in which melody alone largely determined growth (e.g. chants and other monophonic music), while in the thirteenth and fourteenth centuries rhythmic controls such as isorhythm attained an unprecedented sophistication. The gradual dissolution of tonality at the end of the nineteenth century tended to return all stylistic elements to a condition of approximate equality: no single element or combination of one or two could any longer serve as a recognized basis for formal organization and stereotyping—as we can see from trends such as total serial organization as opposed to mere rows, a tacit recognition of the shaping influence of all elements. Amid the many possibilities of confusion through the centuries, the chief responsibility of the style analyst is to keep an open mind about the sources of growth, remembering above all that a theme need not be a melody, and that melodic recurrence may not be the most important determinant of design.

Variation Form

Variation form can offer a tremendous range of freely imaginative possibilities: for example, improvised variations occur in jazz, in monophonic Middle Eastern chant as well as street music, and in recent American and European experiments (Foss, Boulez). Applied another way, in the rigid pattern variations found commonly from the late Renaissance to the early twentieth century, no growth is less imaginative.[2] This feeling of strait-jacketing, the central esthetic difficulty of variation form, results less from set patterns applied to thematic ideas than from the implacable periodic recurrence of articulations controlled by the dimension of the original idea. The inevitable repetition of this dimension turns the growth into a sort of musical link-sausage. Within these linked variations, too, harmonic progressions and melodic goals recur with deadening predictability. These strictures, of course, challenge the capable composer to invent various evasions and alterations in order to relieve tedium. Mozart (or pseudo-Mozart) presents a charming solution in the finale of the symphonie concertante for winds (K. 297b [Anhang C 14.01]), in which a tiny, humorous codetta by the tutti rounds off each variation presented by solo instruments, providing both a recurrent unity of contrast in timbre and relief from a reiterating thematic dimension.

2. See Robert U. Nelson, *The Technique of Variation*, Berkeley, 1948, 2nd ed. 1962.

For timelines and other representations of variation growth, the use of P as a symbol for the initial thematic sentence is desirable, for it retains the possibility of using our full hierarchy of symbols, referring to component phrases of the basic theme as a, b, c . . . and subphrases as x, y, z . . . , with the $1m$, $2m$, $3m$ . . . series available for small details. Mnemonic advantages might tempt us to use temporary symbols such as T and V for theme and variation. Experience shows, however, that it is advisable to adhere to the tested system of symbols, so that we have letter names available for all normal functions in the material under examination. As an illustration, let us suppose that we were to use T for Theme: how would we then symbolize any transitional material that might appear in the course of the piece? Soon we would have to invent a whole new set of symbols. One further reminder about variation symbols: a number of composers return to the initial theme either near the end of the variation structure, or periodically several times during the course of the variations, producing irregular combinations of variation and rondo form. If these returns make only very slight alterations in the theme, one is not justified in symbolizing on the same level—i.e. P^3 in a series beginning with P^1, P^2, connotes a variant of approximately equal weight, which does not properly reflect this quasi-ritornello situation. The solution, worth repeating here for emphasis, is to use P^0, i.e. "Original P" for the theme, thus opening the possibility of representing these slightly varied returns as $P^{0.1}$, $P^{0.2}$, and so on.

Each of the stereotyped musical shapes poses special and differing problems to the composer. The analyst, in turn, will always be particularly interested in observing the degree of resourcefulness with which composers meet these challenges. For all stereotypes discussed below, therefore, it will usefully concentrate our observation to bear in mind a small group of critical points.

CRITICAL STYLE POINTS IN VARIATIONS

1. How many elements does the composer change to obtain fresh sources of variation?

2. Does the composer attempt to weld the set of variations into a unified (even if segmented) whole? Is there a flection or crescendo of rhythmic activity, textural density, harmonic inci-

dents, polyphonic complications, and the like? Are there unvaried (or minimally varied) recurrences of the theme that give a sense of dimension broader than the thematic segment, or possibly a feeling of recapitulation or symmetrical close? (All of these techniques encourage the listener to hear the piece as a totality rather than to listen to each segment as a nearly separate event.)

3. What means, if any, does the composer use to weight the main articulations differently so as to relieve the inevitable repetitions? Does he avoid stereotyped cadences, extend certain variations, insert any codas or transitions between variations? Does he group more than one statement of the thematic sentence under each new variational procedure (as in Lully and Bach chaconnes, for example)?

4. Does the composer risk any genuine mutations, such as fundamental changes in tempo, alteration of basic harmonic plan, or tampering with the phrase dimensions? Do such experiments confuse the impression of variation structure?

Fugue

The fugue represents the final and most sophisticated growth of tonal counterpoint, the end of a long evolution that includes the stages of heterophony, polyphony, *Stimmtausch*, counterpoint, imitation, canon, and rhythmic alteration. Since the fugue necessarily includes many of these techniques, it might be regarded broadly as a loose collection of contrapuntal variations on a central theme. The variations, however, are too disparate in character and too flexibly arranged to be considered as a stereotyped shape. In fact, the fugue occurs in so many shapes that an abstraction like the "school fugue" (see below) represents too great an oversimplification even for the present list of stereotypes. Some theorists have suggested that the fugue is not a form at all, but a texture. Yet again, fugal growths may include many textures, all basically contrapuntal rather than chordal, perhaps, but nevertheless not to be lumped together as a single type of texture. Instead, it may be more enlightening to regard the fugue as a chain of freely selected contrapuntal processes, a flexible arrangement of choices from among a stereotyped repertory of devices, applied to one or two initial ideas or subjects. Successful fugues produce a sense of cumulative, mounting excitement, a crescendo of tension and activity resulting in part from increasing complexity of contrapuntal devices. The analyst must attempt to identify these sources of growing interest. In skillful fugues the heightening tension of contrapuntal development finds confirmation in peaks and underpoints, dissonance quotient, and expansion or compression of tessitura, as well as other less direct sources of stress such as the largely intellectual pleasure of increasingly sophisticated and arcane manipulations. The theorists of the Middle Ages and Renaissance obviously took delight in cataloguing all of the various contrapuntal devices, apparently as much for the sake of categorization as to elucidate music. Today we recognize that such catalogues give us only the merest start toward understanding a piece of fugal music. Nevertheless, as a point of departure that furnishes tested, useful hypotheses (and terminology) for initial analysis, we may keep in mind a stereotyped series of events and devices commonly found in fugues. These include:

Subject. The mature fugue makes use of clearly defined themes, usually called the *subject(s)*, often individualized by a striking *head motive* at the beginning, which arouses the listener's attention to the re-entry of the subject. The head motive also furnishes easily remembered material for later development within the fugue.

Answer. The imitation of the subject, usually called the *answer*, normally takes place at the fifth, often modulating temporarily to the dominant as well. The evolution of the fugue to some extent coincided with the rise of tonality. As a result, pieces based on this special canon with entries alternately on the tonic and at the fifth gradually emerged as flexible yet convincingly unified contrapuntal forms. Two general types of answers occur in fugal pieces, *real answers* (which simply make an exact transposition of the subject to the fifth degree) and *tonal answers* (which attempt to avoid the harmonic dislocations of constant dominant modulations by altering the contour of the subject sufficiently to lead back to the tonic key). The preference of a composer for real or tonal answers reveals something about his feeling for tonal unity and harmonic design in his fugues, since quick modulations back and forth from tonic to dominant imply a small harmonic dimension; also, only by solid stabilization of the tonic at the beginning can we later feel a wide arch of harmonic tension spanning the local excursions.

Countersubject. This is a handy term for any counterpoint that consistently accompanies the subject or answer. Composers often design countersubjects to enliven points of lesser activity (or rest) in the main thematic idea, thereby also supplying attractive secondary material for later stages of the fugal process.

Exposition. The typical fugal exposition cumulates a succession of entries of subject and answer, alternating on the first and fifth degrees, until all the voices of the texture have entered. At this point composers typically make a heavy articulation not unlike the double bar in sonata form, changing texture and dynamics, and moving to a contrasting developmental manner. Fugal beginnings that do not progress beyond the exposition to genuine development of the subject are often called *fugatos*, a useful distinction for style analysis. Thus, if we encounter a series of fugal entries in the development of a sonata form, we would refer to this as a fugato rather than a fugue, unless it actually progressed to further development of the fugal subject.

Episode. Composers of fugue in the Baroque period evolved a nicely ordered process that alternated episodes of sequential treatment (typically motivic fragments from the subject or countersubject) with formal entries of the full subject itself in various new keys. Where episodes do not neatly articulate with other fugal procedures, it may be more satisfactory to refer to these stages simply as successive developments.

Counterexposition. Within the course of the fugue, the composer may decide to make a second exposition of the material, possibly adding a new subject or countersubject. The term *counterexposition* serves to distinguish this event from the initial exposition.

Stretto. The Italian word for tightness neatly describes the shortening of the time interval of the expositional entries, a telescoping of subject entrances in excitingly rapid succession that provides an ideal climax for a fugue.

Head, trunk, codetta. For purposes of detailed analysis of a whole repertory of fugal forms one might wish to make a special study of the subjects themselves. The terms *head, trunk,* and *codetta* (the last borrowed from the French school-fugue terminology) provide names for the chief specializations of function likely to be found in fugal subjects.

CRITICAL STYLE POINTS IN FUGUES

1. *Cumulative power.* Since the fugue depends more on contiguous (*A* to *B*) than on long-range (*A* to *M* to *Z*) relationships, the composer's efforts to pyramid a series of events with rising intensity becomes a major focus for analytical observation. The growing excitement may proceed from any SHMRG element. While it is normal to find strettos associated with increased surface rhythm, subtle composers will add textural and tessitural crescendos as well. The concinnity between various elements, as usual, demonstrates the degree of the composer's control.

2. *Breadth of design.* The extent to which a composer manages to grow beyond contiguous relationships also measures his mastery. Tonal designs that exploit long-range tension, i.e. moving to the dominant and *not* returning immediately; cumulative complexity of contrapuntal devices; recurrent associations of specific timbres with specific functions, such as prominent use of winds in episodes that fragment the subject into tiny motives: all treatments of this sort reveal the breadth of the composer's planning.

3. *Thematic sophistication.* The character of the subject often profoundly affects the success of a fugue, and the greatest composers of fugues typically enhance both internal unity and necessary contrasts by inventing subjects of memorable character combined with maximum contrapuntal and developmental opportunity. On the other hand, in the *Art of Fugue,* Bach showed what could be accomplished with a subject of discouraging stolidity.

Mixtures of Variation and Recurrence

The names commonly given to more complex growths, though traditional and inescapable, reflect the melody-dominated thinking of the nineteenth and early twentieth centuries: theorists of form set up categories mainly according to the recurrence of thematic ideas, too often neglecting important discrepancies created by harmonic plan, weighting of articulations, and other style-analytical criteria of equal or greater importance. Since the shape of any piece emerges from the totality of its SHMRG configurations, the process of understanding this shape must be equally complete. The chief difficulty with stereotypes of growth is this: in order to group a large number of pieces under a single concept, the concept must be so general that it passes over the characteristic points of shape in any particular piece. Such a categorization cannot give more than superficial insight. We notice this inadequacy with new force in considering two- and three-part forms: what an endless variety there are—and how relatively uninformative are these categories, in which specific differences so far outweigh generic similarities. By way of justification, however, we must remember that only by generic groupings can we begin to bring some order out of the chaos of a large repertory; but these initial groupings must never be allowed to obscure the far more vital specific conclusions. (Style *is a particularity, not a generality.) For the more complex forms, though we can begin with loose, stereotyped categories such as two- and three-part forms, better results emerge from a simpler process: allowing the music to create its own categorical stereotypes by following two familiar rules:

　　1. Locate and classify the articulations (heavy, medium, light).

　　2. Within the parts of the piece indicated by these articulations, identify the types of continuation.

EXAMPLE 7-4.　*Au clair de la lune.*

Let us now test this method on a folksong, *Au clair de la lune.* Within this tune, three articulations produce four parts; but is this a four-part form, a two-part form, or a three-part form? These general names do not tell us much, and we may far better describe

* *It does no good to put this in either/or terms. Of course style is also a generality!*

simple pieces by the use of alphabetic abstracts such as AABA. For larger forms as well, providing we remain alert to the danger of oversimplification, the letter abstracts tell us far more than descriptions such as "binary," "ternary," and the like. To return to the folksong, its heavy articulations result from changes of melody and harmony in B, followed by the recurrence of A; the articulation after the first phrase is lighter, since it merely separates a statement and repetition. These articulated relationships can be simplified as AA/B/A, and since there are only three principal parts produced by these articulations, the folk tune is basically a three-part form. Notice, however, that there are many *functionally different* plans that could quite as justifiably be included in this three-part stereotype. The plan AA^{1}A, for example, also articulates in three significant parts, but to group it with AABA adds too little to our understanding: it overemphasizes the function of recurrence and suppresses the difference of the middle part. For purposes of style analysis it works far better to name the categories according to their actual functional configurations. The plan AABA includes the growth functions of contrast and recurrence, so a logical and easily memorable (because functionally descriptive) category to include plans of this sort should simply be named "Repetition-Contrast-Recurrent Forms." The plan AA^{1}A, on the other hand, includes the growth functions of variation and recurrence. The logical category or preliminary stereotype here should be named "Variant-Recurrent Forms." Further, supposing the central portion to be related more distantly, perhaps with a key change to the relative minor, the categorical name might then be "Mutant-Recurrent." These functional labels, though occasionally slightly longer and thus less convenient than catchword oversimplifications such as "two-part form," nevertheless describe more accurately the generic traits of each group, a welcome gain in clarity.

Two-Part Form
(Binary Form; Dance Form)

This formal stereotype can be extremely useful in style analysis if we restrict its meaning to forms similar to the binary plan of suite dances, with central double bars and modulation to the dominant (A::A^1). Here the modulation is important historically, since it creates an arch of harmonic tension essential to the evolution of large forms, such as sonata form. Another justification for this particular stereotype is simply the enormous amount of music that takes this form, not merely thousands of suite dances, but many movements of early sonatas as well. The great variety of these movements raises many questions for the analyst, most of them concerning the degree of differentiation within the parts. All of these movements can trace ancestry to a basic A::A^1 plan; but notice that the traits of style reside in the variants, not in the stereotype. Hence, the more we can reflect these variants in devising subcategories of two-part form, the more clearly we can individuate particular styles and composers.

The form AAB, called "Bar form" particularly by German theorists, probably in sentimental reference to the cult of the Mastersingers, has been frequently explained as a form based on contrast, i.e. closing with something new, creating an unusual, open-ended effect. This conclusion may appear justified by a cursory melodic and textual analysis, but it neglects significant details such as small melodic recurrences at phrase ends, cadential similarities, and unity of key or mode. A representative "Bar form" produces the following growth pattern[3]:

Is this a two- or three-part form? The main articulation (longest vertical on the timeline) indicates a basic division into two unequal parts. On the other hand, the text tempts us to think of three nearly equal parts. Here we can see the difficulty (and the basic uncommunicativeness) of using the well-known stereotypes: clearly this little piece mixes two growth plans. But what a clumsy, non-

3. See Walther von der Vogelweide's *Palästinalied*, in Reese, *Music in the Middle Ages*, New York, 1940, p. 234, Ex. 57.

functional label this produces: "mixed two- and three-part form." (See also the discussion of rondo forms below.) For style-analytical purposes we can describe the piece more precisely and represent its musical functions more fully with an abbreviated review of its growth: repetition and contrast with recurrent terminations. (A repeats, B furnishes contrast, x recurs.) Elsewhere we can partly apply style-analytical methods within the stereotyped categories by discovering functional ways to distinguish between two- and three-part form. Probably the most basic distinction results from the character of the first main articulation, often a double bar: if the articulation is unstable and open (a situation most typically produced by modulation to the dominant), this makes the first part dependent on a second part for completion, resulting in a two-part form. If the first main articulation is stable and closed, however, so that the first section sounds independent and complete in itself (a situation commonly produced by a strong cadence in the original tonic), this creates a typical opportunity for three-part form: the second section must now produce change of some sort (either development or contrast), after which a return of the first section can neatly complete a ternary design.

CRITICAL STYLE POINTS IN TWO-PART FORMS

1. Is the central articulation confirmed by modulation, chord rhythm, surface-rhythmic acceleration?

2. Is the material homogeneous, or can we find some contrast of ideas? If so, are these differing materials articulated and confirmed by other elements? If polythematic, does the composer develop any thematic specialization, such as cadential themes? Is the second part developed motivically and harmonically?

3. What is the balance of the two parts in key rhythm and distance of tonal excursion? Can we detect any relationship of peaks and underpoints between the parts? Is there any recognizable pattern or balance in the arrangement of intensities of texture and rhythmic activity?

4. Can we notice any tendency toward recapitulation? (This tendency, of course, moves toward various combinations of two- and three-part form that gradually evolved into the myriad of magnificently flexible shapes we call sonata form.)

Three-Part Form
(ABA Form; Da Capo Form)

In the historical trend of musical styles toward increasing size and complication, so often noted in the foregoing pages, the "discovery" of three-part form, notably in the design of da capo arias, made possible a considerable extension beyond the two-part structures of dance suites. The three-part form became important also for instrumental music, of course, as the ground plan of minuet-and-trio (actually minuet-trio-minuet) movements. It stimulated new fields of exploration, in search of craftier means of relating the middle section, or in the opposite direction, more striking ways of deepening its contrast. In the immediately preceding discussion we have seen that the first main section of a three-part form will characteristically end in a decisive, stable manner in the original tonic, so that this first section gives a self-sufficient impression, independent of what follows. (*Inter*dependent parts characterize two-part forms.) With this characteristic firmly in mind we can confidently distinguish true three-part forms from those in two parts or in mixed and transitional shapes.

CRITICAL STYLE POINTS IN THREE-PART FORMS

1. Consider points (1) and (2) under "Two-Part Forms" (above, p. 183).

2. Do tempo and meter changes occur in the contrast section? Does a contrasting tempo stimulate harmonic and thematic contrasts as well? Does a new tempo alter thematic dimensions (lengths of phrases or sentences) and weights of articulation? More generally, do slow da capo arias develop types of phrasing and articulation different from fast arias?

3. Can we distinguish between a composer's handling of large three-part forms (such as scherzo-trio-scherzo) and small three-part designs that might occur within one of these sections (such as AA¹A)?

4. Apart from thematic differentiation or specialization, does the composer make any attempts to refine the design of the phrase itself with interior contrasts or tension curves?

Rondo Form
(Ritornello Form; Formes fixes)

NOTE: Though convention has enshrined the use of ABACA symbols for rondos, the *PTSK* scheme, with appropriate subfunctions as required, provides better possibilities for exact description. In place of *P* one can also substitute *R* (for "Refrain" or "Ritornello"), which creates no ambiguities unless we need to refer to the rhythm of a theme. The use of ABACA for main functions would rob us of one whole level of syntactic descriptors.

Rondo forms, typically *R S R 2S R* ($\pm$ Coda), run risks of repetitiveness in dimension similar to those that we often hear in variation forms, but for different reasons: composers tend to use rather square, regular phrasing in rondo themes, perhaps to clarify the theme, making it easier to remember and recognize when it returns. If they then fail to relieve this tendency toward squareness in the contrasting episodes, the rondo may become rather lifeless. As we have seen earlier, flow in middle dimensions seems to depend on phrases of differing tension and emphasis, qualities all the more necessary if the dimensions of the phrases are much the same. Many composers fall into this inherent pitfall of rondo form.

Two subspecies of rondo form deserve special mention:

1. The *modulating rondo*, in which the initial idea occurs in various keys, returning to the tonic only for its final appearance, serves as the basis for the fast movements of many Baroque concertos, especially solo concertos.

2. The *formes fixes* of the Middle Ages, all based on poetic forms involving refrains, obviously produce musical rondos, if the composer follows the poet's scheme (sometimes composers do not: Dufay's *Adieu m'amour*[4] is textually a rondeau, but the refrain verse ends in the dominant). The poetic names of the forms have little relevance for style analysis; but since any discussion of this music will require a reference to the verse forms, it is convenient to list them here. The schemes below use the convention of upper case to

---

4. Willi Apel and Archibald T. Davison, eds., *Historical Anthology of Music*, Cambridge, Mass., 1950, Vol. I, No. 68.

symbolize complete returns of both words and music, with lower case to indicate recurrent music but with changed text. Below the usual *abc* . . . schemes we can compare samples of style-analytical symbols that emphasize growth functions somewhat more clearly.

a) Trouvère *ballade*, troubadour *canzo* (minnesinger Bar is similar if text runs more than one stanza):

ab	*ab*	*cd*	*E(F)*	*gh*	*gh*	*ij*	*E(F)*	*kl*	*kl*	*mn*	*E(F)*
1P	*1P*	*1S*	*R*	*2P*	*2P*	*2S*	*R*	*3P*	*3P*	*3S*	*R*

Note that the letters *mn* convey nothing to us in themselves: we must examine the whole context to understand their function, whereas *3S* immediately tells us that we are dealing with the contrasting couplet of the third stanza. If there should be any need to symbolize further details within *3S*, of course, we have the whole hierarchy of subfunctions available, from *abc* . . . through *xyz* . . . to *1m*, *2m*, *3m*, and so on.

b) French *virelai*, Italian *ballata*:

A	*bb*	*a*	*A*	or	*AB*	*cc*	*ab*	*AB*
R	*ss*	*r*	*R*		*RaRb*	*ss*	*rarb*	*RaRb*

c) French *rondeau*:

$$AB \quad aA \quad ab \quad AB$$
$$PS \quad pP \quad ps \quad PS$$

CRITICAL STYLE POINTS IN RONDO FORM

1. Comparing the rondo statement with the intervening episodes, what sources of contrast does the composer exploit (key, thematic material, orchestration, chord rhythm, dynamic level, textural organization, formal module)?

2. What attempts do we find to conceal—or on the other hand to dramatize—articulations, particularly the preparation for each return?

3. What alterations does the return offer, by way of variety? Are there any extensions, enlargements, compressions, elisions, or other modifications?

4. If there are codas either merely at the end or also internally, how do these achieve stability?

Sonata Form

Composers evolved the powerfully integrated process of development and recurrence that we now stereotype as sonata form rather gradually, combining and adjusting procedures taken from both two- and three-part form. Of the two ancestors, two-part form probably furnished the more decisive genes, since it typically contains the essential modulation to the dominant, a harmonic cantiliver construction that makes the vast arches of sonata form architecturally and psychologically convincing. Almost equally as important, of course, is the ancient principle of recurrence after contrast, the fundamental core of generations of three-part designs. The contributions from these two prime sources may be summarized as follows:

COMPONENTS OF SONATA FORM

from Two-Part Form	*from Three-Part Form*
1. Modulation to the dominant.	1. Principle of full recapitulation.
2. Central double bars, usually with repeats.	2. Contrasting midsection.
3. Motivic development stimulated by more closely integrated parts.	3. Sophisticated phrase control.
4. Thematic differentiation.	4. Thematic specialization.

A summary tabulation such as the above can only reflect general trends; it cannot distill ultimate truths. For example, one can certainly find occasional thematic specialization, i.e. characteristic closing themes, in two-part sonatas of Domenico Scarlatti. But owing to the generally greater control and development of phrase structure in da capo arias, a far larger percentage of such arias shows clear specialization into transitional, secondary, and closing thematic functions than do instrumental works of the same period.

In a similarly generalizing spirit we can review a series of timelines showing the functional evolution of sonata form. This graduated chain of morphological development derives from a conflation of many movements, though in several cases an exact prototype can be cited. Close acquaintance with an evolutionary series of this type shows us how to look for strong and weak points in any sonata form we may encounter:

1. Primitive binary form, with dominant modulation but largely motivic material:

$$\| : Pm \quad m \quad m \quad m \; : \| : Pm^1 \quad m^2 \quad m \quad : \|$$
$$\| : \text{I} \qquad\qquad \text{V} \; : \| : \text{V} \qquad\qquad \text{I} \quad : \|$$

2. Developed binary form, with a more evolved thematic phrase (x and y), but mainly homogeneous material (no S or K ideas) and only slight motivic variation (x^1, x^2):

$$\| : Px \quad y \mid x \quad y \quad y \; : \| : Px^1 \quad x^2 \mid x \quad y \quad y \; : \|$$
$$\| : \text{I} \qquad\qquad \text{V} \; : \| : \text{V} \qquad\qquad \text{I} \qquad : \|$$

3. Polythematic binary, with differentiation of the closing section (K), and some harmonic development (modulation to vi):

$$\| : Px \quad y \mid x \quad y \mid K \; : \| : Px^1 \quad x^2 \mid y^1 \quad y \mid K \; : \|$$
$$\| : \text{I} \qquad\qquad \text{V} \; : \| : \text{V} \quad \text{vi} \quad \text{I} \qquad : \|$$

4. Large binary with full thematic differentiation (P, T, S, K):

$$\| : Px \quad y \mid T \quad \mid Sx \quad y \mid K \; : \| : Px \quad y \mid T \quad \mid Sx \quad y \mid K \; : \|$$
$$\| : \text{I} \qquad \text{V} \qquad\qquad : \| : \text{V} \quad \text{vi} \quad \text{I} \qquad\qquad : \|$$

5. Early sonata form with unevolved development section: brief but specialized thematic functions in the exposition and full recapitulation, but minimal development, often a mere restatement of P in the dominant. This type was frequently used by early composers of the Viennese School. Somewhat later a similar scheme, though with more highly evolved exposition and even briefer development—sometimes none at all, simply beginning after the double bar with $1P$ in the tonic—became popular as the basis for operatic overtures (see Mozart's *Figaro* overture).

$$\boxed{\text{Rec.}}$$
$$\| : Px \quad y \mid Tx \quad y \mid Sx \quad y \mid K \; : \| : Px^1 \quad y^1 \mid Px \quad y \mid Tx \quad y \mid Sx \quad y \mid K \; : \|$$
$$\| : \text{I} \qquad\qquad \text{V} \qquad\qquad\qquad : \| : \text{V} \quad \text{I} \qquad\qquad \text{I} \qquad\qquad : \|$$

6. Early sonata form with incomplete recapitulation after a strongly differentiated exposition and fairly evolved development, a type commonly used by composers of the Mannheim School. The recurrence of $1Px$ at the very end does not represent a reversed recapitulation (which would place T *after* S) but more probably a throwback to the motivic recurrence or closing ritornello principle of the Baroque period:

‖: $1Px$ y $2P$ | T | $1Sx$ y | $1K$ $2K$:‖: $1Px$ x^1 x^2 T^1 |$2P$ $2P^1$ | T | $1Sx$ y | $1K$ $2K$ | $1Px$:‖

‖: I   V‖ :‖: V   vi ii   V |I   I   :‖
                              ped.

7. Full sonata form in its most evolved state often adds an introductory section before $1P$ and a coda emphasizing the sub-dominant after the normal end of the recapitulation.[5]

Intro.

(Exp.) ‖ OP ‖: $1P$ $2P$ | $1T$ $2T$ | $1S$ $2S$ | $1K$ $2K$ $3K$:‖
        V^7 I   mod.   V   v   V   :‖

(Dev.) ‖: $3K^1$ $3K^2$ $2S^1$ $2T^1$ OP^1 | $1T^1$ $1T^2$ |
        ‖: V   v   ii   vi   iii   V   V
                              of V

                                        Coda
(Recap.) ‖ $1P$ $2P$ | $1T$ $2T$ | $1S$ $2S$ | $1K$ $2K$ $3K$:‖ $1P^1$ $3K$ ‖
          I   mod. &   i   I   I   IV   I
              ret. to I

CRITICAL STYLE POINTS IN SONATA FORM

1. Review the questions for two- and three-part forms.
2. Are there any thematic interrelationships, such as a T theme

5. For an extremely illuminating discussion of this whole problem, see Bathia Churgin, *Francesco Galeazzi's Description (1796) of Sonata Form*, in *Journal of the American Musicological Society*, XXI (1968), 181-99. Professor Churgin's article summarizes the views of other experts in this field, such as William S. Newman and Leonard Ratner.

derived from *2P*, or a *2K* theme that reminds us symmetrically of *1P*?

3. Which element(s) does/do the composer alter in the development section? Are there developments in the exposition as well?

4. How complete is the contrast between primary and secondary sections? How well does the development balance the exposition and recapitulation in size and intensity? What changes—omissions and additions—does the composer make in the recapitulation as compared to the exposition?

5. Can we notice genuinely concinnous control of articulations and climaxes? Do the weights of various articulations correspond to the importance of the following material?

6. Is there any evidence of long-range planning such as higher peaks in the recapitulation; longer-sustained preparations and climaxes; more brilliant orchestration?

7. Does the composer concentrate on a few motives in the development, working them out thoroughly (how many mutations?), or move through a number of ideas with only superficial changes, perhaps merely modulations?

Sonata-Rondo Form

This mixed form, frequently found in symphonic finales, deepens the rondo idea by opening with a full sonata-form exposition, then accelerating the events of growth—actually simplifying and abbreviating the form—by returning the primary material in the tonic before setting out into the development. The rondo influence affects the character of the themes, which tend toward square, sharply articulated phrasing. And responding to the sonata influence, the contrast episode often takes the form of genuine development, creating a more highly unified form than the usual rondo. A typical diagram of this form:

Exp.						Ret.	Ep./Dev.				Recap.					Ret.
‖: *1P* *2P*	*1T*	*1S*	*1K* *2K*:	*1P*	*1T¹* *1T²*	*1S¹* *1S²* *1T³*	*1P* *2P*	*1T³* *1S*	*1K* *2K*	*1P¹*
‖ I		V		.V₇	I	mod... iii vi	ii V₇ I	I		

CRITICAL STYLE POINTS IN SONATA-RONDO FORMS

1. Review questions on sonata and rondo forms.

2. What effect does the rondo atmosphere have on the thematic character; on the number and differentiation of theme; on the internal regularity of sentences, paragraphs, sections?

3. Does the curtailment of the development area by the insertion of a return reduce the depth of mutation, key exploration, orchestral contrasts?

4. Is the recapitulation changed or shortened in any way abnormal for sonata forms?

Concerto-Sonata Form

The specialized variety of sonata form used for solo concertos during the Classic and early Romantic periods retains two aspects directly derived from the Baroque period: the opening orchestral introduction and the orchestral tutti at the end of the solo exposition. Historically these both derive from the modulating rondo form of the Baroque concerto, which consisted mainly of tuttis in different keys separated by solo episodes. The Baroque heritage is not an unmixed blessing, for it causes many confusions in concerto-sonata form. Composers do not always understand how to handle a fully separate orchestral exposition as well as a solo exposition; and the entrance of the central tutti gives an entirely different psychology from the end of a normal sonata exposition, which is extremely stable from repeated cadencing and the heavy articulation of the double bar and repeat, usually involving a long rest. By contrast, after the soloist ends his exposition with trill and cadence, the orchestra often embarks on an active episode of its own, modulating through various keys and preparing for the next solo entrance in a contrasting tonality, usually the relative minor. At this point concertos often again revert to Baroque practices and bring in an entirely new theme (N), rather than faithfully develop the expositional material. The flow of these loosely knit pieces is guaranteed by interesting alternations between solo and tutti, a consistent textural polarity that also lends sufficient unity to offset any losses in thematic integration. The influence of sonata form sometimes caused composers to write rather full expositions for both orchestra and solo, often with disastrous results of two kinds: (1) wearing material threadbare by repetition; and (2) losing the power of the dominant tension-arch by modulating twice. The finest concerto composers solved the first of these problems by giving the soloist new themes to expose, particularly new secondary themes. The second problem, apparently much subtler, since more composers fail to solve it, received its best solution in Mozart's works, where the orchestral tutti remains almost entirely in the tonic, leaving the tension and drama of a fresh, untouched dominant to the soloist. Even Beethoven miscalculated this aspect by writing overly interesting modulations in the orchestral expositions of his first three concertos. Where the orchestra brings in remote and fascinating colors, the soloist has a proportionately more difficult time in establishing his own personality.

The threefold presentation of ideas in concerto-sonata form (orchestral exposition, solo exposition, and recapitulation) gives rise to several special situations not found in ordinary sonata forms. In the first place, since the soloist may add several themes of his own, the number of themes tends to become too great for a convincing recapitulation. As a result, most concerto recapitulations omit several themes, possibly ones that receive some attention in either the central tutti or the development. In the second place, the closing section, at least in the works of Mozart, offers a pleasing symmetrical possibility: leave out one K theme until the very end. The following is typical solution (note treatment of $2K$):

Orchestral intro.	Solo exp.	Dev.	Recap. Cadenza	Codetta
1K 2K	*3K 1K	1K^1	*3K 1K	2K

Possibly because of its mixed origins, the concerto never seems quite to stabilize as a form, and the variety of concerto designs may even outnumber the variants of ordinary sonata form. Also, any detailed study of concertos will turn up a number of formal failures; yet the inherent charm of the contrasting timbres and forces overcomes many a formal weakness.

CRITICAL STYLE POINTS IN CONCERTO-SONATA FORM

1. Does the orchestral exposition modulate in a decisive way to the dominant or any other well-defined key?

2. Does the soloist add new themes of his own? If so, are these themes specifically appropriate to his instrument, or equally effective for the tutti? Are any themes shared by means of echoes, or statement and reply?

3. How does the composer treat the central area, as a field for development of expositional material, or as a contrasting episode for the introduction of new ideas?

4. What material, if any, fails to return in the recapitulation?

The foregoing stereotypes represent an important group of initial concepts, and one cannot read the literature of musicology without some knowledge of these conventional forms. From the point of view of style analysis, however, they usually represent generalities too broad to be useful in establishing stylistic differentiation.

CHAPTER EIGHT

EVALUATION

The man who says, "I don't know much about music, but I know what I like," feels justified in expressing everyman's democratic right to his own opinion. He may not realize, however, that this attitude erects an encircling wall of ignorance that may rob him of higher esthetic and intellectual experience. Until now this book has attempted in principle to avoid the problem of subjective values by affirming the final inviolability of personal esthetic judgments, yet at the same time maintaining that an objective analysis of works of music not only reveals important evidence to help in understanding their construction and historical position, but also suggests profiles of intensity in a given work that may directly enhance esthetic experience. The process of evaluation proposed in this final chapter, therefore, necessarily combines subjective and objective judgments.

There is nothing new or strange in regarding music as a combination of subjective and objective elements. On the contrary, the lives of composers confirm the fundamental truth in this dual view by the natural sequence of their self-development: they prepare for self-expression (subjective achievements) by intensive study of objective "rules" and practices originally derived from earlier composers (occasionally sterilized by later theorists). The recognition of counterpoint and harmony as necessary preparations for composition shows that composers themselves have consistently felt the importance of objective conventions as a groundwork for subjective invention. Therefore, when as style analysts we carefully study the objective aspects of a piece, we parallel composers' educational patterns through the centuries: we lay a foundation for subjective judgment by objective study. When Beethoven went to

Vienna, he immediately arranged for counterpoint lessons (*not* composition lessons) with Haydn; and when Haydn proved to be too busy to give him sufficiently detailed criticism, he turned to a much lesser composer who was a stricter and more pedagogically (i.e. objectively) organized teacher, Albrechtsberger. In counterpoint and harmony lessons, the "correct" solutions are conventional abstractions of what composers have evidently found to be the best and most effective solutions; the "rules," therefore, are merely stereotyped statements of objective evaluation. The "right" and "wrong" that Beethoven accepted in Albrechtsberger's criticism was an objective evaluation of a particular passage as "good" or "bad." With these thoughts in mind, one may properly conclude that objective analysis is a significant foundation of musical good taste and an essential educative component in developing sound personal judgment.

Style analysis systematically furnishes much of the basis for objective evaluation, and while we may believe that esthetic judgment should remain as close as possible to intuition, even intuitive judgments imply a scale of response to the varying general intensities and specific characteristics within a piece. (As we have seen above, the idea of "pure" intuition is very rare, since most musical responses rest upon complicated listening habits relating to particular musical systems. Thus the appeal to intuition as a "free" response is misguided: so-called intuition operates within the relatively strict controls imposed by experiences in a single system.) As we list any set of preferences, therefore, we provide material from which it may be possible to deduce predictions of esthetic valuation. By careful stylistic analysis of preferred situations we may be able to identify recurring features that consistently appeal to a particular listener, thereby establishing heuristically his individual scale of values. One primary motivation for the present book emerges from a belief that any refinement of detail in our responses to music, such as the heightened appreciation of organization gained by the complete SHMRG approach, proportionately enriches our esthetic experience. The discussion that follows, rather than attempting to provide a mechanical system for grading music, seeks instead to call attention to the wealth of factors that jointly contribute to our judgments. The weighting of these factors must always remain the responsibility of the individual performer and listener, but the analyst can contribute to the completeness of the areas of choice. While there are many ways in which evaluation could be outlined, for present purposes it is useful to take account of four points, which among them include most considerations of value:

(1) Scope—the size and requirements of the work.
(2) Historical considerations.
(3) Objective values—control of SHMRG.
(4) Subjective values.

Scope

While scope mainly results from size, it connotes at least the possibility of another relevant aspect, complexity. No one would be justified in assuming that a large piece is better than a small piece, of course; but there seems to be substantial, if not total, agreement that a good large piece is more significant than a good small piece. There is considerably less agreement that a complex piece is necessarily better than a simple piece. Furthermore, this brings up the difficulty of defining musical complexity: on the one hand a superficial clarity may conceal extremely involved procedures—the art that conceals artfulness. On the other hand an apparent complexity may result merely from overloading with unnecessary, redundant details. The course of music history itself certainly shows that composers have frequently tended to seek fresh expression by increases in size and complexity. If these two dimensions become exaggerated and oppressive, of course, one may be forced to regard the *absence* of size and complexity as a new direction of value: the record of history provides repeated examples of simplifications developed as a reaction to complications that had progressed beyond reasonable lengths—for example, the polymetric complexities of the late fourteenth century. Considerations of scope, therefore, must always be placed against as broad a background as possible, including both contemporary analogues and surrounding history. It is difficult to see how scope could be defined as an absolute value. Occasionally a piece of large scope may acquire considerable influence, even though it is not well-regarded for its own merits. This rather tortuous aspect of value really belongs with historical considerations.

Historical Considerations

Audiences have always responded strongly to novelties of various sorts, and the musical audience, regarded inclusively, has greeted each new development with mingled cries of delight and alarm. No one would maintain that novelty alone creates value, but the composer who invents new words or syntax to expand the musical language deserves a distinct, if not necessarily high, recognition. Pursuing historical exclusiveness to its logical end, we come to musical uniqueness, an extreme example that combines firstness, lastness, and onlyness as well. (Remember that the values under discussion here are historical more than musical.) Historically and sociologically we may find value in a unique concerto for piccolo and timpani. It may tell something about the fertility of man's imagination and the spectrum of his humor, even if its opportunities for counterpoint are negligible.

Consideration of the values of "firstness" and uniqueness carry us into a broader area of the relation of a musical work to its background. Historically it is important to determine whether a work is conventional or unconventional, since as we study any historical period we are trying first to establish its central conventions and then the outer reaches of its style. We can recognize typical features in any piece simply by comparison with established conventions. A nontypical characteristic, however, requires more careful study to determine whether it indicates progressive or regressive tendencies. We are all familiar with the contrast of generations, if only from our own family experiences of the "generation gap." Possibly as a result of this background, in musical matters we tend to estimate a composer's up-to-dateness largely by his freedom from aspects derived from the immediately preceding generation.

Curiously enough, when composers skip a generation, in borrowing or deriving procedures, we may actually consider them progressive. In the middle of the eighteenth century, for example, up-to-date composers eschewed Baroque counterpoint in favor of the new vertical emphasis; yet by the last quarter of the century, the most advanced and gifted composers, such as Haydn and Mozart, reintroduced contrapuntal subtleties into their works, particularly for thematic development. What had seemed old-fashioned in 1750 appeared fresh and vital in the changed context of 1775.

We should not necessarily equate progressiveness with value, since the convention may have run its course into a condition of decadent exaggeration or of incomplete and therefore somewhat confused transition to a later style. J. S. Bach's language more often looks backward than forward, compared to his contemporaries. Yet how magnificently he handled his old-fashioned procedures. Seen from a broader historical perspective, therefore, he was actually still progressive, in the new depths of experience he evoked from a tradition that had run dry for most other composers. The perfection of his control has impressed and influenced many later generations. By comparison, the early Classic experiments of progressive opera composers such as Leo and Conti seem almost like child's play. Yet the new larger phrase dimensions of these proto-Classicists contained magical potentialities for later development, while Bach had himself fully realized—and exhausted—the potentials of his style.

It is not easy to set up a scale of progressiveness or regressiveness, since the question of familiarity and unfamiliarity affects the strength of the impression that progressive or regressive effects make upon the listener. We may respond quite strongly to a small detail merely because it strikes the ear freshly; we may take a "ho hum" attitude toward a piece of skillful writing simply because its general vocabulary and syntax seem boringly familiar. These subtle determinations we are hardly likely to entrust to computers in the near future: it is hard enough to draw even the most general guidelines. Once again, however, a minimum competence in judgment depends on completeness in our approach: if we consistently review all SHMRG elements, inspecting them for progressive and

regressive traits, we rest our determinations on a broad foundation that precludes raw prejudice or blind overemphasis of a
single perspective.

Among historical considerations, all of them indirect and extrinsic to the musical notes themselves, considerations of general
popularity may seem particularly exterior and inappropriate as part
of esthetic evaluation. Popularity implies various undesirable limitations, since the obviously wider the appeal, the simpler the language
must be; and although there may be strength in simplicity, a skeleton
vocabulary severely limits musical expression. It is unconvincing
to cite Schubert songs and Shakespeare plays as examples of
esthetic greatness achieved by simple means. Works of Schubert
that appear simple on the surface contain hidden refinements and
unsuspected complexities when closely examined. Similarly, with
a knowledge of basic English one may possibly respond strongly to
Shakespeare at a low level, but the layerings and overtones of
meaning in his language have occupied the subtlest critics for centuries. Hence, though for historical or sociological purposes one
might consider popularity as an important criterion of value, its
relevance to esthetic valuation is doubtful. Yet we cannot exclude
popular judgment entirely, for one important historical reason: the
actual physical survival of the music. The more popular works of
any period survive in more numerous copies, both manuscript and
printed. By sheer weight of numbers they tend to become the
pillars of convention in their time. Traditions of performance can
also accumulate an inspiring but partly irrelevant weight of popular
acceptance. As an example of the need to consider this element of
value we can take a practical problem in teaching music history:
let us suppose that we are attempting to evaluate Handel's oratorios in order to choose a single work to illustrate this aspect of his
music. The overwhelming weight of popularity and established
tradition would certainly suggest the choice of *Messiah* as his most
influential and significant oratorio, though it is by no means typical
of his oratorio style; and despite many great moments, it ranks
below *Solomon* and several other oratorios in general balance and
consistency of high quality. Popular appeal, particularly when it
becomes enshrined by long tradition, must inevitably take some

part in the formation of our scale of values, but it should never be permitted an exclusive or decisive weight.

A specialized type of popularity, influence on one's peers, may furnish a more reliable measure of quality. If "imitation is the sincerest form of flattery," then we may in part recognize the influential works of any period by noting those that seem to be imitated by other composers, both contemporaries and those of following generations. In making evaluations of Debussy's and Berg's harmonic styles it is of great interest for us to know that an unusual progression of quartal chords in Debussy's *Pour la danseuse aux crotales* from *Six épigraphes antiques* (1914) occurs at the same pitches and with almost identical vertical distribution in a song of Alban Berg, *Warm die Lüfte* (No. 4, in the *Vier Lieder*, Op. 2), apparently written about five years earlier.[1] The recurrence of these chords in the work of two composers underlines their stylistic importance. No matter who came first (Stuckenschmidt holds to the apparent chronology, making Debussy's work derivative, though in Berg's other early work the influence flowed the other way, *from* Debussy), the coincidence draws attention to a composer's specific choice in a particularly revealing way: these chords, more than others, attracted him sufficiently that he stored them consciously or unconsciously in his memory and turned to them for fresh effect. This observation permits, at least as a general hypothesis, the suggestion that Debussy and Berg regarded quartal chords as the logical next step in vertical formation. The idea seems commonplace to us now, but the passage in question gives vital early evidence of an important change in the direction of harmonic developments.

Far more than popular verdicts, expert opinions such as comments by other musicians, either favorable or unfavorable, help us to recognize the significant aspects in any style. For example, some of the best clues to original accomplishments in any period can be found by studying the works or procedures to which critics and theorists object. The severity of Artusi's criticisms of Monteverdi give us an excellent scale for appreciating the magnitude of the composer's innovations: the more original the stylistic departure, the more strident the objections of the theorist.

1. See H. H. Stuckenschmidt, *Debussy or Berg? The Mystery of a Chord Progression*, in *The Musical Quarterly*, LI (1965), 453–59.

A final extrinsic value, possibly more sociological than historical in nature, concerns the appropriateness of a work to its purpose. This judgment may require some subjective evaluation, such as decisions as to whether a work is in good taste. The question of appropriateness tends to arise more often with regard to pieces of music designed to complement some other activity than in works that set their own objectives. Listeners instinctively recognize appropriate settings of words, suitable music for specific dramatic situations, convincing descriptive backgrounds. We often find conflicting values as a result: a composition that is successful as a piece of musical structure may yet drag out a dramatic scene too long—adjusting the emotional tempo of the two arts requires careful compromises. In large designs of Beethoven, words of the text may repeat inappropriately because the control has passed largely to formal considerations (for example, the repetitions of "Freiheit" in Florestan's Act II aria from *Fidelio*, musically effective but textually excessive). It is sometimes alleged that the intent of the artist should play a part in our evaluation of appropriateness. Quite apart from the difficulty in discovering what the artist's intent really is, as a practical necessity we must judge a work on what it is, not what it may have been intended to be. The idea of approving a magnificent failure belongs more to the area of morals and ethics than to esthetics.

Objective Values—Control of SHMRG

Since so little in human thought can entirely escape personal slant and emotional bias, it would be more cautious, and possibly more accurate, to entitle this section "Supposedly Objective Values." In a common-sense view, however, one must distinguish broadly between a class of mainly objective values that can be represented by symbols, numbers, graphs, analytical words, and other concrete modes of communication, as opposed to a class of mainly subjective values based on personal feelings that one can hardly express at all, except by parallel examples or direct analogies. For purposes of style analysis we must obviously use communicable, i.e. objective, values if we are to share whatever general sense of order we can perceive in the musical works under discussion. Later, as individuals, we may be able to apply subjective values in making various types of final, definitive choices.

As we have repeatedly observed in previous overviews of the course of the history of music, judging by composers' products, they have worked consistently toward increasing control of musical elements (SHMRG), extending this control also into steadily larger dimensions or even, during some periods, into a growing range of dimensions. (For example, comparing two equally competent composers of chansons, A and B, whose longest works are similar in length, if the chansons of composer A range more widely in length, he demonstrates a higher control than B in this respect.) If we now as analysts, with the precious aid of historical perspective, simply apply as standards the goals so clearly implied by the directions in which composers have developed various styles, we reproduce as closely as possible the composers' own points of view, though with an additional advantage of hindsight: composers cannot always have known the final results of their techniques, inventions, and aspirations. With our historical advantage we can use the ultimate plateau of a developing stylistic control as a means of understanding the origins and judging the accomplishments of formative stages leading upward toward the plateau. This deduction of standards from the composers' implied objectives may not establish eternal esthetic truth; but, possibly more important to the understanding of music, it relates analysis as closely as possible to composition.

If we postulate control as the measure of evaluation in style analysis, there are two qualifications that must be kept in mind. First, the relative emphasis of particular musical elements varies significantly from period to period; hence, in setting up standards of control, we must flexibly reflect the contemporary objectives of composers. Obviously, to apply a standard derived from one stylistic era to a preceding or following repertory would produce an entirely false evaluation. For example, judged by dramatic Baroque attitudes toward rhythm, much of Renaissance rhythm seems placid and undifferentiated. Similarly, judged by Classic standards of thematic opposition, many artfully unified Baroque sonata movements seem lacking in contrast. In each case an inappropriate and partly irrelevant standard has been applied. Objective analysis works best, it seems, within the general confines of particular periods. It should pursue the central task of distinguishing the accomplishments and failures of control for specific repertories, identifying the master composers from these concrete accomplishments. The same objective techniques operate much less securely in evaluating eras one against another or in comparing master composers of different times: how can we properly compare Palestrina, Monteverdi, Bach, and Wagner except as masters of their own times? The accomplishments are not parallel in a sufficient number of respects; the differences in circumstances and stylistic resources leave too little common ground. For this broader evaluation, therefore, we must rely on personal preferences and other subjective responses.

A second limit on the use of control as a standard of value emerges from twentieth-century developments. Some of the methods of contemporary composition deny control as an objective. This attitude characterizes *musique concrète*, in which the use of sounds recorded at random specifically excludes much of a composer's control. Chance music, too, aims to avoid normal musical controls. Improvisational elements pose a slightly more complicated problem: by transferring partial responsibility to the performer, the composer does not necessarily abandon control entirely, for in most cases he indicates the approximate parameters of the improvisation. Furthermore, the preferences and habits of the performers exercise an involuntary control on the final result: nothing could be harder than to improvise a genuinely random music, since everything in human experience leans toward repetition, variation, and other chainlike arrangements that show interdependency of ideas—the standard options for continuation hold good for improvisation as well as for more usual forms of composition. And one may doubt whether any of these modern denials of control really attains its goal. The composer of *musique concrète*, after all, must decide which sounds to record and where to cut and splice his tape. More basically, so-called random choice cannot fully exclude the built-in relativities of sounds: one sound must not only be higher, louder, longer, or more colorful than another, it must be with, before, or after. Furthermore, unless composers exclude the listener (a trend apparently approved of by some contemporaries), they must submit to his tendencies to discover order even where it is not intended. How can he entirely suppress a lifetime of listening habits, sweeping the ear clean for one specific piece?

In conclusion, it seems likely that control may still be a useful yardstick for evaluation, since the intentionally disorderly pieces now being discomposed (or decomposed?) actually do not fully accomplish their intent of evading order, though they do achieve a considerable extension and modification of the concept of control. We shall not reach the plateau from which to judge these happenings for some years to come. In the meantime, attempts to apply the evaluations of style-analytical control to these radically new styles will keep the analyst alert, to say the least. Applying another type of evaluation, however, he may find the expenditure of time more fruitful in other areas. Yet listeners (including analysts) owe their contemporaries serious and continuing attention, despite all difficulties. For on this presently one-sided and frustrating dialogue depends the future of the art: if everyone had listened to Artusi instead of Monteverdi, the musical vocabulary would have frozen in place as of 1600.

To return to our analysis of control, the need to unravel intertwining elements sometimes forces us to make artificial divisions of the problem, conquering a seemingly unassailable whole by dividing it into manageable parts. As a starting point, for each musical element we should carefully evaluate three aspects: unity, variety, and balance. Even before we grapple with definitions and criteria, however, we should revive the Rule of Three in a new application to provide a rough working scale of value: good, adequate, poor. For example, it may be extremely difficult to indicate the terms of absolute unity, i.e. at precisely what point, or by satisfying what requirements, a piece becomes fully unified. In a relative way, however, playing through a series of pieces we usually will not find it unduly difficult to establish a relative scale of unity, judging some pieces to be well-unified, others adequately unified, and the remainder poorly unified. By applying this rather coarse scale of relative value in a similar way to a number of other significant characteristics, we can soon establish powerful foundations for judgment.

Objective Evaluations: (1) Unity

The application of the idea of unity to the element of Sound may appear rather obvious, but a little probing quickly reveals noteworthy complications, particularly if we remember to look at all dimensions. Musical unity results from consistency of procedure. During a single movement we may assume that the medium will remain consistent, but we may forget that an instrument or voice nominally in the score may rest so frequently that it hardly participates at all. Unless the changes in the amount of participation follow some plan, the effect may be confusing and inconsistent. A long, gradual reduction in instrumentation to produce a tapered close would not necessarily give a disunified effect, but any abrupt change in general timbre toward the end of a movement would risk giving an unsettled, transitional impression just at the time the movement should be stabilizing. In a piece of several movements, we become even more aware of considerations affecting unity, variety, and balance of Sound. Here any inconsistencies between movements stand out in bold relief, so that their purpose—or purposelessness—strikes the listener with unavoidable force. For example, if after a first movement scored for full symphony orchestra the composer then writes a second movement for string quartet, the inconsistency of medium is so great that it gives an eccentric effect. We tend to hear the two movements as entirely different works because they share so little unity of Sound. Yet if a series of several movements gradually reduces forces, from full orchestra to orchestra without percussion and brass, then without woodwind, then to small string orchestra, we might finally be able to accept a movement scored only for string quartet as part of a consistent (if rather extravagant) plan of reduction.

Consistency of approach can produce a sense of control for other aspects of Sound, such as dynamics. If the characteristic dynamic range of a piece extends from p to f, a sudden shift to frequent markings of *ppp* or *fff* might seem inconsistent, unless its purpose were clear from other aspects of the composition. Similarly, the degree of contrast between timbres can achieve a sense of unity only by following some consistent procedure. This does not eliminate the principle of contrast, for any contrasting idea bears a distinct relationship to preceding ideas—according to the relative degree and complexity of contrast. Unity emerges not merely from sameness but also from consistency, and a well-unified piece can include strong contrasts, providing that the types of contrast give a consistent impression. In the hypothetical sections of a piece diagramed below, (1) to (3) are complex mixed timbres, so that the reduction in size, complexity, and dynamics of (4) will produce so inconsistent (i.e. contrasting) an effect that the piece could not end here without suffering obvious disunity of Sound.

SECTION 1	SECTION 2	SECTION 3	SECTION 4
	Obs., Cls.	Fl.	2 Bns.
	Trps., Trbs.	Tuba	
Tutti			
	Pitched Percussion	K.D.	Cymbal
	Vns., Basses	Vlas. pizz.	Organ

Yet if this startling spectrum of contrast were to be repeated in various ways, the actual contrast itself could then contribute a great deal of unity rather than disordered variety to the piece. Whenever we find a seeming disunity in details, therefore, we must look at the next larger dimension to see if the composer is using a broader control. As a sample of stratified control, notice the planning of dynamics in the paragraphs of the diagram below: phrases 1–2 and 3–4 each maintain a consistent dynamic level, unifying their respective sentences. The sentences, however, make a strong contrast within one paragraph, and only by noting the consistency of paragraph procedures (i.e. high internal contrast) will we appreciate the unity of the section as a whole.

Paragraph 1				Paragraph 2			
Sentence 1		Sentence 2		Sentence 3		Sentence 4	
Phr. 1	Phr. 2	Phr. 3	Phr. 4	Phr. 5	Phr. 6	Phr. 7	Phr. 8
pp	*pp*	*ff*	*ff*	*pp*	*pp*	*ff*	*ff*

Unity of Harmony is more obvious in some ways than unity of Sound; in tonal styles we easily recognize the need for ending in the same key with which we began. But what of nontonal styles? The concept of a final in modal music, of course, parallels the idea of a central tonic fairly closely. But lacking such a clear unifying principle we must fall back on a basic evaluation of procedures: is the piece harmonically consistent? Here we simply follow through all of the aspects of Harmony that we have traced earlier, though with the intent now of evaluating consistent application rather than merely noticing frequencies, spectrums, variations, and the like. Is the piece consistently triadic in its chord structures, or more complex? Does it modulate consistently?—at this stage a more important consideration than whether the goals are direct, indirect, or remote. Does it introduce contrapuntal fabrics according to some perceptible plan, or instead, shift haphazardly from chordal to contrapuntal texture? Does the treatment of dissonance relate consistently to rhythmic stresses or occur at random? Do chord and key rhythms maintain consistent rates of change, arranged logically to support articulations in the form? The aspect of harmonic unity rises high on our scale of values when we contemplate pieces containing several movements: consistency of harmonic procedures can add greatly to the unity of successive movements, not merely in such obvious ways as the use of related keys, but also in the use of a consistent vocabulary of chords and dissonances as well as a consistent syntax and rhythm of modulation. Any movement that strays too far from the group vocabulary runs a risk of isolation, of breaking out of the unity. (The possibility of contrast functions will be discussed below.)

When we must evaluate harmonic procedures in works outside of the tonal period, the measurement becomes more difficult because of the lack of conventional norms of vocabulary such as the triad. The ear is no less aware of consistency, however. In a dissonant serial style, for example, any lapse into triadic procedures strikes the ear nearly as strongly as a diminished seventh in the Renaissance. To be effective, changes in the density of dissonance must relate to a perceptible structural plan. In nontonal just as in tonal styles, a successful sense of harmonic movement results only from a consistent regulation of intensities in vertical combinations.

For Rhythm as well as Harmony, unity has both simple and complex aspects, ranging from meter to rhythmic density. A sense of unity depends on consistency in the handling of some or all of the following elements:

1. Rhythmic vocabulary, including sizes of notes, thematic patterns, and spectrum of rhythmic contrast.

2. Rhythmic modules, from fractions, beats, and meters to characteristic larger modules such as phrases, sentences, and sections.

3. Rhythmic density, including surface rhythm and interactions with other elements (chord rhythm, contour rhythm, textural rhythm).

Since unity in Melody interlocks rather closely with thematic unity (particularly for music with frequent articulations), this source of control will be discussed below as part of unity of Growth. For styles that do not depend on distinct thematic units, however, any unity produced by consistent types of melodic activity comes into full play. During a typical Baroque movement with uninterrupted surface flow, for example, some pattern of repeated figuration generally dominates the melodic action, so that even slight changes in flection may catch our attention. In Bach's Prelude in C♯ Major (WTC I/3; see Example 4-2), bars 1–5 outline a broken triad, an active elaboration of a slow-moving progression. In bars 5–7, however, the line moves diatonically, with much more sense of true flection; we immediately notice a resultant higher melodic intensity and sense the acceleration that it produces. These two types of motion within the eight-bar phrase could leave an impression of disunity; but, much as in the diagram above of paragraph structures containing dynamic contrast, the repetition of internal flection contrast lends a feeling of parallelism and relationship to the successive phrases: stable–moving/stable–moving. Again, therefore, a disunity of details is countered by consistency in a larger dimension.

The relative consistency of melodic vocabulary in a piece or style also helps us to evaluate unity. Nothing could be more disruptive than a chromatic interval in Gregorian chant, for example.

A controlled melodic treatment not only employs consistent range and a well-tried group of intervals but also, the frequency of these intervals should follow a fairly constant pattern, with climactic leaps occurring seldom, so that they may produce a correspondingly great effect. Furthermore, a well-managed melody should maintain a consistent style, either mainly stepwise, skipping, or even leaping, yet always adhering to a consistent manner of disposing steps and leaps. We should feel control in the next larger dimension, too: just as we attain rhythmic unity by the use of recurrent motives, similarly, melodic intervals combine into familiar patterns, such as the broken chords mentioned just above. And just as harmonic phenomena may group around a central chord, similarly, the peaks, underpoints, and cadences of a melody often circumscribe a center of gravity, implied by the unified contour. The unity of melodic tessitura, though affecting dimensions as small as phrase relationships in a sentence, may also take effect on a very broad basis involving several movements, one high, one low, others medial in emphasis, but together leaving an impression of controlled and balanced melodic action.

The most obvious unity of Growth results from articulated melodic similarities: thematic unity. The need for consistency in this type of control affects the listener directly: themes intended to be perceived as related must maintain a consistent scale of similarity. To assist the ear, also, composers tend to exploit constant elements of similarity: if rhythmic similarity unifies thematic materials in one section, we can expect rhythmic unification as a predominating device elsewhere; and the elements used to produce variants, whether orchestration, alteration of intervals, changed harmony, or modified rhythm, recur within the piece, binding it together by the similarity of its procedures quite as effectively as by the family relationships of its materials. This type of procedural unity can be seen most clearly in sets of pieces with distinctive styles, such as dance suites or prelude and fugues. Each piece develops an individual unity by consistent use of characteristic meters, tempos, rhythmic idioms, and fabrics.

A less obvious, but equally important impression of Growth control can be secured by consistency in articulating dimensions.

Master composers create modules in each dimension, characteristic sizes of structural components that give the piece twin values: first, stability produced by fulfilled expectations, i.e. regularly recurring phrase and section dimensions (the larger continuum); and second, the corollary possibility of evaded or delayed expectation, a fundamental source of stimulation and tension to enhance musical movement. Modular expectation applies more loosely as we think in larger dimensions, but unity of Growth always implies considerable regularity in the size of sections, parts, and movements. Where inequalities in large dimensions occur, the deployment of other elements can often compensate—in this potentiality lies the artful unpredictability of music, its imprecise charm; but just as in smaller dimensions, the existence of a norm provides both stability and opportunity for stimulating evasions.

Consistency of formal process may also be considered as a measure for unity of Growth, particularly in the larger dimensions. For example, highly articulated sonata expositions often precede development sections of contrapuntal fabric, which one would expect to be smoothly continuous, almost without articulations. Yet despite all sorts of polyphonic manipulation, the more successful developments contain clear articulations not characteristic of fugal forms, but consistent with the articulated Growth of the expositions. Still more broadly, in a series of movements we begin to feel structural unity mainly as we become conscious of a succession of related or balanced Shapes. A symphony with two sonata-form movements and two fugues would leave an audience puzzled, unless other unifying elements came to the rescue. In the Baroque keyboard suite, composers' preference for a steady succession of modulating two-part forms illustrates this type of large-scale unification by similarity in compositional process. By contrast, the odd assortments of binary, ternary, fugal, and ritornello forms in early concerti grossi often make a frustratingly piecemeal effect, both in size and procedure; yet in many of these pieces, fortunately, the consistent opposition of tutti and concertino provides a compensating unity of textural procedure to balance the inconsistencies of Growth.

Objective Evaluations: (2) Variety

At every point of the discussion above, in seeking measures of unity we have inevitably also implied the need for variety and balance. Unity alone would ossify a musical work, for the fundamental sense of movement depends on changes of all sorts. Once a sufficient change has initiated some perceptible movement, the effective continuation of the piece still depends on the adjustment of later changes to produce a constant flow. Flow alone, however, precious though it is, cannot by itself create a satisfactory result. The articulation and organization of this flow into a successful piece requires finely controlled balances between unity and variety.

If balance is the final controlling value, it might seem sufficient to evaluate this aspect alone. However, relatively few composers achieve a fully rounded balance, since the expression of their individualities guarantees special emphasis (and not infrequently, overemphasis) on particular elements. Furthermore, while some composers excel in unifying their works, others overflow with variety. Where either extreme dominates, we may give low marks for balance; yet we should also give the composer credit for his area of strength. This situation clearly requires separate and distinct evaluation of unity and variety, although the ultimate total judgment may rest mainly on evidence of balance.

The judgment of variety in a composer's works covers much the same ground that one traverses in the course of estimating unity, often in a rather exactly reciprocal way, since a composer's lack of unity may result directly from his overabundance of variety. Thus the same initial hypotheses, or the same working outline of probing questions, will bring out most of the points that the analyst should examine. Again at the start we meet the sticky question of defining degrees of variety, and again the answer lies not so much in absolute theoretical definition as in relative definition by experience: while we may not be able to define in any absolute way a scale of variety, a priori, we can usually separate a repertory of pieces into three general groups, graded according to amount of variety: strong, adequate, weak. Other descriptors for the three categories might be adapted to particular situations such as exaggerated, strong, average (for a composer who had no weak contrasts) or average, weak, absent (for a composer with no strong contrasts). Although any one of these judgments, viewed singly, is obviously almost too general to be helpful, when developed over a broad range of criteria, a cumulative refinement of discrimination emerges from the network of interrelated judgments. Taken together, these judgments exercise a collective strength and validity, making possible a convincing final opinion based on a rich multiplicity of correlations.

As a counterweight to unity, we should now add variety to the characteristics already evaluated. In the process of estimating variety we will find a few new areas and perspectives that do not arise in considering questions of unity. In some ways variety may be even more important than unity for a work of art, because variety concerns change and profile. Unity can be merely static, but variety produces a spectrum of effects to which we can respond. Represented on psychological perception graphs, a straight-line response may be perfectly unified, but it describes only one relationship, with insufficient variation in profile to be perceived as Movement and Shape. Historically, too, searches for variety seem to contribute more advances than do attempts to unify: pursuit of variety leads to experimentation and expansion of resources, a positive direction of achievement for many a composer not gifted with organizing ability.

Applying evaluations of variety to Sound, we must consistently take into account three aspects: (1) degree of variety; (2) rate or frequency of change; and (3) total spectrum of contrasts. These three "measurements" will be judged mainly with respect to timbre, texture, and dynamics, though variety of idiom and range may also be worthy of notice and comment.

Evaluations of variety in Harmony may seem a bit elusive on first thought, but the following points will remind us of ways in which this element can vary:

1. General stability versus instability.
2. Chord and key vocabulary.
3. Chord and key rhythm.

4. Amount and type of dissonance.

5. Types of fabric, i.e. changes between chordal and contrapuntal, simple and complex.

Again, all these five considerations should be judged for degree, frequency, and spectrum of harmonic variety. Some pieces, for example, contain many harmonic changes but within a narrow range; others change less frequently but employ more sharply contrasted modulations and tonal goals, a greater amount as well as a wider spectrum of harmonic variety.

For Rhythm we might start out with the following potentials for variety, again all estimated with regard to degree, rate, and extent:

1. Tempo and meter; inflections such as accelerando, ritardando, meno mosso, a piacere, fermata.

2. Density of rhythmic textures and fabrics, including both contrapuntal intensity and total number of impacts.

3. Patterning.

4. Proportion of action between layers of rhythm (surface, continuum, interactions).

The list above contains several complicated points. For example, to arrive at an estimate of variety in contrapuntal intensity of rhythm requires a good deal of experience and experimentation, and subjective factors play a significant and potentially confusing role. Mentioned here for completeness only, these detailed aspects must be reserved for a more advanced application of style analysis to particular periods, a technique that cannot be adequately treated in the present general discussion. Merely as an illustrative sample, however, we can notice that rhythmic activity makes more impact when combined with linear activity: (b) gives a more intense impression than (a) because both lines move:

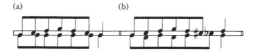

This interactive intensity must be considered most carefully in setting up evaluative spectra of rhythmic contrast. It will not cause us much trouble to observe the degree and rate of patterning, but the phrase "spectrum of patterning" may require a bit more elucidation. Any such spectrum includes not only the vocabulary of patterns in a piece, but also the range of intensity within these pattern types. To make a concrete application of this idea, in the expositions of Sonatas A and B we can observe the following circumstances with regard to rhythmic patterns:

	SONATA A	SONATA B
Length of expositions	40 bars	60 bars
Total no. of patterns	90	132
Types of patterns	10	10
Highest contrast	♪♫ ♩	♩..♬ ♩
Lowest contrast	♩ ♩	♩ ♩

Evaluating this evidence of variety, not forgetting the difference in length of the two expositions, we notice that the amount and thus also the rate of change (reflected in the total number of patterns) is approximately the same. The actual number of pattern types, ten each, is also the same, but the spectrum of intensity in Sonata B is much larger, extending from a short, highly contrasted pattern (♩..♬) to a long, undifferentiated pattern (♩ ♩). The broader spectrum of patterning in B thus contributes a perceptibly richer variety.

Evaluating melodic variety does not seem to produce any special ambiguities: we must simply check through all points of melodic style with respect to degree, rate, and spectrum of melodic variety. As we noticed in earlier discussions of Growth, however, there is an area of overlap between the elements of Melody and Growth with respect to the articulation of small dimensions. For both elements the degree, rate, and spectrum of types of articulation strongly affect our sense of variety and contrast. If one lowers a phonograph stylus at some random point on a recording, the amount of articulation in the melodic line often tells whether the passage is expositional/presentational (highly articulated) or transitional/developmental (fewer articulations). In evaluating Growth articulations, of course, one would have to take all SHMR elements into account; melodic articulation, on the other hand, draws on contour and flection only. From a practical point of view, therefore, we gain a fuller picture of articulation by including it as a part of Growth, where its interactive characteristics can be more fully considered.

The chief sources of variety in Growth are thematic differentiation, contrast in weight and type of articulation, and spectrum of Growth processes. Thematic differentiation utilizes (at least potentially) all the SHMR elements to provide contrast, though each composer tends to prefer one or two elements that he habitually exploits to produce differences between themes (often using the same preferred elements also to unify themes). Our investigation of thematic differentiation must be every bit as systematic as our other analytical techniques. We can never assume that any theme will of itself impress us by its differences in a comprehensive way, for any striking or predominating difference automatically puts other more subtle differences in the shade. Hence, we must seek out the full range of individualities by asking all the usual questions about SHMR. At the end of this checking process we should not omit Growth itself, for which the chief source of variety is change in module. For example, a primary and a transitional theme may share many characteristics, including direct motivic relationships; nevertheless, the tendency of transitional material to break into smaller units effectively differentiates it from primary material. Variety in module furnishes an important means of contrast between movements as well. Many times in Haydn the tempos and meters of first and last movements are not strongly contrasted, but he secures variety in finales by the use of smaller motives, shorter phrases, terser sentences and paragraphs. With more frequent articulations resulting from these smaller units, obviously the articulations must be lighter and smaller, or the flow would be impeded. This leads into the second Growth resource, the whole question of articulations, which also offer the composer a wide range of choice in securing adequate variety in Growth processes. To make only a single comparison, the articulations of slow movements of most composers are constructed rather differently than those of fast movements: the danger of a slow movement falling apart at the point of articulation is greater, so we typically find more stress on the continuum: at least one voice will carry on the basic rhythmic pulse through cadences and other points of articulation—we rarely find complete rest in all parts. Fast movements, by contrast, generate sufficient momentum to carry through a considerable amount of rest, as we can see in almost any work of Beethoven. One can make a revealing test here: play a slow movement at a fast tempo, and immediately the articulations seem obtrusive and hyperactive. It may ultimately be possible to establish an objective determination of tempo by studying quantitative relationships between articulation and the three layers of rhythm. For this purpose we could obviously turn to the computer to digest the enormous amount of data to be controlled in such a study.

Variety in processes is a third major source of contrast and interest in Growth. We have already noted the possibility of contrasting different parts of a piece, for example, by the use of contrapuntal development following a vertically controlled exposition. Now we must expand our thinking to encompass the amount of variety in full movements, the rate at which variety in Growth processes occurs, and the extent of this variety. Notice, for example, that slow movements rarely contain as much contrast as fast movements. Why? Perhaps it is actually a matter of size: looking at exceptional slow movements, such as the very long third movement of Beethoven's Ninth Symphony, we immediately notice that this atypical movement introduces strong contrast between two ideas as the main principle of its structure. No doubt there is (at the least) a general correlation between size and extent of variety in successful pieces. And the way in which a composer handles his sources of variety in all dimensions directly influences both objective and subjective evaluations of his work. We must not forget to look at the variety of Growth types in a series of movements. In the keyboard suite we have noted a sense of cumulative unity produced by the series of similar modulating two-part forms. To obtain variety here composers relied on other elements, such as the contrasts of traditional dance meters and tempos. As composers learned to control longer spans of music, however, we find greater contrasts in patterns of Growth. One of the attractions of the inclusion of the minuet (or scherzo) in Classic symphonies is the strong contrast of its neat, highly articulated sections to the more involved, continuously extended patterns of the other movements. We are not disturbed by the shortness of these movements because they make up for lack of size by extent of contrast. Four sonata-form movements in a symphony, however, in order to be successful, would need to transfer an enormous weight of responsibility for variety to musical elements other than Growth, invoking new and ingenious sources of color and change.

Objective Evaluations: (3) Balance

Just as good judgment occurs comparatively rarely in human beings, good balance occurs surprisingly rarely in music—so rarely, in fact, that listeners immediately comment upon the presence of this quality, often mistakenly calling it symmetry. Semi-*cognoscenti* love to talk about Mozart's symmetry, but what they mean is usually a bit obscure. If they mean numerical equivalence on each side of an articulation, symmetry of this type occurs rather unpredictably in Mozart. What they may be hearing as apparent symmetry is actually a superbly continuous act of balance, controlling several sizes of horizontal dimensions and also the vertical adjustment between components of the texture. By this sleight of sound a balanced 4+5 structure may give a symmetrical 4+4 effect.

In judging the balance of a piece it is often difficult to devise a dual-purpose scale of evaluation that would permit us to compare a section of strong harmonic movement against a following section of strong rhythmic movement. Yet we must nevertheless steadily attempt to determine whether the two sections produce an impression of adequate balance between unity and variety, since this balance requires the highest degree of control and thus supplies the keenest test of value. One of the miracles of music is certainly its power to survive the defects in composers' techniques. An automobile can move slowly with only two or three cylinders firing, and a great many pieces manage to give some impression of movement without much genuine action or internal combustion. What we seek in judging balance is not so much to evaluate the rare cases of complex and beautifully weighted segments—these we will not encounter very often—but rather to become increasingly aware of gross disproportion between the sources of musical stress within a piece. We will find some works that could be described as nonbalanced, rather than balanced or disbalanced, since they consist of sections that move, dispersed between sections that do not move . . . a crude sort of balance, perhaps, but hardly to be described as control. On the whole, the task of judgment will usually not be as critical or as subtle as one could wish: many composers are not so critical or subtle themselves, and they tend to draw upon consistent and recurring resources and procedures. These fortunate habits tend to reduce the severity of the dual-comparison problem mentioned at the beginning of this paragraph, since most of the time comparisons of degrees of unity and variety need concern only one element at a time: only rarely must one compare harmonic balance against rhythm or melody. Also, since the continuity of musical flow furnishes a considerable sense of unity in itself, composers work more in the direction of achieving sufficient variety. A considerable amount of variety, then, can be balanced by a relatively smaller effort at unity, though the strongest pieces seem to stress both qualities. The judgment of balance, therefore, places at the low end of the scale pieces that lack either unity or variety; high achievement is dual: it implies strongly (and diversely) conceived sources of unification and powerfully expressive sources of variety.

At the highest level, judgments of balance, even if based on an objective foundation, may still need to draw on subjective reactions, since the listener as well as the composer develops habits of response that make him more sensitive to unities and varieties emerging from one favored element than from another less favored. Where these preferences coincide with the choices of the composer, a distinct "halo effect" occurs that passes far outside the realm of objective evaluation. Thus, the listener who likes melody will tend to overrate a melodic composer. It is important to recognize the point at which any change from objective to subjective valuation takes place. The mixture is valuable musically but dangerous to clarity in analysis. When we have thought about a piece as clearly as possible and drawn as many conclusions as analysis permits, we then enrich and complete the whole process by turning to the most vital and ultimate standard: personal feeling.

Subjective Evaluation

This aspect of evaluation belongs for the most part to the player-listener himself. The only point in attempting some elaboration of method here is to increase the range of our musical responses. Subjective evaluation should never stop with such primitive determinations as "good/bad," or "best/worst," or "I like/dislike." For one thing, there are many kinds and periods of music, all of which include good things: we do not need to pursue a restrictive "best of all," ignoring the rest of music. On one occasion we will listen to a Bruckner symphony (a large occasion, to be sure); on a different, lighter occasion a Strauss waltz (almost any Strauss) may better fit our needs. Ideally, the practice of subjective evaluation increases our ability to recognize the good in any type of music, rather than merely a narrow, somewhat theoretical "best." In this way we choose from the enormous span of music history the items most meaningful for our own use; and by the material impact of these preferences, such as the purchase of tickets, scores, and recordings, we also contribute to the survival of favored items and to the deepening of their imprint on our culture as a widening audience responds.

Expressing preference entails a complicated collection of responses, and we will understand our own subjective processes of selection (and improve them) by awareness of several layers in the often subtle determinations so oversimplified by the statement, "I like." Putting aside all theoretical esthetics, and concentrating merely on responses that may deepen our understanding of musical style, we can divide subjective evaluation into three aspects: (1) affective range; (2) emotional intensity; and (3) character of appeal.

Affective range describes the number of different moods and the contrast in their effect that we encounter in a piece. To some extent we can approach this response analytically, for example, in the areas of tempo (fast/slow), mode (major/minor), and rhythm (active/stable). But mood is such a personal matter that we must constantly rely upon subjective feelings to guide us. We can apply these feelings to style analysis by making general estimates, as usual divided into three parts: strong, weak, and in between (other descriptors, such as "average," "unremarkable," or "satisfactory" may be useful here to reflect the "in between" state a little better). As we study a group of works by an unfamiliar composer, we will soon come to feel that the composer has a strong, average, or weak musical personality, an impression that rests in turn to a considerable extent on the affective range of his style. Next it may be possible to reach some conclusions about the character of these affects. We recognize a profile by the jut of nose and jaw and the character of its expression; similarly, any forceful, effective piece leaves an impression of its stylistic profile in our memories, of which the affective range forms a highly significant part. For Baroque music we might follow the lead of various contemporary writers, such as Mattheson, cumulating a list of affects as we play through a repertory and dividing our pieces accordingly. In this way we gain a clear idea of the range of affective expression. Some composers remain for life musically in a range of brooding melancholy, while others pass through a wide spectrum of moods. If we find it difficult at first to attach a specific word to a piece, a short list of possible affects may stimulate our reactions in some definite directions:

happy	driving	passive	sad
gay	stately	peaceful	vague (dreamlike)
lively	dignified	pastoral	moody (changeable)
active	funereal	dry	willful (unpredictable)
passionate	reserved	sentimental	humorous (playful)
aggressive	serious	nostalgic	ironic (mocking)

In some periods and for some styles any such list would be almost completely irrelevant, of course; also, certain pieces (or sections of pieces) in any repertory will defy categorization—sometimes the best ones. Yet, if particular affects do not seem appropriate, we may still gain some sense of a composer's ranges simply by applying rough classifications such as rich in mood, average, or monotonous.

Closely intertwined with affective range is emotional intensity: it is difficult to think of a piece with strong affect that would not also transmit an impression of high emotional intensity. Despite this interconnection, however, there is a basic quality/quantity distinction here that generates two related but partly separable questions. To establish the affective range we ask: How different are the moods? To estimate emotional intensity we inquire: How strong are the moods? To put the second idea in musical terms, some composers range emotionally from *ppp* to *fff*, others from *mp* to *mf*. This measurement of intensity obviously plays a vital part in subjective responses. And when considering this range of intensity, we might also remember the rate of intensity: How much of the range do we experience in a given length of time? While we cannot pin down this somewhat general determination in terms of concrete amounts, there is no doubt that composers and pieces have a recognizable IQ (intensity quotient). Though no subjective evaluation can operate on a definite, absolute scale, comparative evaluations of a group of pieces may, nevertheless, establish a relative order of extreme refinement, adjusted far more sensitively than would be possible for objective evaluations, since the subjective responses include unspecified intangible components of total effect. i.e. essential but indefinable correlations of response that we cannot yet describe convincingly, much less measure. For scholar-critics, these subjective nuances contain some dangers, since serious evaluation attempts to establish a generalized, widely acceptable estimate. In making this attempt, the individual must learn to correct his own subjective evaluations as far as possible from the skewing of personal bias: a reserved person might find an emotional piece exaggerated, even vulgar, which to a flamboyant personality would seem quite normal, possibly even a bit tame. The careful evaluator, whether reserved or flamboyant, will make adjustments to compensate the effects of his personal attitudes.

Another resource in deepening our appreciation of emotional intensity can be reached by the old familiar methods: merely check down through SHMRG for range and rate of intensity. Often one can locate the sources of emotional impact by subjective reflection, then confirm them by objective analysis as well. Again we need make no attempt to construct an absolute scale of acoustic, harmonic, melodic, rhythmic, or growth intensity. But we can nonetheless say, more often than not, which phrase or section or piece or composer gives us the impression of highest intensity with respect to particular SHMRG elements. Obviously the musical effect owes something to each of the elements; thus, it may be a waste of time to attempt to isolate any single most important intensifying element. Yet once more, by applying the comparative method we can usually determine which particular two or three elements are significantly more important than the rest in exciting our emotional responses. This rather general determination supplies helpful clues to the direction of our ultimate style-analytical conclusions.

The final subjective aspect, character of appeal, in part belongs with historical considerations of value. Popularity indicates wide appeal, and survival as part of an active repertory indicates continuing strength of appeal. While we may measure these values statistically, however, it may also be worthwhile to attempt to understand the nature of the appeal. The popularity of a piece is a statistical fact; the musical motivation for the popularity is a subjective value that concerns us deeply in understanding a composer, both in relation to his time and as part of an absolute hierarchy of excellence. Any hints that we can discover in historical materials regarding the nature of popular musical responses may provide our most direct and basic insights. For the individual himself, a final part of subjective value proceeds from the immediacy or permanence of a composer's musical appeal. Some composers grow on us slowly but wear well; others charm at first but quickly fade. The permanence of effect seems partly related to complexity of techniques, but the history of music also offers many examples of profound simplicity that permanently maintain the capacity to excite strong responses.

Looking back on the whole elusive process of evaluation we can see that one never arrives at final solutions, even for oneself.

Nor should one try to fix the relationship between art and its devotees. Elusiveness enhances charm in music as well as in women. Like a bottle of new wine to a gourmet, an unknown piece should challenge the listener to fresh refinements of response. Seen in this way, we judge ourselves quite as much as the music in making evaluations. The search for value thus becomes an educative process: the task of distinguishing a hierarchy of excellence in any repertory calls forth a parallel motivation toward excellence of analysis and esthetic appreciation from the player or listener. This continuing pursuit brings a twofold and increasing reward: deepening understanding of a composer's style provides both a growing intellectual communication and an enrichment of emotional experience.

CHAPTER NINE

STYLE ANALYSIS IN
FULL ACTION

Most of the analytical remarks in previous chapters have concerned short examples and illustrations, parts instead of wholes. It remains, then, to put the pieces together, to show the full process in action as we must use it in our daily musical encounters. At the outset, once again we should remind ourselves that even the most sensitive musical analysis artificially freezes a motion art. In this laudable attempt to understand more of the sources of movement than can be grasped during the fleeting impressions of performance, when we stop the motion, we naturally lose some precious flexibilities and subtleties; against these losses, however, we gain new depths of understanding that we could hardly hope to achieve even by repeated hearings. With a somewhat similar intent, a painter closely studies the anatomy of bones and muscles, a knowledge that enables him to understand and later to recreate bodily motion with convincing power.

The approach to a piece may be likened to the approach of a figure from a distance. Inside a distant blur we first distinguish a head and other parts of the body; then we see eyes in the head; and only at close quarters can we observe the color of the eyes. Similarly for style analysis, the general shape of the piece comes first: we must recognize articulations that define the parts, large and small, before we can trace the progress of ideas and the sources of movement. The piece before us now as an illustration of com-

---

EXAMPLE 9-1 (*facing page*).   Purcell, *Golden Sonata*: I.

Violin I

Violin II

Gamba

Continuo

Allegro

prehensive analytical action is Purcell's *Golden Sonata* (first movement), an instructive problem because it conforms to no stereotypes and on first glance presents fewer formal clues than many
other short sonata movements, since it lacks a conventional theme,
and the absence of central double-bars leaves us no immediate hint
as to the general shape. The first search for articulations requires
little more than a broad review: unless an articulation strikes us
in a distinct and obvious fashion, clearly it has no part in defining
the general shape of the piece. As possible sources for gross articulation, therefore, we need only consider macroprocesses such as
change of texture (S), cadences and new keys (H), fresh thematic
material (M), or alteration in surface-rhythmic activity. Purcell's
rhythmic and melodic material remain much the same throughout
the piece, at least when viewed broadly, so more likely sources of
articulation will probably be discovered in aspects of Sound and
Harmony. Exploring Harmony first—it is our most familiar articu-
lator—we find the strongest cadences, V–I in root position, at
bars 11–12 and 16–17. If these heaviest articulations were of approximately equal weight the piece would assume a three-part shape,
but for several reasons the cadence in the dominant gives the more
decisive impression:

1. The full cadence in bars 11–12 climaxes a relatively stabilized
section in the dominant key, further emphasized by an impressive
slowdown in the bass, anticipating and stabilizing the final resolution to C by rocking back and forth between C and G chords. In
comparison, the modulation to D minor, though colorful and fresh,
passes by very quickly, without emphasis: it becomes definite only
with the entry of C♯ in bar 17, and the C♮ in the following bar
turns back decisively toward F. This extremely fluid motion from
minor to relative major characterizes much of the tonality of the
Baroque period.[1]

2. The cadence of bars 11–12 forms a line of demarcation
between two types of rhythmic and contrapuntal texture. While
descending to the cadence the lines smooth out into homorhythmic
eighth- and quarter-note motion with parallel thirds in the upper

1. See LaRue, *Bifocal Tonality, An Explanation for Ambiguous Baroque Cadences, op. cit.*

parts; but just after the cadence the gamba revives the vigorous eighth-and-two-sixteenth figure against slower dialogue in the violins, a notably different treatment than what we heard just before the cadence. In comparison, the degree of activity before and after the D-minor cadence seems much the same, though disposed in different registers; the gamba moves continually during bars 16–19, whereas we can pinpoint the earlier articulation merely by studying the slowdown and sudden surge of surface rhythm in the gamba line, bars 11–12:

3. The dominant cadence precedes a major thematic change, inversion of the opening figures (the violin quarter-notes now fall and the gamba pattern rises). In comparison, although the opening motivic directions return after the D-minor cadence, we cannot feel a consistent principle, since the second violin persists with an inversion (compare bars 6 and 18), so that the whole effect is one of continuing exploration of motivic possibilities rather than decisive, articulative change.

As a result of these impressions, the cadence in the dominant should be regarded as the prevailing articulation, hence producing a basic shape in two parts. Within the two parts we can find a number of less emphatic cadences, each confirmed by new textural dispositions of the opening motives, so that the shape of the piece suddenly becomes very clear. (See Example 9-2, next page.)

And Purcell confirms the importance of the central dominant cadence in still another way by inverting the procedures of phrases 1 and 2 to produce 1a and 2a, first establishing an unmistakable (though variant) parallelism, then unifying the end by elaborating (instead of inverting) the ideas of phrase 3 to produce 3a.

Once the heavy and lighter articulations have clarified the shape of a piece, we possess defined areas in which to study the sources of movement. To stimulate our powers of observation we must carry in mind at all times a rather elaborate range of possibilities. Good analysis requires an active imaginative approach: we

EXAMPLE 9-2.

1a

2a

3a

look and listen to improve an evolving hypothesis concerning the growth of a piece, testing, correcting, and replacing one possibility after another. The more experience we acquire, the larger our fund of hypotheses becomes, since obviously the hypotheses one uses for Purcell will be both more and less detailed than those needed for Stravinsky; furthermore, each person excels in response to particular elements, so that personal hypotheses will vary, even with regard to the same piece. (Remember that analysis is really a very special kind of performance that seeks to bring out as many qualities of a piece as possible.) As initial equipment we can start with the following list:

BASIC COMPONENTS FOR ANALYTIC HYPOTHESES

Sound

Timbre: selection, combination, degree of contrast of instruments and voices.

Range, tessitura, gaps, special effects, exploitation of idiom, surface articulation.

Texture and fabric: doubling, overlap, contrast of components; homophonic, cantus firmus, contrapuntal, polarized (polychoric; melody / figured bass or 2+1; melody / accompaniment; solo / ripieno).

Dynamics: terraced, graduated, implied by instrumentation or range; types and frequency.

Harmony

Main functions: color and tension.

Stages of tonality: linear and modal, migrant, bifocal, unified, expanded, polycentric, atonal, serial. Analysis of nontonal, nonserial styles as structures of variant stability / instability.

Movement relationships, interior key schemes, modulatory routes.

Chord vocabulary (direct, indirect, remote), alterations, dissonances, progressions, motifs, sequences.

Harmonic rhythm: chord rhythm, inflection rhythm, key rhythm.

Part exchange, counterpoint, imitation, canon, fugue / fugato, stretto, augmentation / diminution.

Melody

Range: mode, tessitura, vocal / instrumental.

Motion: stepwise, skipping, leaping, chromatic; active / stable, articulated / continuous, chromatic / level, etc.

Patterns: rising, falling, level, wave, undulating, sawtooth (RFLWUS).

New or derived: function as primary (thematic) or secondary (cantus firmus, ostinato).

Middle and large dimension: peaks and 'lows.

(See also *Growth*: options for continuation.)

Rhythm
  Surface rhythm: vocabulary and frequency of durations and patterns.
  Continuum: meter (regular, irregular, additive, heterometric, syncopated,
    hemiolic); tempo; module or dimensions of activity (fraction, pulse,
    motive, subphrase, phrase, sentence, larger grouping).
  Interactions: textural rhythm, harmonic rhythm, contour rhythm.
  Patterns of change: amount and location of stress, lull, and transition
    (SLT).
  Fabrics: homorhythmic, polyrhythmic, polymetric; variant rhythmic
    density.

Growth
  Large dimension considerations: balance and relationship between move-
    ments in dimensions, tempos, tonalities, textures, meters, dynamics,
    range of intensity.
  Evolution of control: heterogeneity, homogeneity, differentiation, specializa-
    tion.
  Sources of Shape:
    Articulation by change in any element; anticipation, overlap, elision,
      truncation, lamination.
    Options for continuation: recurrence, development, response, contrast.
  Sources of Movement:
    Conditions: stability, local activity, directional motion.
    Types: structural, ornamental.
  Module: the pervading or characteristic growth segment.
  Text influence: choice of timbre; exploitation of word-sound for mood and
    texture; word evocation of chord and key change; clarification of
    contrapuntal lines by forceful keywords; influence of word and sen-
    tence intonation on musical line; limitation by awkward vocables;
    influence of word rhythms on surface rhythms and poetic meter
    on musical meter; degree of adherence to text form (line, stanza,
    refrain, da capo, etc.) in articulations and options for continuation;
    concinnity or conflict in mood changes, fluctuations of intensity, loca-
    tion of climax, degree of movement.

Using a fundamental checklist of this sort, we can construct
initial analytical frameworks for particular pieces or composers. For
example, we could eliminate "polytonality" from the outline when
considering Purcell; but what about "polymetric"? This observation
might seem irrelevant, if we restrict the meaning to simultaneous
3/4 and 7/8, for example, as found in twentieth-century compositions. But a hemiola in two violins that the gamba does not confirm
produces a polymetric result also. On the whole, therefore, it saves
time to work through all hypothetical possibilities just as they come,
keeping an open mind. And in any case, before departing very far

from the outline above, we should remember that it has passed through dozens of revisions and years of testing and use. The power of the style-analytical approach comes from its combination of a systematic framework with an inherent flexibility of emphasis: by relevant adjustments, the basic framework can furnish a valid approach to many different styles. When adjusting our hypotheses to attain any required flexibility, therefore, we must be particularly careful not to lose the invaluable organizing effect of the SHMRG routine. Notice that if we consistently employ this framework, the comparison and evaluation of any two works, of any two composers, and even of two entirely different eras can be accomplished without lost effort on preliminary sorting of characteristics: the SHMRG approach effectively groups stylistic observations in advance.

At this point a fair question might be: are we working on Movement or Shape? The answer once more reflects the characteristic ambiguity of music: we must observe both aspects at once; since so many musical effects produce both Movement and Shape, only in a final summing-up can we decide which function prevails. As a minimal reminder to assure comprehensive observations it may now help to use a sheet divided into appropriate boxes somewhat as follows:

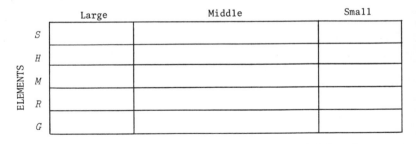

The method of filling-in can proceed in two ways: (1) by observing each SHMRG element individually in all three dimensions before proceeding to the next elements, i.e. filling in the chart horizontally, or (2) by observing each dimension individually as it emerges from SHMRG, before examining another dimension, i.e. filling in

the chart vertically. If any box remains blank or difficult to fill in—
a common circumstance—this merely indicates a dimension or
element that is not stylistically relevant for a particular piece or
composer. In most boxes we will normally make several comments,
sometimes more than we can handle. Even from this rather general
approach, therefore, we will easily discover at least fifteen functional points of style. At the present time very little writing about
music furnishes any such amount of concrete observation and
commentary.

Throughout the centuries most composers have attempted to
coordinate stylistic elements, though not necessarily the same elements nor with the same emphases. For music that correlates
stylistic elements the vertical approaches to the chart more nearly
parallel the growth process than do the horizontals. If we think
of a superbly coordinated composer such as Mozart or Beethoven,
we immediately see how much understanding we gain by watching
the elements working together, far more significant insights than
we obtain by singling out one element and tracing its isolated
course. The core of Classic music is coordination, and a revealing
analysis must reflect this core. As a contrast, consider the music of
Debussy, in which carefully graduated color contrasts often produce more sense of movement than do harmony, rhythm, or melody.
In Romantic concentration of this sort (S emphasis)—and in early
music such as plainsong (M emphasis) and recent music such as
electronic tapes (S emphasis)—the predominance of one or another
single element demands horizontal analytic procedure developed
to illuminate the controlling element rather than a coordinated
analysis by dimensions. Returning to Purcell, the signs of coordination already noted in his *Golden Sonata* cadences suggest that
a dimensional approach will yield the more meaningful sequence of
observation.

Confusion of Dimensions

At times we will unavoidably experience difficulty in assigning
points of style to one particular dimension or another. Sometimes
the composer himself may be slightly confused or inconsistent. More

often the style component exercises a double function, affecting Movement or Shape on two different levels. (Note the comments below on H in large and middle dimensions: the D-minor modulation, which lends a new type of movement to the second half as compared with the first half, more coloristic than tensional, definitely affects large dimensions; yet at the same time, because of its brevity, the modulation creates an indecisive local harmonic relationship between phrases—i.e. a middle-dimension uncertainty). We must bear in mind also that the three-dimensional approach is a methodological abstraction designed to increase the comprehensiveness of our observations. Not every piece moves in all three dimensions, and in the other direction, we can conceive of movement on more than three levels. Hence, if we occasionally encounter difficulty in locating a particular observation dimensionally, no great damage can result, and we will often reach a clarification as we draw our final conclusions.

Significant and Accessory Observations

Just as we speak of structural and ornamental changes, so we must distinguish significant observations, which collectively reveal a distinctive stylistic profile, from accessory observations—stylistic truisms or details too small to justify mention. For example, we communicate little of Purcell's style if we comment that he uses many passing dissonances. So do thousands of composers; the comment is true but uninformative. A more useful observation would call attention to Purcell's anticipations as the only sharp dissonances of the piece. Yet even here we commit a vagueness: *the fully valuable comment on style must always go beyond description to show function.* A genuinely significant presentation of these anticipations as style clues, therefore, should mention that they occur only in connection with the most important cadences, as additional sources of articulation. Stressing function wherever possible, therefore, rather than mere description or enumeration, we can now proceed to examine the *Golden Sonata* systematically in the three usual dimensions (see the charts on the following pages).

Large Dimensions

S	1+2 grouping of texture, with a large gap between gamba and violins. Violins move frequently in parallel thirds. Contrapuntal independence of parts increases through the piece, culminating in phrase 3a, where each part develops a different motive (1+1+1 texture). Conservative instrumental treatment: no unusual demands in range or technique. Not idiomatic—flutes or oboes could play the piece.
H	Full cadence in the dominant accomplishes a main tensional goal at bar 12, fixing the approximate size of the piece, since we expect approximately the same amount of music to establish a convincing return to the tonic, if the Growth develops as a varied parallel type (one of the commonest types for Purcell's listeners; see G below). Short modulation to D minor gives fresh harmonic color to the second half (increasing harmonic movement, yet without sufficient organization to be felt as key rhythm). Long pedal on C at the end furnishes sufficient emphasis to stabilize the whole piece; it is not merely a cadence for the second half, since it extends two bars beyond the symmetrical length of twelve bars expected to balance the first half.
M	Recurrence of violin peaks on upper C (compare bars 1 and 4 with 20, 21, and 24) produces a slightly inexact long-range symmetry. Interior peaks on G (phrase 3) and B♭ (phrases 1a and 2a) furnish a series of varied melodic limits, i.e. some movement but not much sense of direction.
R	Rather small durational vocabulary: half to sixteenth, with few dotted values. Avoids static sameness of surface rhythm by a gradual rise in activity, though we sense this action-crescendo more within each half considered by itself (i.e. in middle dimensions) than as an intensity mounting through the piece as a whole.
G	Progressive intensification of textural and contrapuntal procedures (broadly confirmed by greater melodic flow in second half) gives a consistent flow of movement. Impressive harmonic stabilization at end shows large-dimension concern. Inversion of both opening motives (and also of the general line-direction from downward to upward) immediately after the decisive dominant cadence in bar 12 confirms the structural importance of this cadence; the inversion initiates a variant parallel growth of approximately equal length. This combination of thematic variation and harmonic tension creates effective movement without loss of unity.

Middle Dimensions

S	Phrasing made completely clear by part exchange: active figure in texture (gamba line) moves into violins and back: A B A A /B\ A B A B (This observation concerns S only so far as the location of textural activity is concerned.) Stretto imitation changes texture from 1+2 to 1+1+1 (bars 10 f.), a more active fabric.
H	Carefully graded cadences articulate phrases and subphrases: vii–I (bars 3 f.), IV⁶–I (bars 5 f.), ii⁶–V (bars 7 f.), ii⁶–V in the dominant (bars 9 f.), V–I in the dominant (bars 11 f.). These cadences increase in weight up to the middle, an important directional influence. Contrapuntal intensity grows as the stretto imitation between violins (bars 6 f.) extends to gamba as well (bars 10 f.). Similar build-up in second half begins with dialogue entries in violins (bars 12 f.), then returning to the 1+2 texture, but with imitative entry of violin II (bar 14) rather than immediate parallel thirds, telescoping this two-beat distance of imitation to one beat (bars 19 f.), finally also involving gamba in the stretto. Immediate return to F (bar 18) after D minor creates indecisive, nondirectional effect (bifocal tonality).
M	Each successive phrase articulates clearly by contrast of skips and leaps following stepwise motion (compare end of bar 3 with beginning of bar 4). Changes in tessitura for each phrase give a distinct sense of melodic movement beyond the single phrase and a long line, balanced more between than inside of phrases.
R	General growth in surface activity within each half: compare bar 1 (nine impacts) with bar 11 (twenty-two impacts) and similarly, bar 13 (fifteen impacts) with bar 20 (twenty-six impacts). Dotted halves and eighths (high-contrast pattern of distinctive effect, 3:1 compared to the 2:1 relationships of quarters plus eighths, or eighths plus sixteenths) occur only at the most important points: the three full cadences (bars 12, 17, 26) and the activity climax (bars 20 f.—here violin II has an even higher contrast pattern: tied quarter followed by sixteenths.
G	The increasing breadth of phrasing within each half confirms other sources of mounting interest, and the final phrase contains the broadest gestures of all, descending from an upper C to middle F, then rising majestically again to C over two bars and descending with equal breadth to the final F.

Small Dimensions

S	[No significant observations]
H	Basic contrapuntal orientation shows in double passing-tones (falling in bar 4, rising in bar 15); integrity of lines even when they produce fifths (bar 21); shape of motive preserved even when it produces inconsistently sudden, rapid chord rhythm (note effect of the second eighth-notes in bars 15 and 16) or sharp dissonances between the violins (bar 19).
M	Sensitivity to melodic climax: literal sequencing of the motive in bar 20 would have carried the first violin up to D, obscuring the effect of C as a climax and balance to the C's in bars 1 and 4. Skillful melodic development: the three thematic motives (quarter-note, eighth-note, and eighth-and-two-sixteenths) are interrelated: compare violin I in bars 3 and 6 with gamba in bars 1–6. (See Example 9-3.)
R	Largely undifferentiated rhythm: repeated durations or repeated patterns of adjacent rather than contrasted values. Lack of differentiation makes small changes correspondingly effective, as in the slight acceleration from the eighths in the violins and the slight deceleration of the simultaneous quarter in the gamba, which together produce a clear rhythmic articulation, thrown further into relief by the halves in the gamba part at the beginning of phrases 1–3. Several cadences show systematic deceleration: the gamba line in bars 9 and 11; violins in bars 16 f.; rhythmic relaxation of whole texture after bar 20.
G	Concinnity of details, particularly confirmation of articulations by harmonic stabilization, rhythmic slowdown, textural exchange of material.

EXAMPLE 9-3.

(a) Motivic interrelationships

(b) Inversions

Conclusions

The charts above provide a detailed foundation for many types and levels of discussion about the first movement of Purcell's *Golden Sonata*. For many purposes, however, they may actually provide too much evidence. We can readily imagine the embranglements of any attempt at a general conclusion about fifty such sonata movements based on correlations of fifty such charts. To compare these fifty movements (or even five), we need to isolate the salient points of style in each piece. For these distilled observations the familiar rubrics of growth can again provide functional headings: *Sources of Shape* and *Sources of Movement*. To these we may add a useful category of comparative observations: *Conventional and Innovative Features*. These three headings can now be used to guide the winnowing process for the Purcell movement:

1. *Sources of Shape.* The large-dimension shape divides into two parts, so it could be identified with the familiar labels of two-part or binary form. A more informative category can be derived from the actual processes of continuation: the second part is a contrapuntally and melodically varied parallel of the first part. In middle dimensions the same process of varied parallelism applies, but the sources of variance are textural and harmonic, while in small dimensions many of the continuations are exact parallels, i.e. sequences of small motives. Purcell extracts an astonishing variety from extremely simple materials, and at points of articulation his coordination of elements, particularly texture and harmony but also melodic and rhythmic activity, seems unusually advanced for a trio sonata.

2. *Sources of Movement.* Though the central dominant cadence establishes the usual tensional expectations of return to the tonic, an unusual power of movement comes from successively more elaborate contrapuntal treatments that Purcell invents for the second half, culminating in the extended series of close imitations from bar 19 onward. Within each half the level of rhythmic activity rises perceptibly, and the fundamental harmonic plan—modulation to V, excursion to vi, and return to I—gives further clear direction.

Within the phrase, the clarity of melodic direction balances the lack of rhythmic differentiation.

3. *Conventional and Innovative Features.* A first hearing of Purcell's *Golden Sonata* (first movement) may leave memories of typically Baroque characteristics such as 1+2 texture, iterative rhythmic motives, and cadences with clashing seconds, much like Corelli sonatas. On each further hearing, however, we become more aware of the individual qualities of this finely crafted movement. Purcell seems almost willfully to have chosen neutral melodic material in order to emphasize the variety of treatments he can invent: inversion, compression, stretto, dispersion in dialogue, extension in double sequence. Equally unusual is the activity crescendo found in the first half and paralleled on a slightly higher level in the second half. Artistically the most satisfying touch may be the return to the peak C (not heard since bar 4) at the point of climax in bar 20 coupled with the superbly graded reduction in activity over the stabilizing dominant pedal at the end. By these evidences of long-range conception Purcell showed his vision of things to come.

INDEX

Entries preceded by asterisks contain the more important material. Single capitals (S, H, M, R, G) refer to Sound, Harmony, Melody, Rhythm, and Growth as in the text. Lower-case "n" following a page number indicates a footnote; "f" and "ff" signal a continuation on one or two following pages, respectively. In lists of works the following abbreviations occur: conc. (concerto); pf. (pianoforte); son. (sonata); sym. (symphony); vn. (violin). In the entries for S, H, M, R, and G, references for dimensions, Movement, and Shape are collected at the end, for convenience.

Sound

Timbre: selection, combination, degree of contrast of instruments and voices.

Range, tessitura, gaps, special effects, exploitation of idiom.

Texture and fabric: doubling, overlap, contrast of components; homophonic, cantus firmus, contrapuntal, polarized (polychoric; melody/figured bass or 2 + 1; melody/accompaniment; solo/ripieno).

Dynamics: terraced, graduated, implied by instrumentation or range; types and frequency.

Harmony

Main functions: color and tension.

Stages of tonality: linear and modal, migrant, bifocal, unified, expanded, polycentric, atonal, serial. Analysis of non-tonal, non-serial styles as structures of variant stability/instability.

Movement relationships, interior key schemes, modulatory routes.

Chord vocabulary (direct, indirect, remote), alterations, dissonances, progressions, motifs, sequences.

Part exchange, counterpoint, imitation, canon, fugue/fugato, stretto, augmentation/diminution.

Melody

Range: mode, tessitura, vocal/instrumental.

Motion: stepwise, skipping, leaping, chromatic; active/stable, articulated/continuous, chromatic/level, etc.

Patterns: rising, falling, level, wave-form, sawtooth, undulating (abbrev. R, F, L, W, S, or U).

New or derived; function as primary (thematic) or secondary (cantus firmus, ostinato).

Middle and large dimensions: peaks and lows.

(See also "Growth": Options for continuation.)